WINNING WITH HONOUR

In Relationships, Family, Organisations, Leadership, and Life

WINNING WITH HONOUR

In Relationships, Family, Organisations, Leadership, and Life

SIONG GUAN LIM

Lee Kuan Yew School of Public Policy,
National University of Singapore, Singapore

JOANNE H. LIM

The Right Perspective, Singapore

 World Scientific

 Imperial College Press

Published by

World Scientific Publishing Co. Pte. Ltd.

5 Toh Tuck Link, Singapore 596224

USA office: 27 Warren Street, Suite 401-402, Hackensack, NJ 07601

UK office: 57 Shelton Street, Covent Garden, London WC2H 9HE

Library of Congress Cataloging-in-Publication Data
Names: Lim, Siong Guan, 1947–   author. | Lim, Joanne H., author.
Title: Winning with honour : in relationships, family, organisations, leadership, and life / by
    Siong Guan Lim (Lee Kuan Yew School of Public Policy, National University of Singapore,
    Singapore) and Joanne H Lim (The Right Perspective, Singapore).
Description: New Jersey : Imperial College Press, 2016. | Includes index.
Identifiers| LCCN 2015049911| ISBN 9789813108639 (hardcover : alk. paper) |
    ISBN 9789813108646 (pbk. : alk. paper)
Subjects: LCSH: Honor--Singapore. | Branding (Marketing)--Singapore. | Success--Singapore.
Classification: LCC BJ1533.H8 L56 2016 | DDC 170/.44095957--dc23
LC record available at http://lccn.loc.gov/2015049911

British Library Cataloguing-in-Publication Data
A catalogue record for this book is available from the British Library.

First published 2016
Reprinted 2016, 2017

Printed in Singapore

CONTENTS

AFFIRMATIONS

SMU
SINGAPORE MANAGEMENT
UNIVERSITY

12-6-16

My dear Siong Guan,

Thank you for sending me your Book "Winning with Honour". I had a quick browse through it and admired the numerous quotations about Honour throughout the Book. That itself must have been a long & tedious exercise that brings out the wisdom in them. But so many, is really unbelievable by itself.

With age my attention span is no longer the same. After the stroke I sometimes feel tired and stop reading. The past is still very clear but yesterday is often forgotten. So reading the cross roads is indeed enlightening to me.

Please thank Joanne for a wonderful 2nd Book - will she do one for children. Epigram Books do well in Cartoons. Edmund, previously of the ST, does it.

With warm regards
Sincerely
Nathan

My dear Siong Guan,

Thank you for sending me your Book "Winning with Honour". I had a quick browse through it and admired the numerous quotations about Honour throughout the Book. That itself must have been a long & tedious exercise that brings out the wisdom in them. But so many, is really unbelievable by itself.

With age my attention span is no longer the same. After the stroke I sometimes get tired and stop reading. The past is still very clear but yesterday is often forgotten. So seeing the crossroads is indeed enlightening to me.

Please thank Joanne for a wonderful 2nd Book — will she do one for children. Epigram Books do well in Cartoons. Edmund, previously of the ST owns it.

With warm regards

Sincerely

N ... n

Nathan

AFFIRMATIONS

WHAT OTHER LEADERS ARE SAYING ABOUT THIS BOOK

"This book is a labour of deep commitment to contribute to the sustenance of human existence in our society and on this planet. It deals with the pressing need for honouring our word and honouring the values that transcend time. Reminders from such a wonderful book are timely as moral relativity is becoming more apparent today. An excellent read for leaders at all levels from individuals, families, and organisations, to the community, society, and state."

Ambassador Mohammad Alami Musa
Head of Studies in Inter-religious Relations in Plural Societies
S Rajaratnam School of International Studies
Nanyang Technological University
Singapore

"*Winning with Honour* is the second book by Siong Guan Lim and Joanne H. Lim after *The Leader, the Teacher & You*. Honour to the authors could be described as the virtue of virtues. It embraces responsibility, duty, trust, integrity, compassion, courtesy, and many more good values. The authors argue that Honour can be lived in one's life and the way one deals with others, and can be acted out at a personal level and national level."

Professor Chan Heng Chee
Chairman, Lee Kuan Yew Centre for Innovative Cities
Singapore University of Technology and Design
Singapore

"*Winning with Honour* is a book for both educators and families because it shows how the practice of Honour weaves teachers, students, parents, and children into an organic whole that supports each other and builds each other up. As a result, the authors call on each sector of society to see significance in each other by honouring each other, the way we are made, and the universal laws under which we operate. Furthermore, they show how honouring the different seasons in our lives can help us weather the storms of life more effectively."

Mrs Belinda Charles
Dean, Academy of Principals
Singapore

"This is another hugely impressive and highly original book by Siong Guan Lim and Joanne H. Lim. It deals with values and virtues as the key to a rewarding life—whether in relationships, in business, or in the life of the nation. *Winning with Honour* celebrates winning but at the same time challenges the modern, consumerist ideal of success. The book will challenge everyone regarding the meaning and purpose of our lives. It deserves to be widely read."

Lord Griffiths of Fforestfach
Vice Chairman, Goldman Sachs International
United Kingdom

"This is a deeply wonderful book, best read with a pencil. There is scarcely a page on which one will not take notes and later return to the wisdom contained. It draws attention to Singapore 'punching above its weight' and an explanation as to why—a well-defined concept of Honour. The case for this and future work is made with excellent analysis and supporting anecdote. The book is not only a worthy successor to its predecessor, in many ways it surpasses it. Read it. Digest it. Base your important decisions on it."

Mr Francis Hartmann
Adjunct Lecturer in Public Policy
Originator of the Harvard Kennedy School course on Effective Implementation
Harvard Kennedy School of Government
United States of America

"Siong Guan Lim and Joanne H. Lim have written another remarkable book. It is suffused with wisdom. I agree with the central thesis of the book that the success of an individual, company, institution, and country depends on trust, and trust is founded on Honour."

Professor Tommy Koh
Ambassador-At-Large, Ministry of Foreign Affairs
Professor of Law, National University of Singapore
Singapore

"This second book by Siong Guan Lim and Joanne H. Lim is about the virtue of Honour in one's life. No one can address this question better than Siong Guan. With his varied experience and legacy of the Public Service, industry, business, and corporate affairs, he brings to life what drove him; Honour became the creed of his life.

At a young age, with no past experience and none of the 'policy-making' experiences of others, he had many insights about the problems facing our young nation and he was moved to find solutions, but always with Honour as the guiding spirit.

He was a remarkable product of our history, with insights into our problems and appreciating at each stage the growing pains we faced. Thus he became an institution in our midst. But always taking upon himself to get things done and getting them completed.

Anyone wanting to learn his values and experiences, will find much in the book to learn from."

Mr S R Nathan (3 July 1924 – 22 August 2016)
Former President of the Republic of Singapore
Singapore

"How did Singapore ascend the global economic ladder to be a model for emerging economies? In *Winning with Honour*, Siong Guan Lim and Joanne H. Lim put forth that Lee Kuan Yew's visionary leadership also saw through the weaving of a fabric of Honour into the good governance instituted. Honour and honouring have made Singapore exceptional and need to be sustained for a bright future. This book is a primer in conducting our everyday lives in Honour and with Honour that we may, putting others before ourselves, emerge winners in the race of life."

Mr Philip Ng
Chief Executive Officer, Far East Organization
Singapore

"*Winning with Honour* speaks deeply to those who care about the survival, success, and significance of individuals, families, communities, and nations. The authors argue persuasively that Honour is the secret to why nations and businesses thrive, and why some leaders continue to attract more trust and respect than others, over the ages. The wisdom contained in these pages reflects the need for an examined life and the importance of incorporating Honour in our daily being. *Winning with Honour* is a book that honours the good of our past, our present, and our future. I encourage you to read it and share it."

Ms Denise Phua Lay Peng
President, Autism Resource Centre (Singapore)
Singapore

"*Winning with Honour* explores the meaning of Honour and its importance for building strong individuals, families, communities, organisations, and nations. Seen from the story of Singapore's independence, we learn how Honour was crucial in establishing transparent and accountable institutions, building strong and credible businesses, and nurturing a harmonious society. Siong Guan Lim and Joanne H. Lim impart useful advice for individuals seeking to learn and practise a culture of Honour in their relationships, leading to happy and fulfilling lives."

Dr Stephen Riady
Executive Chairman, OUE Limited
Singapore

"Successful countries—and companies—must have people who understand they are part of something bigger than they are. *Winning with Honour* captures the virtues and values that have allowed Singapore to become a whole that is far greater than the sum of the parts. Honour forms a foundation that provides for today's success and tomorrow's potential in Singapore; in all great, time-tested companies; and in life."

Mr John Rice
Vice Chairman of General Electric
United States of America

"This is a timely book written as Singapore enters another period of transition in a difficult local and global environment. A year after the death of Lee Kuan Yew, it is opportune to reflect on the key aspects of his philosophy that allowed Singapore to develop from a poor outcast from Malaysia into probably the world's most successful city state. Sensibly, the authors have not tried to analyse all the various components of success. They recognise that the future is going to require different skills but have picked the umbrella quality of Honour to enable a wide discourse on the individual and collective attributes that are most likely to ensure that the next generation continues to innovate, develop, and together, succeed."

Sir John Rose
Chairman, Holdingham Group, and former CEO, Rolls Royce Inc.
United Kingdom

"This is in many ways an exceptional book. It provides an insider's view of Singapore, the success story as well as the challenges the city state faces in a rapidly changing world. It is up to date on management issues, but at the same time rooted in profound knowledge of history. It contains pragmatic assessments of economy and society. Above all, it is a spiritual book satisfying the need of the reader to look beyond the fleeting material success and to focus on ever-lasting values, of which Honour is certainly the most important one."

Mr Urs Schoettli
Consultant on Asian Affairs and former Asia Correspondent of Neue Zürcher Zeitung (Switzerland) in Beijing, Hong Kong, Delhi, and Tokyo
Switzerland

"To reach the top is relatively easy. To stay at the top, that is the real challenge, and this is true for nations, companies, and also for individuals. In *Winning with Honour*, the two authors focus on this most delicate question and offer the concept of Honour as a basis for reputation, trust, reliability, well-being, and success. Particularly in this time of constant change, this study is a must-read for responsible leaders in politics, business, and society as a whole to prepare for the future."

Dr Toni Schönenberger
Member of the Board, UBS Wolfsberg, and Executive Chairman
stars Foundation Board
Switzerland

"Siong Guan Lim has played a significant role in the Singapore 'miracle'—now the wealthiest nation in the world per capita. As an insider, his analysis is that undergirding Singapore's material and economic success has been its culture of Honour. Honouring one's word, the rule of law, intellectual property, integrity, and transparency. This culture of Honour is the reason investors have trusted Singapore with their investments. He argues however that this needs to be renewed by each generation of Singaporeans for Honour to continue to be Singapore's 'brand'. This highly readable book is not just an anatomy of Singapore but of why nations rise and fall."

Dato Dr Kim Tan
Chairman
SpringHill Management Limited
United Kingdom

"People should have a mindset of honouring their past, present, and future without any arrogance or any complacency in order to move forward. Each person and each country must make every effort to become reliable and trustworthy. This book analyses Singapore's past and present, and discusses what is required for Singapore's continued success and survival into the future. The authors are and will continue to be shining 'Red Dots'."

Mr Hiroshi Watanabe
Governor and Chief Executive Officer
Japan Bank for International Co-operation
Japan

"It is easy for us to bemoan how messed up our world is! We can lambast political self-interests, corporate greed, or human shortsightedness as much as we want, but it is a completely different proposition for us to do the right things and do them right at the same time. Once again, Siong Guan Lim and Joanne H. Lim teach us how! Reflecting the lessons of great leaders and not least, his own, Siong Guan paints a practical vision of what a better tomorrow looks like. This prophet cries, 'Honour!'"

Tan Sri Dato' Francis Yeoh
Managing Director, YTL Group of Companies
Malaysia

"Siong Guan Lim and Joanne H. Lim's new book, *Winning with Honour*, proposes that Honour has a key role to play as an enabler of constructive, respectful debate in our muti-racial, multi-religious, increasingly plural, and potentially contentious Singaporean polity.

As a committed supporter of a multi-ethnic and multi-faith, as well as a more fully democratic polity, I cannot agree more. Honour, as defined by Mr Lim and Joanne, goes beyond mere tolerance of banner differences, beyond even the necessary mutual respect that has to be the bedrock of sound multi-cultural policies. It also introduces the key element of caring for the other as a fellow citizen irrespective of differences, and thus injects compassion, dare I say love, into the equation. This is at once both radical but profoundly liberating if we are to create the space to have frank public debate on important issues and evolve fully into one of the most diverse democracies in the world."

Mr Yeoh Lam Keong
Social commentator and former GIC Chief Economist
Singapore

APPRECIATION

___

APPRECIATION

The usefulness of history does not lie in dates and figures—it lies in events and ideas that offer lessons and wisdom for the future. While context is important, perspective is even more critical.

The ideas behind this book would not have been conceived if not for the interactions with the many people we have met, who had concerns about what the future will bring for all of us, and what Singapore could be in the future. There are far too many people who have offered their hindsight, insight, and foresight for us to list. We are grateful for the intellectual challenges they have offered, which have helped us develop clarity and focus in our thoughts.

Particularly for this book, we would like to thank the following leaders who have taken the time to review the book:

- **Ambassador Mohammad Alami Musa**, Head of Studies in Inter-Religious Relations in Plural Societies, S Rajaratnam School of International Studies, Nanyang Technological University, Singapore

- **Professor Chan Heng Chee**, Chairman, Lee Kuan Yew Centre for Innovative Cities, Singapore University of Technology and Design, Singapore

- **Mrs Belinda Charles**, Dean, Academy of Principals, Singapore

- **Lord Griffiths of Fforestfach**, Vice Chairman, Goldman Sachs International, United Kingdom

- **Mr Francis Hartmann,** Adjunct Lecturer in Public Policy and Originator of the Harvard Kennedy School course on Effective Implementation, Harvard Kennedy School of Government, United States of America

- **Professor Tommy Koh**, Ambassador-at-Large, Ministry of Foreign Affairs, and Professor of Law, National University of Singapore, Singapore

- **Mr S R Nathan**, Former President of the Republic of Singapore, Singapore

- **Mr Philip Ng**, Chief Executive Officer, Far East Organization, Singapore

- **Ms Denise Phua**, President, Autism Resource Centre (Singapore), Singapore

- **Dr Stephen Riady**, Executive Chairman, OUE Limited, Singapore

- **Mr John Rice**, Vice Chairman of General Electric, United States of America

- **Sir John Rose**, Chairman, Holdingham Group, and former CEO, Rolls Royce Inc., United Kingdom

- **Mr Urs Schoettli**, Consultant on Asian Affairs and former Asia Correspondent of Neue Zürcher Zeitung (Switzerland) in Beijing, Hong Kong, Delhi, and Tokyo, Switzerland

- **Dr Toni Schönenberger,** Member of the Board, UBS Wolfsberg, and Executive Chairman, stars Foundation Board, Switzerland

- **Dato Dr Kim Tan**, Chairman, SpringHill Management Limited, United Kingdom

- **Mr Hiroshi Watanabe,** Governor and Chief Executive Officer, Japan Bank for International Co-operation, Japan

- **Tan Sri Dato' Francis Yeoh,** Managing Director, YTL Group of Companies, Malaysia

- **Mr Yeoh Lam Keong**, Social commentator and former GIC Chief Economist, Singapore

Joanne H. Lim
Siong Guan Lim
April 2016

INTRODUCTION

What exactly does it mean to win in life and how can we win ... and win with Honour?

Singapore had to find its own way to survival, security, and success, despite thinking it impossible in 1959.

Under the leadership of Singapore's founding Prime Minister, Mr Lee Kuan Yew, Singapore built a brand of Honour centred on integrity, trustworthiness, dependability, determination, tenacity, hard work, and adaptability.

We all like to win.

But what exactly does it mean to win in life and how can we win … and win with Honour?

We all want to be satisfied.

But what exactly makes a satisfied life?

If you want to win in life, win with Honour, and be satisfied, this book is for you!

WHY THIS BOOK CAME TO BE

Singapore celebrated 50 years of independence in 2015. For many countries around the world, 50 years is not such a big deal. But it is a big deal for little Singapore, which has been described as a "little red dot" on the world map.

The government of Singapore in 1959 had not believed that Singapore could survive as an independent sovereign state on its own. Singapore was still a British colony, and with no natural resources to call its own, Singapore needed a contiguous economic hinterland; merger with Malaya to its north seemed the obvious solution.

This happened in 1963 with the formation of Malaysia made up of the Federation of Malaya with Sabah, Sarawak, and Singapore.

But the marriage did not last long for Singapore. Independence came suddenly and unexpectedly on 9 August 1965. Singapore had to find its own way to survival, security, and success, despite thinking it impossible in 1959.

There was nothing in Singapore, apart from its people hungry for work and life. Even the earth was not fertile. The solution, under the leadership of Singapore's founding Prime Minister, Mr Lee Kuan Yew, was to build a brand of Honour centred on integrity, trustworthiness, dependability, determination, tenacity, hard work, and adaptability.

It was a brand about being a people and a government who delivered on promises we made, and who left no doubt that we would honour our

This book is about life and living, and is not just about the survival and success of Singapore.

Honour is valuable to all who would care to reflect on how to sustain success in one's life, family, community, organisation, and/or nation.

Most of us live full lives—but do we live fulfilled lives?

word whenever we gave our word, no matter what. Success followed the courage and the imagination.

But celebrating 50 years of independence will not make the future for Singapore unless the virtue of honouring our word is understood and sustained by succeeding generations. The genesis of this book was a sense, almost of compulsion, to share our convictions on the utter criticality of Honour to make Singapore's future.

But as we studied the literature and developed our arguments, it struck us that Honour was not just about explaining Singapore's journey from Third World Economy to First World Economy in a generation, but was an essential virtue that undergirds purposefulness in life, satisfaction in family, stability in society, advantage in business, success in leadership, and security in the nation.

Thus it came about that this book became one about life and living, and not just about the survival and success of Singapore.

One final comment in this short backdrop to the book: This book is written from the perspective of Singapore and Singaporeans, but it draws wisdom from history, geography, culture, religion, the wisdom of the ancients, as well as writings and examples from all over the world. We believe there is a universality in the message of Honour that can prove valuable to all who would care to reflect on how to sustain success in one's life, family, community, organisation, and/or nation.

PURPOSE OF THIS BOOK

Most of us live full lives—but do we live fulfilled lives?

In the course of our work, we have met many top leaders of global multinational companies. While many of these senior executives are high flyers in the corporate world and superstars at their workplaces, many live painful personal lives marred with divorce, terse relationships with their children, strained relationships with their families, and/or fractured friendships.

They are abundant on the outside, but empty on the inside. Often, they try to fill the void in their lives with workaholism and addictions, but these stop-gap measures only bring about more brokenness and distress,

Many people spend their whole lives running and striving to get "there", but once they get "there", they find that "there" is really not where they wanted to get to.

Win in life and work by practising and promoting Honour, particularly in the two dimensions of:

- Honouring Our Word
- Honouring Each Other

In a world powered by technology, and infiltrated by materialism and consumerism, most of us find ourselves living full but unfulfilling lives.

Fulfil the calling that only you can fulfil ... for there will only be one edition of you in the entire history of humanity.

and often results in poor health physically, emotionally, mentally, and spiritually.

Many people spend their whole lives running and striving to get "there", but once they get "there", they find that "there" is really not where they wanted to get to. To their dismay, they find that they were either busy running the "rat race" in a wheel—furiously running but getting nowhere no matter how hard they tried—or climbing the "ladder", only to realise that the ladder was leaning against the wrong wall!

The purpose of this book is to invite you to think about what "winning in life" actually means. What is success? How do you define success? What makes for a successful life?

This book seeks to raise consciousness about the virtue of Honour in our lives, and posits that a good way and the best way to win in life and work is to practise and promote Honour, particularly in the two dimensions of:

- **Honouring Our Word**
- **Honouring Each Other**

The book draws wisdom from the ancients and religion, as well as from recent research and contemporary commentators. We do not claim to have all the answers, but we share what we ourselves have learnt so that you can come to your own conclusions and convictions of what makes a successful and worthwhile life.

WHO THIS BOOK IS FOR

This book is for anyone who wants to live a satisfied, healthy, and meaningful life.

In a world powered by technology, and infiltrated by materialism and consumerism, most of us find ourselves living full but unfulfilling lives if we do not regularly take a pause to reflect over our lives and our actions.

We hope that you will explore this book and find insights and foresights about how you could conduct your life differently, so that you make the most out of your life, and fulfil the calling that only you can fulfil … for there will only be one edition of you in the entire history of humanity.

Honour is important for strong:

- Individuals
- Families
- Communities
- Organisations
- Nations

Honour has played a fundamental role in the Singapore story since its independence in 1965.

Singapore's history over 50 years illustrates what is possible when imagination and human enterprise are coupled with Honour.

Make your future by honouring Honour.

STRUCTURE OF THE BOOK

There are ten parts to this book:

- **Part I: Honour: Small Thought, Big Idea.** In this part, we explore what Honour is and why Honour is important for strong individuals, strong families, strong communities, strong organisations, and strong nations.
- **Part II: Honour for a Satisfied Life:** Honouring our humanity
- **Part III: Honour for the Future:** Honouring our chances for success
- **Part IV: Honour in Relationships:** Honouring the building blocks of our life
- **Part V: Honour in Individuals:** Honouring our identity
- **Part VI: Honour in Families:** Honouring our first relationships
- **Part VII: Honour in Communities:** Honouring our responsibility
- **Part VIII: Honour in Organisations:** Honouring our potential
- **Part IX: Honour in Leadership:** Honouring our people
- **Part X: A Study of Singapore, A Study of Honour: Small City, Small State.** In this part, we describe the fundamental role that Honour has played in the Singapore story since its independence in 1965, and how its history over 50 years illustrates what is possible when imagination and human enterprise are coupled with Honour, even if there might be a lack of natural and human resources. We also consider the current state of values in Singapore, and the possible scenarios should Honour not be honoured.

We end the book with

- **Closing Thoughts: Honour Honour:** Making our future

HOW TO READ THIS BOOK

We are all different and have different needs. In a time-starved world, you might like to select the bare minimum to read, while honouring your individual needs.

The left hand pages summarise the critical points on the right hand pages. If anything on the left hand pages interests you, read the right hand pages.

To live with Honour is to live!

"Mine Honour is my life;
 Both grow in one;
 Take Honour from me,
 and my life is done."

- For those who would like to get a **rough gist** of the book:
  - ✓ Scan through the left hand pages—these pages summarise the critical points on the right hand pages. If anything on the left hand pages interests you, read the right hand pages, which will discuss the topics in depth.
  - ✓ Read the Closing Thoughts

- For those interested in **"Winning in Life"**:
  - ✓ Read Parts I – IX
  - ✓ Read the Closing Thoughts

- For those interested in **"The Singapore Story"**:
  - ✓ Read Parts I, III, and X
  - ✓ Read the Closing Thoughts

LIVING AND WINNING WITH HONOUR

To live with Honour is to live! As William Shakespeare, widely regarded as the greatest writer of the English language, wrote:

> **"Mine Honour is my life; Both grow in one; Take Honour from me, and my life is done."**

Happy reading, and may you **WIN WITH HONOUR** in relationships and leadership in families, communities, organisations, and most importantly, in life!

PART I

HONOUR
SMALL THOUGHT, BIG IDEA

Honour defines our humanity—we have Honour because *we are*.

Honour is like a muscle—we are born with it, but whether it maintains its functionality and grows depends on whether we choose to exercise and train it.

Honour is ours to lose.

Honour is living by the virtues.

When you are honourable, you keep your word. You do the right thing regardless of what others are doing.

WHAT IS HONOUR?

Many people, when challenged with the proposition of Honour and honouring, react by saying: "I agree that 'Honour' is important, but what exactly do you mean by 'Honour'?"

As a verb, honour means to ascribe value, esteem, regard, or respect to a person or thing. As an adjective, it is the quality of knowing and doing what is morally right. As a noun, Honour is something that symbolises recognition and privilege.

Whether it is used as a verb, adjective, or noun, practically everyone agrees that Honour is an important virtue for life and living.

Honour defines our humanity—it is a universally recognised and esteemed value not defined or confined by religious or cultural mores. **We have Honour because *we are*.**

Deep within each of us there is a sense of something that makes us worthy as a human being, and that something is Honour. It is like a muscle—we are born with it, but whether it maintains its functionality and grows depends on whether we choose to exercise and train it. **Honour is ours to lose**.

HONOUR, THE VIRTUE OF ALL VIRTUES

The Virtues Project[1] was founded in Canada in 1991 by Linda Kavelin-Popov, Dr. Dan Popov, and John Kavelin, and was honoured by the United Nations during the International Year of the Family as a "model global program for families of all cultures".

The Virtues Project conducted research across religions, ethnicities, beliefs, and cultures to find the meaning of life; their research found that virtues (which are values in action) are "the very meaning and purpose of our lives", "the content of our character", "the elements of the human spirit", "the truest expression of our souls", and "the essence of authentic success".

According to their research: "**Honour is living by the virtues**. It is showing great respect for yourself, other people and the rules you live by. When you are honourable, you keep your word. You do the right thing regardless of what others are doing."

Values only become virtues if they are lived out. As Honour is the

Honour can be said to be the virtue of all virtues.

Honour is something we *offer* someone simply because they are fellow human beings, whereas trust or respect is our *reaction* to someone.

The point of reference for "trust" or "respect" is ourselves, whereas the point of reference for "Honour" is the other person.

Honour is an offer we initiate not because of reward, but because it is the right thing to do.

virtue of living by the virtues, **Honour can be said to be the virtue of all virtues**.

HONOUR IS SOMETHING WE OFFER

Some people have wondered why we choose the word "Honour" rather than a simpler and less abstract word such as "trust" or "respect". The reason is that there is a critical point about Honour that would be lost if it were replaced with trust or respect.

Think about it in this way. **Honour is something we *offer* someone**, whereas trust or respect is our *reaction* to someone.

If people behave in a way which makes us believe in them, or demonstrate skills and abilities that impress us, we give them our trust and respect. In contrast, **Honour is what we offer others simply because they are fellow human beings**.

To understand the point about Honour being a matter of giving, think about the difference between "liking" and "loving" someone. Much too often, people use the words "like" and "love" as though they are interchangeable. But they are not the same in a very important way.

When we "like" something or someone, it is because there is something about the thing or person that pleases us. So when we "like", the point of reference is, in fact, ourselves.

The situation is quite different when we "love". If we "love" someone, we will always be thinking of doing what we can to make the other person happy, comfortable, or satisfied. It may be giving presents, spending time together, giving words of praise or encouragement, serving them in some way, or simply hugging them. The focus is the other person.

Clearly then, the focus of "liking" is ourselves, while the focus of "loving" is the other person. The first is "me" centred, while the second is "others" centred. In the same way, the point of reference for "trust" or "respect" is ourselves, whereas the point of reference for "Honour" is the other person.

Of course, when we honour someone, we are likely in turn to get their trust, respect, or regard. Nevertheless, Honour, like love, is an offer we initiate not because of reward, but because it is the right thing to do.

To offer Honour is an act of humility, kindness, courage, and initiative.

If what we want or what we need are long-term relationships (whether they be personal, public, or professional), trust is what we must have.

The foundation of trust is Honour.

Honour should be a way of life and cannot be left as an ideal ... it is the way to a satisfied life.

Some people feel that to honour someone is a sign of weakness and subservience that results in losing out or losing face. No doubt, to offer Honour is an act of humility and kindness, and is also an act of courage and initiative; there are good reasons for doing so, and, at worst, it would simply be an act of "enlightened self-interest".

Think of how we choose our friends. Friends are people whom we can trust, who can keep our secrets, and who care about us as we care about them. The friendship is sustained if there is a mutual expression of Honour. But as soon as one party dishonours the friendship, trust is lost and the friendship is threatened.

In the same way, think of a business. If all we want is to make a quick sale, we may simply charge a high price or knowingly provide a defective product to get rid of existing stock. But we can be sure that that will be the first and last time the customer will deal with us. If what we want is not just the first sale, but for the customer to come again in the future and to introduce his friends as new customers, we will be interested in forging long-term relationships built on good service, honesty, and trustworthiness. We have to start by treating the customers with Honour.

If what we want or what we need are long term relationships (whether they be personal, public, or professional), trust is what we must have. And **the foundation of trust is Honour**.

Honour should be a way of life and cannot be left as an ideal … for as we see in the next part, it is the way to a satisfied life.

PART II

HONOUR FOR A SATISFIED LIFE
HONOURING OUR HUMANITY

The Harvard Grant Study revealed a few secrets to a satisfied life:

- Secret #1: Value Love Above Everything
- Secret #2: Relationships Matter a Lot
- Secret #3: Beware Alcohol and Cigarettes
- Secret #4: Be Content
- Secret #5: It is Never Too Late to Change
- Secret #6: It is Mostly Up to Us

Men who had a meaningful connection to their work were happier than those who achieved traditional success.

Early relationships are significant.

Ask any human being, and he or she will tell you that they want to be satisfied.

But what exactly makes a satisfied life?

HARVARD STUDY ON SATISFACTION

Harvard University conducted an epic study over 75 years to determine what human beings need to live a satisfied life and to flourish in life.

The Harvard Grant Study began in 1938 and followed 268 Harvard undergraduate men who came from all walks of life. Over 75 years, researchers followed developments in the men's lives and tracked a wide range of psychological, anthropological, and physical traits, including intelligence levels, alcohol intake, relationships, income, and even the hanging length of their scrotums!

Dr George Vaillant led the study from 1972 to 2004 and published the fascinating findings of the study in 2012 in a book entitled: "Triumphs of Experience: The Men of the Harvard Grant Study" (Belknap Press 2012).

The study revealed a few secrets to living a satisfied life, which we list here:

- **Secret #1: Value Love Above Everything**
  In Vaillant's own words, the most important finding from the Grant Study is: "Happiness is love. Full stop." Vaillant writes that there are two cornerstones of happiness: "One is love. The other is finding a way of coping with life that does not push love away."

- **Secret #2: Relationships Matter a Lot**
  According to Vaillant, the study revealed that relationships with other people matter more than anything else in the world. This finding not only applied to overall life satisfaction but also career satisfaction—men who had a meaningful connection to their work were happier than those who achieved traditional success.

  The study also revealed that early relationships are significant. Men who had warm childhood relationships with their mothers were more effective at work in their later years, and they earned about USD 87,000 more per year compared to men who had

While we cannot do anything about our past, we can take steps to help the children in our spheres of influence be the best that they can be.

Beware alcohol and cigarettes.

One should aim for contentment, not cash.

Money matters only up to a point.

It is possible for those experiencing hard situations or challenging change to find happiness, and turn suffering into lessons.

Family background has no correlation to one's happiness.

uncaring mothers; they were also less likely to develop dementia later in life. In addition, men who had warm childhood relations with their fathers were less anxious as adults, enjoyed vacations more, and had increased life satisfaction at age 75. While we cannot do anything about our past, we can take steps to help the children in our spheres of influence be the best that they can be.

- **Secret #3: Beware Alcohol and Cigarettes**
  The study found that mental illness followed alcoholism, and that there is a strong correlation between alcohol abuse and neurosis, as well as alcohol abuse and depression. Alcohol, coupled with cigarette smoking, significantly contributed to morbidity and early death. In addition, alcoholism was found to be the leading cause of divorce.

- **Secret #4: Be Content**
  The Harvard Grant Study revealed that when it comes to work, the only thing that matters is that one is contented with one's work—hence, one should aim for contentment, not cash. This finding is aligned with a 2010 study by Angus Deaton, a British-American economist who was awarded the Nobel Memorial Prize in Economic Sciences in 2015. According to Deaton's 2010 study, increases in annual income beyond USD 75,000 do not increase emotional well-being. Hence, money matters…but only up to a point.

- **Secret #5: It is Never Too Late to Change**
  The study highlighted that one cannot assume one's tomorrow based upon what one sees today, and that it is possible for those experiencing hard situations or challenging change to find happiness, and turn suffering into lessons, with the appropriate coping mechanisms. For example, men who did well in old age did not necessarily do so well in mid-life, and those who did well in mid-life did not necessarily do well in old age. In addition, the background that one was born into also had no correlation to one's happiness.

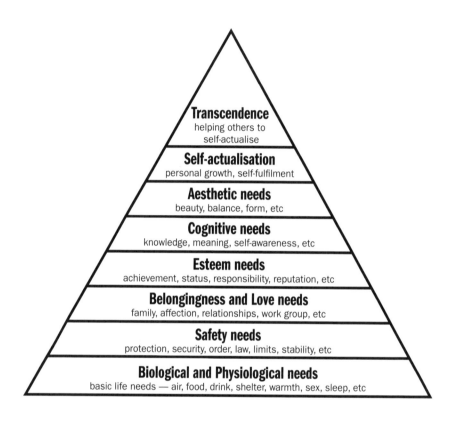

Maslow's Hierarchy of Needs Extended

- **Secret #6: It is Mostly Up to Us**

  The study found that physical health after age 80 is less determined by our genes and more by our habits prior to age 50. According to Vaillant: "The credit for growing old with grace and vitality, it seems, goes more to ourselves than to our stellar genetic makeup."

TRANSCENDENCE, OUR HIGHEST NEED

While the Harvard study highlights the human need to feel loved and to love, it is also important for us to recognise that we have other needs as human beings.

Abraham Harold Maslow (1908–1970) was an American psychologist who hypothesised that the needs of human beings lie in a hierarchy where once one level of needs is met, the next higher level of needs gains prominence.

Maslow identified five levels of needs:

- Biological and Physiological Needs (e.g. food, air, water, shelter, etc.)
- Safety Needs (e.g. security, stability, law, etc.)
- Belongingness and Love Needs (e.g. family, friends, etc.)
- Esteem Needs (e.g. status, reputation, achievement, etc.)
- Self-Actualisation Needs (e.g. the realisation of one's potential, etc.)

Further research in this field concluded that the list is incomplete, and human beings have three more needs:

- Cognitive Needs (e.g. understanding, etc.)
- Aesthetic Needs (e.g. beauty, balance, form, etc.)
- Transcendence Needs (e.g. helping others realise their potential)

The need for Transcendence—that is, helping others realise their potential—is ranked as the highest of all needs in the human psyche. Hence, the highest need we all have is to move beyond just thinking of ourselves to contributing to the lives of others by doing good for their lives.

To put it simply, if we want to live a satisfied life, we have to remember that it is not about ourselves, but about others.

Transcendence (ie. helping others realise their potential) is our highest need as human beings.

If we want to live a satisfied life, we have to remember that it is not about ourselves, but about others.

Honour is necessary for every relationship to thrive, be it in the

- Personal space
- Professional space
- Public space

Trust is the currency of all long-term relationships, and Honour is the Foundation of Trust.

HONOUR & SATISFACTION

Relationships are what define life. We were not meant to live life alone. We are born into relationships with our father and our mother, and we then form relationships with other human beings through our family, schools, workplaces, and other stations as we journey in life.

After our material needs have been met, the quality of our relationships have a large impact on the quality of our lives. Unfulfilling, dysfunctional, and abusive relationships have a negative impact on our lives, while honourable, meaningful, and positive relationships empower us to fulfil our potential.

What we have learned from the Harvard Grant Study and Maslow's Hierarchy of Needs is that

- **Relationships and love matter more than any other thing**
- **Material things and money matter only up to a point**
- **Our habits and mindsets determine our lives**
- **It is never too late to change**
- **We must take self-responsibility for our happiness and satisfaction**
- **Transcendence is our highest need as human beings**

Hence, we live satisfied lives when

- We have loving relationships
- We help others

Honour is necessary for every type of long term relationship to thrive, be it in the

- **Personal** space (e.g. families, friends, relatives, etc.)
- **Professional** space (e.g. customers, bosses, colleagues, etc.)
- **Public** space (e.g. government, communities, charities, etc.)

This is because **trust is the currency of all long-term relationships, and Honour is the Foundation of Trust**. For a system of Honour to work, Honour must first be offered by one party and reciprocated by the other party, and then only may a relationship of trust be established.

THE HONOUR CIRCLE

We build trust most fundamentally by

- **Honouring Our Word**
- **Honouring Each Other**

By consistently keeping our promises and thinking about others, we build stable and trusting relationships that make for a satisfied life. And this results in a virtuous cycle that impacts all aspects of our lives, namely families, communities, organisations, and nation. This is illustrated by the Honour Circle on the left.

Honour Honour for a satisfied life … honour to win!

PART III

HONOUR FOR THE FUTURE
HONOURING OUR CHANCES FOR SUCCESS

It is important that each individual in every society takes responsibility for their own future, and not expect their parents or the government to prepare for their future and provide for all of their needs.

We are at a point in history where humanity will change more in the next twenty years than in the previous 300 years. There is an urgent need to look into the future and prepare for it.

With regard to future thinking, we not only need to think exponentially, but also in combinations.

C onfucius said: *"Success depends upon previous preparation; without such preparation there is sure to be failure."*

While this saying of Confucius rings true, it is also important to note that no matter how much each generation of leaders makes things secure and comfortable for subsequent generations, it will never be adequate or even satisfactory. Each generation is different in terms of expectations, aspirations, and circumstances. Each generation has its own issues, its own challenges, and its own opportunities. Each generation wishes to determine its own destiny.

Hence, it is important that each individual in every society takes responsibility for their own future, and not expect their parents or the government to prepare for their future and provide for all of their needs.

However, before we can prepare for the future, we need to know:

- **What the future is going to be like**
- **Why Honour is critical for a good future**

DIGITAL TRANSFORMATION OF BUSINESS AND SOCIETY

At a recent KPMG Robotic Innovations event, futurist Gerd Leonhard delivered a keynote titled: "The Digital Transformation of Business and Society: Challenges and Opportunities by 2020".

Leonhard opined that we are at a point in history where humanity will change more in the next twenty years than in the previous 300 years. There is thus an urgent need to look into the future and prepare for it— it is important to shift from a focus on "what is", to a focus on "what could be"; a "wait and see" attitude translates into a "wait and die" result, as the question is no longer "what if", but "what when".

With regard to future thinking, Leonhard mentioned that we not only need to think exponentially, but also in combinations.

Consider the digital disruption in the music business: the music industry changed from selling CDs for $20 per CD to earning a few cents per play; as the digital revolution invaded the industry, the industry lost over 70 percent of revenue in slightly over a decade, and protectionist behaviour did not save it at all. In fact, the winners were not the traditional winners in the music industry, and were instead companies such as Spotify,

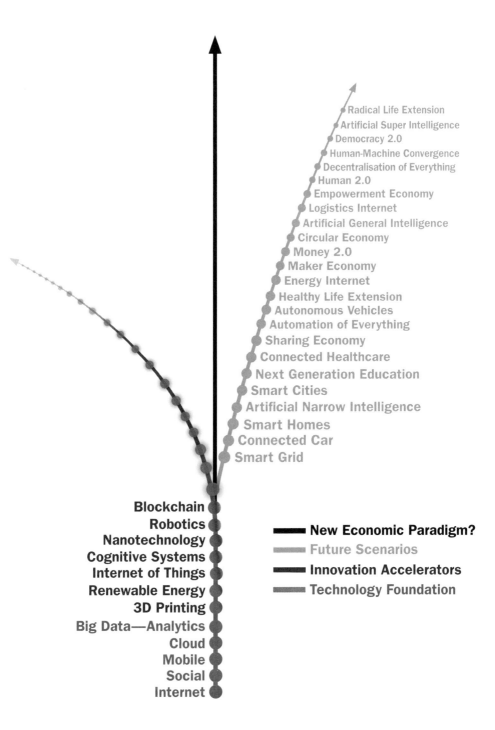

Radical Life Extension
Artificial Super Intelligence
Democracy 2.0
Human-Machine Convergence
Decentralisation of Everything
Human 2.0
Empowerment Economy
Logistics Internet
Artificial General Intelligence
Circular Economy
Money 2.0
Maker Economy
Energy Internet
Healthy Life Extension
Autonomous Vehicles
Automation of Everything
Sharing Economy
Connected Healthcare
Next Generation Education
Smart Cities
Artificial Narrow Intelligence
Smart Homes
Connected Car
Smart Grid

Blockchain
Robotics
Nanotechnology
Cognitive Systems
Internet of Things
Renewable Energy
3D Printing
Big Data—Analytics
Cloud
Mobile
Social
Internet

New Economic Paradigm?
Future Scenarios
Innovation Accelerators
Technology Foundation

FUTURE SCENARIOS by Frank Diana

Apple, Facebook, and Google.

Automation will also become more widespread. As reflected in the future scenario diagram by consultant Frank Diana on the left, anything that can be automated will be automated—there is just too much to be gained by automating as robots do not need to have unions, do not need to be paid benefits, etc. However, **the acceleration of automation has ethical implications… but technology does not have ethics**.

In most of the futuristic industries such as nanotechnology, genetic engineering, regenerative medicine, robotics, artificial intelligence, brain sciences, and synthetic biology, technology can take two paths that Leonard terms as "**Hellven**", as meaning a situation where the technology can be "heaven" (where technology is used to increase the well-being of people) or "hell" (where technology brings about bad unintended consequences).

Leonhard also makes the point that **while technology has progressed explosively, humanity has only progressed linearly**. As commented by Diana in his blog: "As we pursue exponential technologies, we must do it in a way that avoids negative consequences…A world of super intelligence requires super humanity—**technology does not have ethics, but society depends on it**."[2]

Collectively, automation, robotics, intelligent assistants, and artificial intelligence will reframe business, commerce, culture, and society. We need a new social contract for the big data world. **Whether this new world is heaven or hell depends on whether humanity is honoured and whether humanity has Honour**.

ABUNDANCE ON THE OUTSIDE, SCARCITY ON THE INSIDE

Leonhard opined that the exponential and intersecting growth of "Digitisation, De-Materialisation, Automation, Virtualisation, Optimisation, Augmentation, and Robotisation" will result in inter-dependency, job displacement, and abundance that comes about due to dramatic cost reduction.

In a world of abundance, there is too much to use. But **while there is a physical manifestation of abundance outside, there is a spiritual,**

While there is a physical manifestation of abundance outside, there is a spiritual, emotional, and mental scarcity inside, which sparks individuals to search for:

- Trust
- Experience
- Purpose

As digitalisation increases, anything that is not digitalisable will become more valuable.

There will be a growing need to focus on the right side of our brain, which cannot be replicated by an algorithm.

About 40 to 60 percent of jobs will be lost to automation and digitalisation.

emotional, and mental scarcity inside, which sparks individuals to search for what they feel they lack, namely:

- Trust
- Experience
- Purpose

Leonhard believes that algorithms can only go so far. In accordance with the economic laws of demand and supply, **as digitalisation increases, anything that is not digitalisable will become more valuable,** which means that people will seek more intuition, love, trust, understanding, creativity, etc.

There will thus be a growing need to focus on the right side of our brain, which cannot be replicated by an algorithm. Examples of right brain characteristics that will grow in importance are:

- Intuition
- Values
- Imagination
- Creativity
- Randomness
- Synthesis
- Emotions
- Humour
- Empathy
- Beliefs

According to Leonhard, unemployment is real and increasing exponentially—about 40 to 60 percent of jobs will be lost to automation and digitalisation, as robotics and artificial intelligence are increasingly used to perform repetitive tasks.

HONOUR IN THE EXPERIENCE ECONOMY

In the world of automation and abundance, experience will become extremely valuable, and an industrial and services economy will be transformed into an "experience economy".

In an "experience economy", people will be more willing to pay for bespoke and innovative services. What would thus be demanded are superior customer service and adept skills in innovation.

After total efficiency is achieved, the value of the business will be contingent on the human and non-digitalisable aspects of a purpose-driven company, namely:

- Purpose
- Design
- Brand

Organisations must not only excel at technology, but also at humanity.

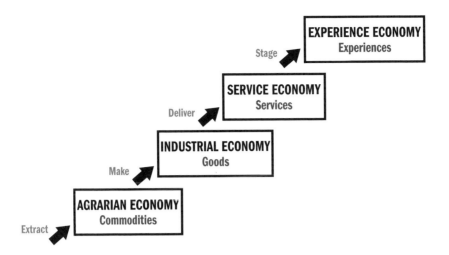

In an experience economy, people will be more willing to pay for bespoke and innovative services. What would thus be demanded are superior customer service and adept skills in innovation. Hence, creativity, innovation, social intelligence, and customer focus will be very important for businesses, and people will need to develop skills in creative problem-solving and constructive interaction if they still want to be employed.

In the world of big data, efficiency and productivity are part of the process, but are not the end goals. According to Leonhard, while value will be created through productivity gains and cost savings along the way, the value from total efficiency through automation will be reached in five to ten years. **After total efficiency is achieved, the value of the business will be contingent on the human and non-digitalisable aspects of a purpose-driven company**, namely:

- Purpose
- Design
- Brand

What this means is that **organisations must not only excel at technology, but also at humanity**. This is particularly important in a "switching economy", where consumers are empowered to switch providers should they not trust their current provider, not feel convicted about the purpose of the organisation, and/or if a competitor provides a

We must honour our humanity.

Organisations must dare to think differently and innovate to create new value that cannot be easily automated.

We need stronger values, ethics, standards, principles, and social contracts in an automated world.

We need Honour to honour these stronger values, ethics, standards, principles, and social contracts to avoid hellish outcomes.

In the VUCA world, there are three key challenges:

- **Challenge #1: The Need for Clear and Strong Leadership**
- **Challenge #2: The Need for Individuals to Think for Themselves, not of Themselves**
- **Challenge #3: The Rise of Relativism**

tailored or personalised experience that meets their needs better.

In a nutshell,

- We must honour our humanity.
- Organisations must dare to think differently and innovate to create new value that cannot be easily automated.
- We need stronger values, ethics, standards, principles, and social contracts in an automated world.
- We need Honour to honour these stronger values, ethics, standards, principles, and social contracts to avoid hellish outcomes.

VUCA WORLD

While life has always been volatile, uncertain, complex, and ambiguous, it has become increasingly so over the past decade with the progress of technology, and the rise of the digital age and globalisation.

The acronym VUCA (Volatile, Uncertain, Complex, and Ambiguous) was the term used by the US military as they faced increasingly volatile, uncertain, complex, and ambiguous warring tactics in Iraq and Afghanistan. It has since been adopted pervasively in the business community due to many financial and economic fiascos that have erupted over recent years.

In the VUCA world, there are three key challenges:

- **Challenge #1: The Need for Clear and Strong Leadership:**
- **Challenge #2: The Need for Individuals to Think for Themselves, not of Themselves**
- **Challenge #3: The Rise of Relativism**

Challenge #1: The Need for Clear and Strong Leadership

Leaders are human, and humans like to be popular. Leaders, whether it be of nations or companies or any organisation, need to be aware of the wishes and desires of their people, but more importantly, they have to judge what would be good for the people, the organisation, the company,

Leaders must have the moral courage to do the right thing, regardless of what others are doing, even if it costs them their popularity.

Leaders cannot avoid making the moral judgment as to what would be good for the people because they have to "create the future", and not simply follow what people want today.

If we are to be responsible members of society, each one of us must think for ourselves as to what would be good for future generations.

In the age of the selfie and the internet, the desire for more public recognition and admiration leads one to take deceptive and self-destructive paths.

or the nation for the years to come. **Leaders must have the moral courage to do the right thing, regardless of what others are doing, even if it costs them their popularity.**

Leaders have to be clear about what kind of organisation they want to leave for the next generation to inherit, and what kinds of values the next generation will need to ensure the continued success and survival for the organisation. Leaders cannot avoid making the moral judgment as to what would be good for the people because they have to "create the future", and not simply follow what people want today.

Challenge #2: The Need for Individuals to Think for Themselves, not of Themselves

On the lack of thinking, this has become more serious with the advent of the internet. In the age of the internet, information is so easily searchable that people need not think for themselves, but simply look for the website or blogsite that offers information and opinions that they find agreeable.

But in such convenience lies the danger of not bothering to think. If we are to be responsible members of society, each one of us must think for ourselves as to what would be good for the generations to come.

Think about the internet: there are many ideas available from all kinds of people. The internet is neutral but the views and perspectives are not. People have virtual personalities with multiple avatars. We often have a hard time figuring out what is real and what is not, especially if it does not come from a known or credible source.

And even when it comes from a known or credible source, the information may not always be accurate. For example, American journalist Brian Douglas Williams was the anchor and managing editor for NBC Nightly News, the evening news program of the NBC television network, for about a decade. Williams was considered to be one of the country's most popular and well-respected news anchors before he was suspended from his position for misrepresenting events that he claimed happened while he was covering the 2003 Iraq War.

In the age of the selfie and the internet, the desire for more public recognition and admiration leads one to take deceptive and self-destructive paths—news, photos, and posts are tweaked, comments are taken out of context, etc.

In a world of instant gratification, few individuals pause to verify the facts and the research; many simply go along with people's opinions.

People should not make decisions based upon what is easy and convenient, but on what is right and good.

The rise of relativism has resulted in a situation where concepts of right and wrong, good and bad are not anchored to the absolutes.

The stability of societies lies in trust and a presumed standard of goodness and rightness.

In a VUCA world, the best preparation is not rules and processes, but values.

In a world of instant gratification, few individuals pause to verify the facts and the research; many simply go along with people's opinions, which oftentimes are based on rumour, whims, guesses and/or untruths.

When important decisions are being made that affect the future, people have to think for themselves what is good for not only this generation, but also for future generations. People should not make decisions based upon what is easy and convenient, but on what is right and good.

Challenge #3: The Rise of Relativism

The rise of relativism has resulted in a situation where concepts of right and wrong, good and bad are not anchored to the absolutes, such as those found in the wisdom of religion or ancient cultures, but are based simply on what is convenient or what is popular.

Relativism is when people take short cuts and tell lies but do not feel bad or ashamed about it so long as someone else cheats more or lies more. For example, there was a senior banker who justified his own bank's regulatory infringement in the Libor scandal[20] as "not that bad" since the submissions from his bank were "closer to the truth" compared with its competitors, who were "more untruthful"!

The stability of societies lies in trust and a presumed standard of goodness and rightness. Trust is the currency for all long term relationships, and Honour is the foundation of trust.

HONOUR O.T.T.L.L.S.S. TO SURVIVE AND THRIVE IN THE VUCA WORLD

But how does one best prepare oneself to deal with these three challenges in an automated world that is increasingly Volatile, Uncertain, Complex, and Ambiguous (VUCA)?

In a VUCA world, the best preparation is not rules and processes, but values. In a fast-changing world, there are no "maps" because no one has gone that way before; when there are no "maps", we need a good "compass". The "compass" comprises the values we hold to be important for our lives. So the best preparation we can make in the VUCA world is values-based.

In a VUCA world:

- Honour a "life compass" based on absolute values and principles
- Develop self-confidence and sound judgment
- Have the courage to be different from others
- Adopt a realistic view of people
- Nurture a capacity to build relationships

We can survive and thrive in the VUCA world by learning to honour O.T.T.L.L.S.S., which stands for:

- **O**bserve
- **T**hink
- **T**ry
- **L**earn
- **L**ead
- **S**tand
- **S**erve

In a VUCA world, we need to:

- Honour a "life compass" based on absolute values and principles
- Develop self-confidence and sound judgment
- Have the courage to be different from others
- Adopt a realistic view of people
- Nurture a capacity to build relationships

We can survive and thrive in the VUCA world by learning to honour **O.T.T.L.L.S.S.**, which stands for:

- **O**bserve
- **T**hink
- **T**ry
- **L**earn
- **L**ead
- **S**tand
- **S**erve

Observe

The first step in getting things done is to take time to Observe. Before you offer an answer, be clear what the question is. Before you offer a solution, be clear what the problem is. Observation is the first step.

Observing does not simply mean looking. It is seeing with curiosity and seeking to understand. It is seeing what is happening, who is doing what, what is being done step by step, what the surrounding is like, how people are reacting, and so on. This is the "What", "Who", "Where", "When", and "How" part of observation.

But we must not stop there. We must go on to the "Why" part of observation. Why are things being done as they are? Why this way and not some other way? Indeed, a wise rule of thumb is to ask "Why?" five times!

Never be satisfied till you get to root causes. Too many people are satisfied with just the immediate, superficial answers. Ask questions. Seek clarifications. Understand motivations.

Never be satisfied till you get to root causes. Ask questions. Seek clarifications. Understand motivations.

We must not only ask questions, but strive to be a good listener.

Being a good observer often means that we need to roll up our sleeves and try to do the task ourselves

The purpose of observing is to understand.

We cannot improve things, and we cannot do better, if we do not fully understand the fundamentals.

There is the story of the experiment with five monkeys that were placed in a cage with a banana. Whenever any of the monkeys reached out for the banana, all five monkeys were doused with cold water. Soon, any monkey that tried to reach out for the banana was stopped by the other monkeys.

One of the monkeys was taken out and replaced with a new monkey. The new monkey instinctively reached out for the banana, and was immediately pounced on by the other monkeys. It did not know why, because by that point the cold water had already been turned off. But the new monkey soon learned not to go after the banana.

Next, a second new monkey was introduced into the cage to replace one of the original monkeys. When it tried to reach out for the banana, it got beaten up by all the other monkeys. Thus, there were now two monkeys who had learnt the hard way not to go for the banana, though the reason was not apparent to them other than that they would get beaten up if they did so.

In due course, three more new monkeys were introduced one after the other, and the remaining three original monkeys were taken out. Now there were five monkeys who never experienced being doused by cold water, but who had all learnt to leave the banana alone, without knowing why the banana was out of bounds in the first place!

This is what happens when questions are not asked and we do not question why we do what we do. We should be better than the monkeys!

However, we must not only ask questions, but strive to be a good listener.

And being a good observer often means that we need to roll up our sleeves and try to do the task ourselves, in order to fully appreciate what is going on. As the adage often credited to Confucius goes:

If I hear, I forget.
If I see, I remember.
If I do, I understand.

The purpose of observing is to understand. We cannot improve things, and we cannot do better, if we do not fully understand the fundamentals. Humility will speed up our ability to understand. This requires us to be

In general, people do not think enough about issues for themselves, and end up adopting the views of the herd. This has become worse with social media.

If people are not careful and questioning of the information they receive, they could end up "talking to themselves".

We should not, unthinkingly, allow others to think for us.

The world is lacking in ideas because there is a lack of desire and commitment to think, and a lack of willingness to try and to risk failure in the process.

prepared to honour others who know more than us, and who are willing to explain and to teach us.

After we have observed well, we can go on to the next step, which is to Think.

Think

In general, people do not think enough about issues for themselves, and end up adopting the views of the herd. This has become worse with social media where people choose the sites they like because these sites appeal to them in tone, approach, and substance. Algorithms too have been programmed to "feed" people with information that they are more likely to like. Thus if people are not careful and questioning of the information they receive, they could end up "talking to themselves".

People should question propositions, and ask for facts and research data as necessary and appropriate. We should not, unthinkingly, allow others to think for us.

Thinking is a discipline. It requires open mindedness, effort and energy to explore different views, gather information, sort out facts from assumptions, and come to conclusions on how things could be better. The world is lacking in ideas because there is a lack of desire and commitment to think, and a lack of willingness to try and to risk failure in the process.

Jack Ma, Executive Chairman of Alibaba, mentioned in a speech in South Korea that we are now moving from the Information Technology period (IT) into the Data Technology period (DT): IT is about making big companies and yourself stronger. However, the DT period is opposite of IT. IT is "I have, you don't have", while DT is "You have it, I don't have it, but I don't need to have it". Data Technology is about sharing, taking responsibility, and having a passion for the future.

The wonderful thing about the DT period is that everyone starts from the same line as there is no expert in DT. The internet and data are neutral—it is the user that determines whether the information is used for good or for bad. Ma highlighted the point that in the DT period, it is particularly important to question: *"Is that true? Is there an opportunity inside? Is there anything I can do to make a difference?"*[3]

So let us not be found wanting here. While our views may not be

While our views may not be original thought, may they be our own thoughts, which are the result of our own convictions and beliefs.

Children learn so much because in their vocabulary the word "failure" does not exist—they only know the word "try".

We need to change our mindset, and look at trying as a journey of discovery and adventure.

"The only way to avoid making mistakes is not to do anything. And that, in the final analysis, will be the ultimate mistake."

Failure lies in not thinking and not trying.

original thoughts, may they be our own thoughts, which are the result of our own convictions and beliefs.

After putting in the effort to understand through deep and careful thinking, we need to move on to the next stage, which is to Try.

Try

Children learn so much because in their vocabulary the word "failure" does not exist—they only know the word "try". For children, learning a new skill or discovering a new fact is fun! They discover failure only when their parents, friends, and relatives introduce the words "fail", "dumb", and "stupid" into their vocabulary. Then the children begin to withdraw and stop trying, so as to avoid the next failure and avoid being called "stupid".

It is apparently true that the Japanese discover more comets than any other group of people. Why is this so? A Japanese professor offered a good answer: "Because Japan has more people looking and they have better instruments!" So that is the short answer: more well-equipped people are looking and trying.

We all need to relearn how to try. We need to change our mindset, and look at trying as a journey of discovery and adventure.

Dr Goh Keng Swee, the First Deputy Prime Minister of Singapore, underscored this point when he was the Minister of Defence, faced with the daunting task of building a relatively large, fully capable Singapore Armed Forces that can effectively deter military aggression against Singapore. He had to encourage his officers to think beyond their experience, and even beyond their imagination. He declared: *"The only way to avoid making mistakes is not to do anything. And that, in the final analysis, will be the ultimate mistake."*

In other words, failure lies in not thinking and not trying. The Singapore Armed Forces would never have built its strength and capability so quickly without Dr Goh's endorsement of this spirit of asking, trying, and learning from everywhere, daring to imagine, and exploring unexplored territory.

Of course there is no credit in making mistakes that could have been avoided if we had thought through things more carefully. But failures are often unavoidable despite our best efforts, because we simply did

"Learning by Doing" is often the only way to learn fully and understand deeply.

Adults learn much less and much more slowly because we have become afraid to ask questions.

If we do not allow or do not encourage our children to take on the journey, we undermine the future for them.

It is the process, not the answer, that helps a child develop his/her ability to tackle problems in his/her life.

The best way to learn is to ask questions and to confront reality, but always to do this with humility to learn from any situation and from anyone.

not know everything, and mistakes are the way to discover what we do not know. "Learning by Doing" is often the only way to learn fully and understand deeply.

Learn

After trying, we need to learn from what had gone well and what had not gone well, so that we can do better the next time round.

Learning must be for a purpose, and that purpose is to make things better. Children learn so much and so fast because they ask a lot of questions. Adults learn much less and much more slowly because we have become afraid to ask questions.

Between pride and ignorance, so many of us sadly prefer pride and hope to bluff our way out of problems instead of confronting our problems head-on. Adults become afraid to ask because we fear others may think us.stupid, or sometimes because we fear others may think we are trying to show how smart we are—the former is human nature, while the latter is often a cultural issue, where the common expectation, especially in Asian contexts, is not to stand out.

Often, adults stand in the way of learning. Sometimes it is because we are protective and provide our children with all the answers, thus preventing them from exploring and building up their self-confidence and capacity for sound judgment. At other times, it is because the adults criticise and discourage too much, out of fear that their children may disgrace them. Adults often fail to realise that the journey of learning is the whole point, and not the answers. And if we do not allow or do not encourage our children to take on the journey, we undermine the future for them.

It is the process, not the answer, that helps a child develop his/her ability to tackle problems in his/her life—the answer can only solve a particular problem in a particular situation, but it is really the thinking process, as well as the self-confidence and courage built along the way, that can be multiplied as the child faces the myriad of situations in his/her life.

So the best way to learn is to ask questions and to confront reality, but always to do this with humility to learn from any situation and from

THE PARADOXICAL COMMANDMENTS

By Dr Kent M. Keith

People are illogical, unreasonable, and self-centred.
Love them anyway.

If you do good, people will accuse you of selfish ulterior motives.
Do good anyway.

If you are successful, you win false friends and true enemies.
Succeed anyway.

The good you do today will be forgotten tomorrow.
Do good anyway.

Honesty and frankness make you vulnerable.
Be honest and frank anyway.

The biggest men and women with the biggest ideas can be shot down
by the smallest men and women with the smallest minds.
Think big anyway.

People favour underdogs but follow only top dogs.
Fight for a few underdogs anyway.

What you spend years building may be destroyed overnight.
Build anyway.

People really need help but may attack you if you do help them.
Help people anyway.

Give the world the best you have and you'll get kicked in the teeth.
Give the world the best you have anyway.

anyone. **Learning is the heart of progress and the heart of improvement, and therefore the heart of success.** Be open, be humble, be intentional.

Lead

After the steps of Observe, Think, Try, and Learn, we finally come to Lead.

Leadership is making good things happen that on their own would not happen. Everyone has it within himself or herself to lead. **We are all leaders in our own right because we all have our own spheres of influence.** We lead because we are not satisfied with ourselves when we know we can do better. And we lead because we want to make things better for the world and the people around us.

An Apple commercial in 1997 states: *"The people who are crazy enough to think they can change the world are the ones who do."* This phrase aptly describes Steve Jobs, the spirit behind the creativity and audacity of Apple.

While you and I are unlikely to have the audacity of Steve Jobs to change the whole wide world, **all of us can be leaders who make a positive difference in our own spheres of influence**, our "smaller worlds" of our family, our workplace, or our society. We should not let the opportunity to do good for the lives of others pass us by.

As leaders, our intention must always be to do good. If our intentions are purely selfish, to draw the attention of the world to ourselves, or simply to feed our own interests or our own egos, we should not be surprised if others turn against us. We must thus always ensure that our hearts are pure.

Leaders are not distracted by cynics because leaders are motivated by unselfish purpose—they clearly understand the saying: *"If you don't live by the praise of men, you won't die by their criticism."*

Take encouragement from "The Paradoxical Commandments" (reproduced on the left) by American writer, Dr Kent M. Keith, which Mother Teresa had adapted and written on the wall of her home for children in Kolkata, India.

Leaders have the courage to think, to be different, and to pursue a dream by backing it up with action. A leader must always be motivated to do good, to create something new, to do the best possible, and to never be satisfied if there is a better way or a better thing to do. Aspire to lead.

"If you don't live by the praise of men, you won't die by their criticism."

Leaders make good things happen that on their own would not happen.

In a world of too much information and too little conviction, the world requires people with clear convictions in their lives.

Seek to serve and not to be served. Seek to serve the needs of society and to make a positive difference in your spheres of influence.

The essence of leadership is other-centredness.

You fail to honour your abilities and talents if you choose not to lead.

Stand

Leaders make good things happen that on their own would not happen. The presence of the word "good" means leaders have to make the moral judgment of what is good and right as opposed to what is bad and wrong. Leaders must thus be willing to stand up and be counted for their convictions. They must be prepared to be different in order to make a difference.

Remember that there are always among your bosses, your peers, and your subordinates, people who are afraid to stand up for what is good and right because they are afraid to stand out from the crowd.

In a world of too much information and too little conviction, the world requires people with clear convictions in their lives, who can bring about change and improvement in a world lacking in leadership. Be prepared to stand tall, stand apart, and stand with courage.

To stand is to be seen. To stand is to not be moved. Detractors will try to move you, either by intimidating, taunting, or teasing. When they do these, it reflects more of their character and personality than what you are doing.

Serve

Even while you are prepared to stand out from the rest, you should never forget why you are leading and why you are standing up. It is because you seek to serve and not to be served.

Seek to serve the needs of society and to make a positive difference in your spheres of influence. It is a privilege and an honour to serve the needs, the hopes, and the dreams of the people around you.

Examine your heart to ensure that you stand not out of pride, but out of service. Examine your heart to ensure that what drives you is not arrogance, but humility. Examine your heart to ensure that what you seek is change for the good of the community around you, and not fame for yourself.

The essence of leadership is other-centredness. The people around you

Serving your followers has to be your continual frame of mind.

The future is one in which the unseen becomes much more important than the seen. It is important for us to address the scarcity on the inside, and not focus on the abundance on the outside.

The world needs people who think for themselves, not of themselves.

What we need is a compass of values, principles, and beliefs of what can and should be.

Reach out for the opportunity to do good by following the steps: Observe, Think, Try, Learn, Lead, Stand, and Serve.

and following you are not toys or tools for you to play around with or to push around. They are human beings who also have their own interests, dreams, ambitions, and responsibilities. And when they are convinced you want the best for them and for others, and that you want to help them reach their hopes in life, they are the more likely to come together to help you reach your dreams.

First them, then you. Serving your followers has to be your continual frame of mind.

SUMMARY: WINNING YOUR FUTURE WITH HONOUR

We live in a world where we have too much information, but too little conviction. Even though we are technologically connected, our souls are disconnected from each other and from our work.

The future is one in which the unseen becomes much more important than the seen. Hence, it is important for us to address the scarcity on the inside, and not focus on the abundance on the outside.

The world craves leaders who seek to serve the good of the many. The world needs people who think for themselves, not of themselves. The world awaits leaders who have their own convictions of good and bad, right and wrong, and who are not content to follow the crowd in the wrong direction.

Success is never certain and the path is not predefined. If you are simply following others, you can use their maps and their tools, but your possibilities are then limited by what they have done in circumstances that will never be the same as yours.

While we can refer to what has been done by those who have gone before us, what we need is a compass of values, principles, and beliefs of what can and should be. We also need energy and stamina to keep going despite detractors and distractions.

O.T.T.L.L.S.S. Reach out for the opportunity to do good by following the steps: Observe, Think, Try, Learn, Lead, Stand, and Serve. These are not difficult steps, though they may not be easy to do due to lack of discipline, laziness, fear, or simply a lack of desire. Everyone can be a leader by following these steps—everyone, including kids, teenagers, youths, and

Everyone can be a leader, wherever they may be.

Honouring others is what will give you the power and energy to stand apart, stand tall, and stand to serve others.

seniors, wherever they may be.

Honouring others is what will give you the power and energy to stand apart, stand tall, and stand to serve others within your family, your school, your workplace, your society, and your country.

WIN

WITH

HONOUR

IN YOUR

FUTURE

BY ASKING YOURSELF:

- Am I preparing myself for the future not only in terms of my knowledge and skills, but also my attitude and mindset?
- Am I taking every opportunity to **O.T.T.L.L.S.S.?**
  - Observe
  - Think
  - Try
  - Learn
  - Lead
  - Stand
  - Serve

PART IV

HONOUR IN RELATIONSHIPS
HONOURING THE BUILDING BLOCKS
OF OUR LIFE

In order to build honourable and healthy relationships in every area of our lives, we need to:

- Honour Our Word
- Honour Each Other

To honour each other in any type of relationship, be it in the personal, professional, or public spaces, we need to:

- Honour Love
- Honour Self-reflection
- Honour Forgiveness
- Honour Cause and Effect
- Honour Conflict
- Honour Disappointments
- Honour Time
- Honour Cycles

Honour Love.

Life is all about relationships and all relationships start with Honour. Honour enhances, endears, and empowers in a wish for the good of collective well-being.

When we honour others, we acknowledge people for being fellow human beings—not for who they are or who they are not; not for what they have or do not have; not for what they do or do not do. We accept them as they are and want the best for their long term well-being. We may disagree with what they think or what they do, but that does not diminish our concern for their long-term well-being.

As mentioned earlier, in order to build honourable and healthy relationships in every area of our lives, we need to:

- **Honour Our Word**
- **Honour Each Other**

And to honour each other in any type of relationship, be it in the personal, professional, or public spaces, we need to:

- **Honour Love**
- **Honour Self-reflection**
- **Honour Forgiveness**
- **Honour Cause and Effect**
- **Honour Conflict**
- **Honour Disappointments**
- **Honour Time**
- **Honour Cycles**

Honour Love

Regardless of race, religion, language, nationality, and/or culture, and whether we are young or old, single or married, we all need to feel loved and to love. When there is a love deficit, we feel pain, inferiority, and rejection, which might negatively manifest in materialism, addictions, mood swings, depression, mental illness, and rebellion.

If we want to love and be loved, we must first learn how to express love to others in a way that they understand, just as we need love to be expressed to us in a way that we understand.

Often we misunderstand the intentions of others because the way they express and understand love is different from the way we ourselves express and understand love.

There are five "love languages":

- **P**hysical Touch
- **R**eceiving Gifts
- **A**ffirmative Words
- **T**ime meaningfully spent together
- **A**cts of Service

We should honour others by taking the effort to find out their love language and communicate using the love language of the other party, and not our own love language.

Gary Chapman, author and well-known speaker at marriage conferences, published a New York Times bestseller called "The Five Love Languages" (Northfield Publishing 1995) that has sold more than 10 million copies. The term "languages" is used because we each have a way of expressing our love that means the most to us, and our "love language" may be quite different from the love language of others.

Often we misunderstand the intentions of others because the way they express and understand love is different from the way we ourselves express and understand love—the resulting miscommunication can be as bad as when we do not understand others because they speak a different language.

According to Chapman, there are five "love languages":

- **P**hysical Touch
- **R**eceiving Gifts
- **A**ffirmative Words
- **T**ime meaningfully spent together
- **A**cts of Service

Chapman suggests that each person often has one primary and one secondary love language that may be deciphered by observing:

- How one expresses love to others
- What one complains the most about
- What one requests the most from others

We all naturally tend to give love in the way we want to receive love, but we have to recognise that the way that we understand love is not necessarily the way that others understand love. When the love language used is not the same for the two parties, it gives rise to misunderstanding and perceived lack of appreciation, as often happens when we speak to someone of a different culture and language group.

Hence, when interacting with other people, whether it be within the family or at the workplace, we should honour others by taking the effort to find out their love language and communicate using the love language of the other party, and not our own love language.

Honouring with love requires one to do the right thing, and not the nice thing, for the long term well-being of the collective whole.

"Failure is the mother of success" (失败是成功之母), only if we adopt a spirit of reflection and honour our mistakes by learning from them, without stooping to blame others for our failures or sinking into depression out of shame.

Self-reflection is important as we all make mistakes in life.

When our days are packed and our lives are full, it is particularly important for us to take time out to pause and think about whether our lives are headed in the right direction.

Apart from communicating in the right love language, we also need to be clear that honouring with love requires one to do the right thing, and not the nice thing, for the long term well-being of the collective whole. For example, when a father disciplines a child, while it might not be a comfortable thing for the child in the short-run, the father is demonstrating love to the child out of concern for the long-term future of the child, and for the survival and success of the family.

Honour Self-Reflection

Life is a process of learning by doing. Experience has to be the master teacher. Aspiration alone is never enough. Success upon the first attempt is extremely rare. In any event, we often learn more from failures than from successes.

Failures help us pinpoint where the mistakes and weaknesses have been, so we know what we should look out for the next time. As the Chinese say: "Failure is the mother of success" (失敗是成功之母). However, this is only true if we adopt a spirit of reflection and honour our mistakes by learning from them, without stooping to blame others for our failures or sinking into depression out of shame.

Self-reflection is important as we all make mistakes in life. Some mistakes are small, and others are life-changing. While we can never change the past, it is important for us to apologise for our mistakes, self-reflect, take self-responsibility for our actions, learn life lessons, and respond in a positive way that will enhance our future, not subtract from it.

To help us self-reflect, here are a few questions that we can **ask ourselves every night before we go to sleep**:

- What are three things that I am grateful for today?
- What went well today and why?
- What did not go so well today and why?
- Do I need to apologise to anyone for hurting their feelings?
- If I made a mistake, how can I avoid making the same mistake again in the future?

Self-reflection is also very important as time passes quickly. When our days are packed and our lives are full, it is particularly important for

To ensure that our lives are headed in the right direction, perhaps we could ask ourselves:

- Am I honouring my core values and living them out?

- Am I honouring my word?

- Am I honouring my talents by using them?

- Am I fulfilling my calling?

- Am I honouring myself by taking care of my physical, emotional, mental, and spiritual needs?

- Am I conducting myself in an honourable way such that others will respect me?

- Am I meeting the expectations I set for others?

- Am I honouring my time by investing it in people and worthy activities that matter?

- Am I giving my best?

- Am I kind?

- Am I positively contributing to the lives of those around me?

- Am I becoming the person that I want to be in the next 10–20 years?

us to take time out to pause and think about whether our lives are headed in the right direction.

To ensure that our lives are headed in the right direction, perhaps we could ask ourselves the following questions on a monthly basis:

- Am I honouring my core values and living them out?
- Am I honouring my word?
- Am I honouring my talents by using them?
- Am I fulfilling my calling?
- Am I honouring myself by taking care of my physical, emotional, mental, and spiritual needs?
- Am I conducting myself in an honourable way such that others will respect me?
- Am I meeting the expectations I set for others?
- Am I honouring my time by investing it in people and worthy activities that matter?
- Am I giving my best?
- Am I kind?
- Am I positively contributing to the lives of those around me?
- Am I becoming the person that I want to be in the next 10–20 years?

Honour Forgiveness

Hari Raya Aidilfitri, which signifies the end of *Ramadan*, the month of fasting every year for Muslims, is a time where Muslim families and friends seek forgiveness from each other, visit their ancestors' graves, recite prayers at the mosque, and visit relatives and friends to feast on traditional delicacies.

The most common greeting used by Muslims in Singapore is "Selamat Hari Raya". Another greeting is "Maaf Zahir Dan Batin", which translates loosely to "I seek forgiveness (from you) physically and spiritually".

As the latter greeting suggests, Hari Raya Aidilfitri is a time of forgiveness within the Muslim community. In particular, many Muslims make it a point to forgive others and to ask forgiveness from their father and their mother for the wrongs they have committed over the past year.

Honour Forgiveness.

Not choosing to forgive is akin to us drinking poison and expecting the other person to die.

Learning to forgive is good for both your mental and physical well-being, and your relationships.

No one is perfect in this world, including you!

To forgive does not mean to forget, but to deliberately choose to not remember, so that it does not poison our future.

Forgiveness is actively choosing not to be a "grave digger".

This is a laudable act of Honour to one's father and mother that conveys gratitude, respect, and concern. It is an act of Honour that wipes the slate clean and enables one to move forward and live life light.

Not choosing to forgive is akin to us drinking poison and expecting the other person to die. When we do not forgive others, they become a burden that we carry around in our minds, souls, and spirits.

In his book, "Forgive for Good" (HarperOne 2001), Dr Fred Luskin, the co-founder and director of the Stanford University Forgiveness Project, shared that research has emerged over the past decade to show that "learning to forgive is good for both your mental and physical well-being, and your relationships", as forgiveness "has been shown to reduce depression, increase hopefulness, decrease anger…increase emotional self-confidence, and help heal relationships."

All of us should thus make a daily effort to forgive those who offend us and seek forgiveness from those we have wronged till it becomes a natural, authentic part of ourselves—not as a show of false goodness, but as an authentic outpouring of love and Honour—if not for the sake of others, then at least for ourselves!

In order **to practise forgiveness**:

- First, we need to recognise that no one is perfect in this world, including ourselves! Each one of us needs to humbly recognise that of ourselves before we judge the imperfections of others. And for those with many regrets in life or those who are prone to self-blame, we need to remember to forgive ourselves.

- Second, we need to recognise that to forgive does not mean to forget, but to deliberately choose to not remember so that it does not poison our future. Oftentimes, each time we are offended by a person, we dig up the whole list of the person's past offences—this often does not bring us any comfort and only adds to our bitterness.

  Forgiveness is actively choosing not to be a "grave digger": what is buried is buried, and if we keep digging it up, we will keep churning the rotten and the rotting. When we forgive, we are committing to dismiss the offence each time it comes to mind, to take our eyes off the bad of the past, and to refocus on the good

Forgiveness is a decision and not an emotion, hence we should not wait until we feel like forgiving to forgive. Forgiveness is an act of the will, and the person who benefits most from it is you.

Start with the intention to bless rather than curse.

The weak can never forgive. Forgiveness is the attribute of the strong. Choose to forgive and ask for forgiveness!

Honour the law of cause and effect. We reap what we sow.

Every human thought, word, and deed is an "invisible seed" that in turns reaps a "physical fruit" that is either desirable or undesirable.

of the present, and the possibilities of the future. Forgiveness is to not hold the offence against the other person any more, and to not allow the past to poison our future. As the theme song in the popular Disney movie, *Frozen*, goes: "Let it go".

- Third, we need to remember that forgiveness is a decision and not an emotion, hence we should not wait until we feel like forgiving to forgive. Forgiveness is an act of the will, and the person who benefits most from it is you—by choosing to forgive, you gain freedom from the past abuses. As long as you hang on to the past, you will keep yourself a prisoner of the past.

Forgiveness does not mean that we ignore the fact of the offence, nor does it mean passively tolerating abuse, whether physical or emotional—rather, it is choosing a perspective to seek change for the better and start with the intention to bless rather than curse.

As Mahatma Gandhi said: *"The weak can never forgive. Forgiveness is the attribute of the strong."* So, let us be strong, and choose to forgive and ask for forgiveness!

Honour The Law Of Cause And Effect

Ralph Waldo Emerson, the famous American poet, commented that the Law of Cause and Effect is the "law of laws". The universal Law of Cause and Effect basically recognises that there is a consequence for every action and "we reap what we sow".

Hence, poor dietary habits result in poor health, uncontrolled spending results in debt, while honouring people in your life with respect, love, and honesty will enable you to experience loving relationships that beget happiness and fulfilment.

According to this law, every human thought, word, and deed is an "invisible seed" that in turns reaps a "physical fruit" that is either desirable or undesirable. As the Chinese saying goes: "善有善报，恶有恶报，不是不报，时辰未到" (It is only a matter of time for good to beget good, and evil to beget evil).

So, if we want ourselves to live happy lives, and for our children to live

Choose to plant good thoughts, words, emotions, and deeds daily.

We need to take responsibility for our thoughts, choices, actions, and lives. It is important for us to be proactive in our relationships with others.

Honour Conflict. Arguments and disagreements between individuals are common and should be expected.

To enhance communication during terse times:

- Fight honourably
- Fight fairly
- Speak honourably

in a better world, it is important that we choose to plant good thoughts, words, emotions, and deeds daily. We need to take responsibility for our thoughts, choices, actions, and lives.

What this law implies is that it is important for us to be pro-active in our relationships with others. If we are passive in our relationships with others, we will only be nice to those who are nice to us—this means that we are subject to the decisions of others to be nice to us. So instead of waiting for others to take the initiative, we can choose to be the initiator of an act of kindness…after all, it is only a matter of time before the good that you sow returns back to you!

Honour Conflict

Arguments and disagreements between individuals are common and should be expected— each of us grew up in a different family environment, each organisation has a different culture, and everyone has a different way of doing things.

In fact, if individuals want to develop their relationships, they should welcome conflict that comes from diversity as it reveals how individuals feel about various situations, what perspective each one holds, what needs they have, etc. As the Chinese say, "不打不相识" (If you don't fight, you don't get to know each other) and "好事多磨" (The road to happiness is strewn with hardship).

But while there will always be tension in any relationship, there are a few principles that we can note in order to enhance communication during terse times:

- **Fight honourably**
- **Fight fairly**
- **Speak honourably**

Fight Honourably

Mark Gungor[4], one of the most sought after speakers of communication in the United States, suggests noting the following when communicating during times of conflict:

- **Honour the time and place:** It is important that you do not start

In order to fight honourably during times of conflict:

- Honour the time and place
- Honour different beliefs and expectations
- Honour differences in style
- Honour commitment

Fighting is useful to establish "meaningful, mutually respected boundaries"; otherwise needs continue to go unmet and the relationship might break down irretrievably.

talking simply when you want to as it might not be an appropriate time and place for the other person—make the effort to ascertain whether the moment is right for the other person. Carve out a special time and appropriate place for you to communicate with the other party when you are both emotionally and psychologically calm.

- **Honour different beliefs and expectations:** According to Gungor, various studies in medicine, psychology, and law have shown that people tend to see what they expect to see, resulting in self-fulfilling prophecies. For example, if you believe that the other party is incompetent, you will see him/her through that filter. Hence, if we want to truly understand the other person, we should be humble enough to be suspicious of our own biases, and choose to engage every conversation with an open mind.

- **Honour differences in style:** While you might be very quiet, the other party might be very loud; while you might be very direct, the other party might be more passive-aggressive. It is thus very important that both individuals work hard to objectively identify and address the conflict at hand without allowing differences in styles to complicate conflicts.

- **Honour commitment:** Start off the conversation by confirming your commitment to solve the problem and assure the other party that you are not attacking or rejecting him/her personally. This is an important concept as human beings naturally crave acceptance and love, and flee from rejection and pain. According to Gungor, a study from the University of California has shown that rejection registers in the area of the brain that responds to physical pain. Hence, if an individual feels rejected, he/she feels pain and is likely to have to choose "fight or flight"—this makes conflict resolution extremely difficult.

Fight Fairly

According to Gungor, fighting is useful to establish "meaningful, mutually respected boundaries"; otherwise needs continue to go unmet and the relationship might break down irretrievably. But while there is a need to

How to Fight Fairly:

- Pick the right time and place
- Affirm your commitment to resolving the issue
- Espouse honesty, care, and vulnerability
- State the issue without placing blame
- Encourage dialogue

Speak honourably to each other during conflict by considering how your words will make the other party feel before actually saying it.

Honour Disappointments.

During downturns, choose to believe that things will work out for the good, and that instead of being rejected, you are actually being redirected to something even better!

fight, it is also necessary to fight fairly!

Gungor offers the following points on **how to fight fairly**:

- **Pick the right time and place** to clarify the issue at hand when both parties are emotionally and psychologically stable
- **Affirm your commitment** to resolving the issue and finding a solution
- **Espouse honesty, care, and vulnerability** when communicating
- **State the issue without placing blame** on anyone by using "I feel" or "I think" statements rather than "you always" or "you never" statements
- **Encourage dialogue**

Speak Honourably

It is also important to remember to speak honourably to each other during conflict by considering how your words will make the other party feel before actually saying it. As Gungor states: *"flooding each other with criticism in the name of 'honesty' and 'openness' is guaranteed to put enormous strain on your relationship"*, as not everything you think and feel is kind and/or enhances the well-being of the other party.

Honour Disappointments

Disappointment arises when reality does not match up with expectations, especially unrealistic expectations. When life does not turn out the way we had hoped, we need to re-evaluate and re-adjust our expectations, so that our disappointment does not turn into a bitter seed that reaps fruits of bitterness. It is particularly during the down times that we must keep our spirits up and choose to believe that things will work out for the good, and that instead of being rejected, you are actually being redirected to something even better!

It is also important for us to guard against "what if" and "if only" thoughts. These thoughts are dangerous as they keep our focus on the past or on external factors and people that we cannot change or control. Examples of such thoughts include "what if I had chosen to work at the

We have to dare to face the facts for what they are, and not live in remorse, regret, fantasies, or imagination.

Use the "SBS" method to deal with disappointments:

- **S**tart with what is right
- **B**e positive
- **S**tay resilient

Honour Time. Time is the only asset that we cannot buy. It is thus important for us to honour the time of others by arriving on time for appointments, and giving others our full attention.

Honour cycles. We reap what we sow.

For the individual to survive and succeed, the nation and society must first survive and succeed.

other company", "if only my father had spent more time with me", "if only my mother had a better temper", etc.

Such thoughts are useless as there are no real answers to hypothetical questions—we have to dare to face the facts for what they are, and not live in remorse, regret, fantasies, or imagination. More importantly, such thoughts take our focus off the things that we can control, which will affect our future either positively or negatively.

When disappointments hit us, let us honour them by using the **"SBS" method**:

- **S**tart with what is right (look at what you have, rather than focus on what you do not have)
- **B**e positive (perceive the disappointment as a redirection to something better, not a rejection)
- **S**tay resilient (believe that all things work out for good)

Honour Time

Time is the only asset that we cannot buy; our lives have a limited and finite amount of time. It is thus important for us to honour every relationship by honouring the time of others by arriving on time for appointments, and giving others our full attention when we are with them. So put away those mobile devices when you are conversing or eating with someone!

The Japanese are well known for their punctuality. It is a matter of Honour for them. Neither too early nor late is their dictum. As explained by a Japanese teacher—if someone cannot even do something as simple as honouring the time of an appointment, they cannot be trusted to do more important things. Again, trust is the currency of every relationship, and Honour is the foundation of trust.

Honour Cycles

It is important for us to realise that life moves in cycles and circles. We all reap what we sow. Often we do not reap, because we do not sow in season.

In the circle of life, for the individual to survive and succeed, the nation must first survive and succeed. Hence, it is in our own best interest

Every individual has to take responsibility for their own happiness and well-being, and not expect others or the government to make them happy.

We are the masters of our own destiny... it starts with us.

to actively increase the quality of the relationships within our families, communities, and organisations. This requires every individual to take responsibility for their own happiness and well-being, and not expect others or the government to make them happy.

We must always remember that we are the masters of our own destiny... it starts with us.

WIN

WITH

HONOUR

IN

RELATIONSHIPS

BY:

- Honouring Love
- Honouring Self-reflection
- Honouring Forgiveness
- Honouring Cause and Effect
- Honouring Conflict
- Honouring Disappointments
- Honouring Time
- Honouring Cycles

PART V

HONOUR IN INDIVIDUALS
HONOURING OUR IDENTITY

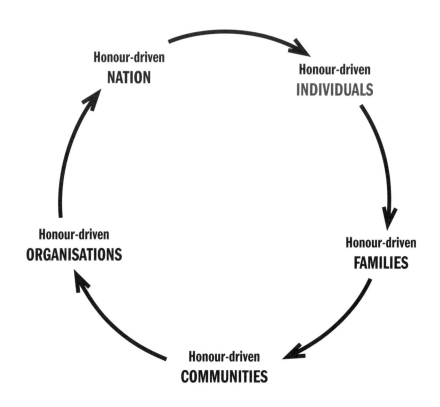

THE HONOUR CIRCLE

We tend to think of Honour basically in terms of how others treat us, when in fact the starting point of Honour is ourselves. **Honour is something that we offer someone simply because they are a fellow human being, and is not our reaction to the actions of someone else.**

HONOUR YOURSELF

It is unfortunate that many people do not honour themselves—this manifests in self-loathing and self-pity or, on the other extreme, narcissism. Instead of celebrating and building on their strengths, they are constantly comparing themselves to others and are preoccupied with keeping up with their neighbours. They complain and make comments such as: "If only I had her charisma…", "If only I had his bank account…", "If only I looked like her…", etc.

If we do not start with an acceptance of ourselves, live with self-respect, and believe that we are living for a unique purpose that only we can fulfil, we deny ourselves the ability to be the best that we can be. In addition, because we are not happy with ourselves, we would likely make life stressful and miserable for those around us.

We need to honour ourselves by identifying our unique talents and abilities, accepting our weaknesses, failures, and celebrating our best efforts and successes. And we need to have the courage to be original and different from others.

However, it is also **important for us to differentiate between self-love and the love of self.** Self-love is healthy and positive, while love of self (narcissism) is unhealthy and negative. Self-love honours the self as important but not all-important, while the love of self honours the self above all else and everyone else.

Life is about balance. Hence, it is important that we regularly reflect whether we are in the healthy self-love sphere, or are in the unhealthy self-pity or self-focussed sphere. If you are not able to objectively evaluate yourself, ask a trusted family member or friend. It is important to honour yourself with truth.

Every human being is made up of three parts:

- **Body**
- **Soul**
- **Spirit**

If any of these three parts of a person is "deficient" in any way, a person feels that there is a void and that he or she is incomplete. If the individual does not take steps to address these deficits, it would lead to dysfunctional behaviour.

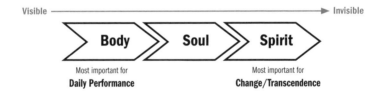

Visible ————————————————————————→ Invisible

Body ⟩ Soul ⟩ Spirit

Most important for
Daily Performance

Most important for
Change/Transcendence

HONOUR YOUR BODY, SOUL, AND SPIRIT

Every human being is made up of three parts:

- **Body:** This is the physical part of our human self that grows, matures, decays, dies, and then decomposes back into its constituent elements and remains a part of the dust of the earth. The body is what gives us "world consciousness".

- **Soul:** The soul is our individuality and is what people often refer to as the "heart", which symbolises the centre of our intellectual, moral, and spiritual life. The soul gives us "self consciousness". It can be said to have three aspects:

  ✓ Our intellect (what we think)

  ✓ Our emotion (what we feel)

  ✓ Our will (our power to decide and take decisive action)

- **Spirit:** The spirit is our innermost being—it is the source of power and control for the body and the driving force that nudges one to do good or do bad. One of the most important aspects of the spirit is the conscience. The conscience is our "built-in compass" that gives us our sense of what is good or bad in thought and behaviour, as well as what is right or wrong in our action.

If any of these three parts of a person is "deficient" in any way, a person feels that there is a void and that he or she is incomplete. If the individual does not take steps to address these deficits, it would lead to dysfunctional behaviour (e.g. overeating, overspending, sexual indulgence), stress, insecurity, frustration, fear, apathy, and/or self-destruction.

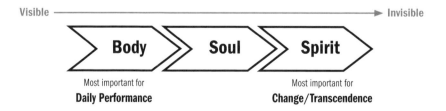

Visible ————————————————————→ Invisible

Body >> Soul >> Spirit

Most important for
Daily Performance

Most important for
Change/Transcendence

The invisible needs are often neglected because of unawareness or ignorance.

As the spirit and soul control our thoughts, which then affect our decisions and our actions, it is important for us to address what is "invisible" so that we may best live out the "visible".

Honour our thoughts as they affect our choices and actions, which then affect our destiny.

It would be useful to recognise the increasing importance of our soul and spiritual needs as we consider our development on a personal, community, organisational, and national basis.

The visible and bodily needs are easily identified and are thus the easiest to address; however the invisible needs are often neglected because of unawareness or ignorance. For example, if we cut our finger, we can usually see the wound and feel the pain, and depending on how serious it is, we know what to do next. But, if we are emotionally and psychologically hurt, we can feel the pain even though we do not see the wound, and as it is an "invisible hurt", others might not know that it exists and thus are less likely to offer any support or comfort unless it is articulated by the individual.

However, as the spirit and soul control our thoughts, which then affect our decisions and our actions, it is important for us to address what is "invisible" so that we may best live out the "visible".

HONOUR OUR THOUGHTS

Even though we may not all agree exactly on what is good and what is bad, or what is right and what is wrong, the point simply is that each of us has an inner compass. Our thoughts affect our choices and actions, which then affect our destiny.

We each have the power to decide either rationally (using our minds), or emotionally (using our hearts), or usually through some combination of the two. The way we decide may simply be to follow what others do, in which case we are allowing those elements of our senses that connect with what we see and hear around us to determine our course forward.

Alternatively, we may make our decisions based on values and the sense of morals and ethics we each hold in our spirit. The spirit is what gives us "inner-consciousness" or "god consciousness". It is what makes each of us different from others in the way we think, feel, and act.

What we see from Maslow's hierarchy of needs is that the basic needs at the bottom of the pyramid are mostly "body" needs, which develop into "soul" needs, and then "spirit" needs. It would be useful to recognise the increasing importance of our soul and spiritual needs as we consider our

Think honourable thoughts. If we focus on the good, we will think good, be good, do good, and will naturally reap good!

75 to 98 percent of mental, physical, and behavioural illness comes from one's thought life.

It is the quality of our thinking and choices (our consciousness), and our reactions that determine our "brain architecture".

It is in our best interest to make a conscientious effort to think honourable, positive, and life giving thoughts!

development on a personal, community, organisational, and national basis.

THINK HONOURABLE THOUGHTS

We also need to be mindful about what we focus on because that will determine our thinking, which will then determine our choices, which will then determine our actions, and ultimately shape our destiny. So if we focus on the good, we will think good, be good, do good, and will naturally reap good!

In her book, "Switch on Your Brain" (Baker Books 2013), Dr Caroline Leaf wrote: *"Research shows that 75 to 98 percent of mental, physical, and behavioural illness comes from one's thought life. This staggering and eye-opening statistic means only 2 to 25 percent of mental and physical illnesses comes from the environment and genes."*

We may have a fixed set of genes in our chromosomes, but which of those genes are active and how they are active have a great deal to do with how we think and process our experiences. Our thoughts produce words and behaviours, which in turn stimulate more thinking and choices that build more thoughts in an endless cycle. So it is the quality of our thinking and choices (our consciousness), and our reactions that determine our "brain architecture"—the shape or design of the brain, and the resultant quality of our minds and bodies.

Our thinking not only affects our choices and reactions, it also affects our DNA! In an experiment done by the Institute of HeartMath, it was found that the DNA changes its shape according to the feelings of the researchers—when the researchers felt anger, fear, frustration, or stress, their DNA responded by becoming shorter and many DNA codes were switched off; however, when feelings of love, joy, gratitude, and appreciation were felt, the shutdown was reversed and the codes were switched back on.[5]

It is thus in our best interest to make a conscientious effort to think honourable, positive, and life-giving thoughts!

That
which you
love

Passion

Mission

That
which
you are
good
at

Ikigai

That
which
the world
needs

Profession

Vocation

That which
you can be
paid for

HONOUR YOUR CALLING
FIND YOUR *IKIGAI*

HONOUR YOUR CALLING

Oprah Winfrey, one of the world's most famous talk show hosts of all time, has said: "*There is no greater gift you can give or receive than to* **honour your calling.** *It's why you were born. And how you become most truly alive. We're all called. If you're here breathing, you have a contribution to make. The real work of your life is to figure out your function—your part in the whole—as soon as possible, and then get about the business of fulfilling it as only you can*"[6].

As you live your calling, you will find your purpose in life. Most people who are not happy are not living their calling, and thus have not found their *ikigai* (生き甲斐), which is a Japanese concept meaning "reason for being".

According to the Japanese, **everyone has an *ikigai*, and it is important for everyone to find it as it brings satisfaction and meaning to life**.

Ikigai is also used to refer to a mental and spiritual mindset in which individuals feel that their lives are valuable. It is not linked to one's economic status or the present state of one's life—even if someone is in a seemingly hopeless situation, if the person has a goal that they are working towards, they possess *ikigai,* although they might feel like they are groping in the dark and cannot see the light at the end of the tunnel.

In the article titled "*Ikigai—jibun no kanosei, kaikasaseru katei*" ("*Ikigai*—The Process of Allowing the Self's Possibilities to Blossom"), Kobayashi Tsukasa, a psychiatrist at Sophia University's Institute of Counselling, states that "*people can feel real* ikigai *only when, on the basis of personal maturity, the satisfaction of various desires, love and happiness, encounters with others, and a sense of the value of life, they proceed toward self-realisation.*"

According to Kobayashi, neither work nor most hobbies can be considered as *ikigai*; he opines that despite Japan's wealth, **"*most people do not feel happy because they try to attain happiness through material acquisitions rather than through freedom of the spirit,* *without which true* ikigai *can never be found.*"

You know that you have found your *ikigai* if you are:

- Doing something that you truly like
- Doing something that the world needs

People who are secure and self-assured consider the needs of others as if they were their own wants and desires.

Honour the "Golden Rule":

- "Do unto others what you would have them do to you" (Christianity)
- "Do not impose on others what you do not desire others to impose upon you" (Confucius)
- "Let no man do to another that which would be repugnant to himself" (*Mahabharata*, sacred Hindu literature)
- "Hurt not others in ways you yourself would find hurtful" (*Udanavarga*, sacred Buddhist literature)

Work on attaining a sense of self-worth and purpose.

Without the ability to love unconditionally, you miss out on one of the most incredible experiences in life.

- Doing something that you are good at
- Doing something that you can be paid for

If you are missing out on any of the above, you are probably missing out on your potential and missing out on a satisfied life! So take steps to find your *ikigai* today.

HONOUR THE GOLDEN RULE

People who have a healthy sense of self-love and *ikigai* have a strong sense of identity and are very comfortable in their own skin. Due to their strong sense of self-worth and sense of purpose, these people are able to receive love and give love to those around them in a non-manipulative way.

People who are secure and self-assured consider the needs of others as if they were their own wants and desires. By doing so, they honour the "golden rule" that can be found in various ancient cultures and religions:

- "Do unto others what you would have them do to you" (Christianity)
- "Do not impose on others what you do not desire others to impose upon you" (Confucius)
- "Let no man do to another that which would be repugnant to himself" (*Mahabharata*, sacred Hindu literature)
- "Hurt not others in ways you yourself would find hurtful" (*Udanavarga*, sacred Buddhist literature)

If you do not have a healthy sense of self-love and sense of purpose, you will not be able to give unconditional love, since you give love in order to get love back. And without the ability to love unconditionally, you miss out on one of the most incredible experiences in life. It is thus important for each individual to work on attaining a sense of self-worth and purpose.

HONOUR BOUNDARIES

Conceited, narcissistic, and self-focussed individuals get what they want

Honour Boundaries.

If there are self-focussed people in your life, it is important to honour them and to honour yourself by establishing boundaries and communicating these boundaries to them clearly, so that they understand that there are consequences to their actions.

If we are truly concerned about the well-being of others, it is important that they are taught the law of cause and effect.

Honour by learning from the regrets of others.

at the expense of others—they only give their time, money, and attention when there is something in it for themselves. These people may have been wounded or scarred by life, and need help to establish a healthy sense of self-worth.

If there are such self-focussed people in your life, it is important to honour them and to honour yourself by establishing boundaries and communicating these boundaries to them clearly, so that they understand that there are consequences to their actions.

Too often, people fail to discipline self-focussed individuals as they fear being labelled as negative or judgmental—but if we are truly concerned about the well-being of these individuals, it is important that they are taught the law of cause and effect, and that they learn that unconditional love requires a conditional relationship, so that they do not continue to self-destroy and can develop to their full potential as a human being.

HONOUR BY LEARNING FROM THE REGRETS OF OTHERS

As we consider whether we have found our *ikigai*, we should also consider the regrets of the dying to know what mistakes we should avoid while we still can.

Bronnie Ware was an Australian palliative care nurse who cared for patients in the last 12 weeks of their lives. She put her observations on dying into a book called "The Top Five Regrets of the Dying: A Life Transformed by the Dearly Departing" (Hay House 2012).

In her book, Ware writes of the common themes that come up again and again as her patients faced death. Here are the top five regrets of the dying, as witnessed by Ware:

Regret #1: I wish I'd had the courage to live a life true to myself, not the life others expected of me
The most common regret people had was that at the end of their lives, they had not honoured many of their dreams, and "had to die knowing that it was due to choices they had made, or not made. Health brings a freedom very few realise, until they no longer have it."

Top Five Regrets of the Dying:

Regret #1: I wish I'd had the courage to live a life true to myself, not the life others expected of me

Regret #2: I wish I hadn't worked so hard

Regret #3: I wish I'd had the courage to express my feelings

Regret #4: I wish I had stayed in touch with my friends

Regret #5: I wish that I had let myself be happier

Only a fool learns from his own mistakes. The wise man learns from the mistakes of others.

Regret #2: I wish I hadn't worked so hard

According to Ware, every male patient that she nursed regretted that they had worked so hard as "they missed their children's youth and their partner's companionship". Some women also mentioned this regret, but as her female patients were from an older generation, most of them had not been breadwinners and thus most did not have this regret. However, all of the men she had nursed had been breadwinners and they all deeply regretted spending so much of their lives "on the treadmill of a work existence".

Regret #3: I wish I'd had the courage to express my feelings

"Many people suppressed their feelings in order to keep peace with others. As a result, they settled for a mediocre existence and never became who they were truly capable of becoming. Many developed illnesses relating to the bitterness and resentment they carried as a result."

Regret #4: I wish I had stayed in touch with my friends

"Often they would not truly realise the full benefits of old friends until their dying weeks and it was not always possible to track them down. Many had become so caught up in their own lives that they had let golden friendships slip by over the years. There were many deep regrets about not giving friendships the time and effort that they deserved. Everyone misses their friends when they are dying."

Regret #5: I wish that I had let myself be happier

"Many did not realise until the end that happiness is a choice. They had stayed stuck in old patterns and habits. The so-called 'comfort' of familiarity overflowed into their emotions, as well as their physical lives. Fear of change had them pretending to others, and to their selves, that they were content, when deep within, they longed to laugh properly and have silliness in their life again."

As Prussian German statesman and aristocrat, Otto von Bismarck (1815-1898), sagely noted: *"Only a fool learns from his own mistakes. The wise man from the mistakes of others."* May we choose to be wise!

Honour by thinking for yourself and asking:

- Why do we do this?
- Why do we do it this way?
- Is there a better way to do this?
- Is it necessary?

Start questioning anything that has become routine to you.

Honour by not feeling entitled.

A false sense of entitlement leads to the offender feeling good but living life badly with a lack of work ethic, a denial of responsibility, as well as a plethora of relational and emotional issues.

The person who chooses to feel entitled is ultimately the one who loses in life.

HONOUR BY THINKING FOR YOURSELF

It is tempting to live a life of routine by doing things the same way every day. But if you live mindlessly and do everything out of habit, you run the risk of letting your habits erode your ability to think critically and question why you do what you do, and why you do things in the way that you do.

The best way to break out of this rut is to start asking:

- Why do we do this?
- Why do we do it this way?
- Is there a better way to do this?
- Is it necessary?

Start questioning anything that has become routine to you—operating procedures, company policies, techniques, etc. Often, once you start reflecting, you awaken your creativity and come up with better ways of doing things that increase your well-being and the well-being of those around you.

HONOUR BY NOT FEELING ENTITLED

Many people have noted that there is an increasing sense of entitlement, especially among younger people. There is a feeling that just because they are born, they are entitled to an easy and convenient life, a job with a good pay, promotions that come with time and not contribution, etc.

Some people think that just because they have a title in someone else's life (e.g. father, mother, son, daughter, sister, brother, friend, boss, employee, etc.), the title makes them special and gives them a claim to whatever benefit they expect. Some others think that the universe owes them big time and that they deserve special treatment because life has thrown them a curveball. Yet others refuse to accept responsibility for their lives and fail to consider the impact of their actions on the lives of others.

A false sense of entitlement leads to the offender feeling good but living life badly with a lack of work ethic, a denial of responsibility, as well as a plethora of relational and emotional issues. Aligned with the law of cause and effect, the person who chooses to feel entitled is

We can choose to react by letting the abuses from the past negatively affect our future, or we can choose to respond maturely by learning from the past to forge a better future.

Life does not owe us anything. No one owes us anything. We are not entitled to anything.

At the end of the day, it is really not about ourselves, but about other people.

Our highest need in life is helping other people fulfil their potential.

We all have something to offer to this world, regardless of our station in life.

It is important for the "rich" to sow into the lives of those who are "poor" so that we can all help each other level up and live to our full potential.

ultimately the one who loses in life.

Most of us have been abused in our lives in one way or another at some point in our lives, be it psychologically, mentally, emotionally, physically, etc. What has happened has happened. There is nothing that we can do about the past. We can choose to react by letting the abuses from the past negatively affect our future, or we can choose to respond maturely by learning from the past to forge a better future.

Remember that life does not owe us anything. No one owes us anything. We are not entitled to anything. We reap what we sow in thoughts and deeds.

SUMMARY: HONOUR IN INDIVIDUALS

While it is important to reach self-actualisation and be satisfied with our lives, it is also important for us to always remember that at the end of the day, it is really not about ourselves, but about other people.

As Maslow's Hierarchy of Needs reflects, our highest need in life is really that of transcendence, which is helping other people fulfil their potential. It is thus in our best interest to choose to honour others and help them realise their potential.

We are all rich in some ways and poor in some ways. Some of us are outwardly rich but inwardly poor, while some of us are poor on the outside but rich on the inside. Some of us have abundance of time, some of us face a scarcity of time, etc.

While we are all equal in birth and death, we are born into unequal circumstance. It is thus important for the "rich" (be it physically, mentally, emotionally, and/or spiritually) to sow into the lives of those who are "poor" so that we can all help each other level up and live to our full potential. We all have something to offer to this world, regardless of our station in life.

When we think about "Winning with Honour", let us keep in mind the words of Mother Teresa, who was awarded the Nobel Peace Prize in 1979:

"At the end of our lives we will not be judged by how many diplomas we have received, how much money we have made or how many great things we have done.

"At the end of our lives we will not be judged by how many diplomas we have received, how much money we have made or how many great things we have done.

We will be judged by: I was hungry and you gave me something to eat. I was naked and you clothed me. I was homeless and you took me in."

—Mother Teresa

"We will be judged by: I was hungry and you gave me
something to eat.

I was naked and you clothed me. I was homeless and
you took me in.

Hungry not only for bread—but hungry for love.

Naked not only for clothing—but naked of human dignity and
respect.

Homeless not only for want of a room of bricks—but
homeless because of rejection."

WIN

WITH

HONOUR

IN YOUR

INDIVIDUAL LIFE

BY ASKING YOURSELF:

- Am I helping myself live with self-respect and developing my talents by taking responsibility for my own life, thinking the right thoughts, making sound decisions, and responding appropriately?
- Am I living my unique purpose?
- How am I helping others in my spheres of influence fulfil their potential and be the best that they can be?

PART VI

HONOUR IN FAMILIES
HONOURING OUR FIRST RELATIONSHIPS

THE HONOUR CIRCLE

Abraham Lincoln, the 16th President of the United States, has often been quoted as having said: ***"The strength of a nation lies in the people—in the homes of the people."***

While it has been noted that Lincoln never really said it, the wisdom behind the words is priceless. Healthy and positive relationships formed within the family unit lead to healthy and positive relationships in the public space, and result in healthy and successful communities and organisations, and ultimately a strong nation.

The most important institution in the world is the family unit. It is in the home that character is moulded and formed, values are infused and espoused, and lifetime attitudes are set. If character, values, and attitudes are not sown correctly, a lifetime of poor patterns will be reaped—patterns that often last a lifetime unless one goes through a life-shaking or life-shattering encounter that inspires transformation.

It is important for us to honour each and every part of the basic family unit that comprises:

- **Parents (our father and our mother)**
- **Marriages (our own, our parents', and our relatives)**
- **Children (our own and our relatives)**

HONOUR OUR FATHER AND OUR MOTHER

Apart from honouring ourselves, we most need to honour those who gave us life. We all have a father and a mother. Without them, we will not exist. Even if they might have been terrible parents who abused or neglected us, we should still honour them because without them and their decision not to kill us, we would not have our life. Just as we are not perfect, our parents are not perfect. **Honour to our father and mother should thus be unmerited and should be initiated by us.**

If you observe those around you, you will notice that those who are not so filial tend to be not so successful in life. Why is this so?

We think it is because being the child of our father and our mother is the most fundamental identity that we assume from birth, and as **with every identity there comes responsibility.** Hence if we have not learned or have not been committed to being responsible to our parents from

Honour our father and our mother.

Honouring our responsibility towards our father and our mother helps us to be responsible in other areas of our life, and this maturity then helps us to fulfil our potential.

This principle of honouring our father and mother is universal across religions and cultures.

Honouring our father and our mother does not mean to always agree with them or to obey blindly. It is an active act of regard.

a young age, this irresponsibility spills over into other areas of our life, resulting in us being less successful than we can actually be.

Honouring our responsibility towards our father and our mother helps us to be responsible in other areas of our life, and this maturity then helps us to fulfil our potential.

This principle of honouring our father and mother is universal across religions. For example, in Hinduism, a Hindu is directed to never forget one's father and mother. In Christianity, a Christian is commanded to honour one's father and mother. In Islam, Allah asks his believers to respect their parents till the day they die.

Similarly in China, which has historically had a diverse range of religious beliefs, historian Hugh D.R. Baker from the University of London's School of Oriental and African Studies notes in his book, "Chinese Family and Kinship" (Macmillan, Columbia University Press 1979), that respect for the family is the only element common to almost all Chinese across religions.

Filial piety is a key virtue in Chinese culture and Confucian philosophy. The character for filial piety is the Chinese character *xiao* (孝), which is a combination of the character *lao* (老, meaning old) above the character *zi* (子, meaning son), signifying an elder being carried by a son. **Generally, filial piety means:**

- Taking care of one's parents
- Engaging in good conduct in the public space to bring good repute to one's parents and ancestors
- Performing well in one's job so as to support one's parents
- Choosing not to be rebellious
- Showing love, respect, and support
- Displaying courtesy
- Ensuring peace in the family
- Dissuading parents and family members from moral unrighteousness

Honouring our father and our mother does not mean to always agree with them or to obey blindly. It is an active act of regard, where even to disagree is the result of being concerned for the well-being of

Filial piety is not only expressed in terms of money, but more importantly in terms of time and concern.

By choosing to honour our fundamental responsibilities in an unchangeable relationship of being the child of our mother and our father, we become better human beings.

Honour Marriage.

our parents. Actively considering their needs and delivering on our promises to them are similarly acts of honour towards them. Filial piety is not only expressed in terms of money, but more importantly in terms of time and concern.

Honour is expressed for our mother and our father through living out the virtues of love, respect, esteem, and caring for them in the spirit of authenticity, integrity, other-centeredness, and responsibility. By choosing to honour our fundamental responsibilities in an unchangeable relationship of being the child of our mother and our father, we become better human beings.

HONOUR MARRIAGE

According to Greek mythology, human beings were originally created with four arms, four legs and a head with two faces, looking in opposite directions.

The humans were fast and powerful. One day, they decided to go up Mount Olympus, which the ancient Greeks believed to be the abode of the gods. The gods were upset that the creatures sought to attack them in this way, but they could not kill the humans as they would be destroying their worshippers.

Zeus, the father of the gods, had a brilliant idea. With the help of his son, Apollo, Zeus cut the creatures in half, and condemned humans to spend the rest of their lives desperately looking for their other halves—their "soul mate"—to make them whole again.

And thus was born the whole idea of "soul mates" and the belief that every human being has only one other half somewhere out there with whom they can naturally reconnect, and that they would always be less happy with any other person. Hence, when relationships fail, it is not because they have done something wrong, but because they have not yet found their one-and-only "soul mate".

Such a concept about "soul mates" keeps the blame elsewhere, and life becomes an unending round of coupling and decoupling, or perhaps of no coupling at all. The trends of multiple sexual partners, pre-marital sex, cohabitation, late marriages, as well as increasing rates of divorce, are a

The idea of "soul mates" can be considered a preposterous idea.

The success of a marriage is not so much the result of marrying the right person, but is the result of choosing to do the right things regardless of one's feelings and emotions.

Trust is what couples value the most in their marriages, and Honour is the foundation of trust.

Love is not an emotion, but is a choice.

In love, the focus is the other person.

reflection of the idea of hunting for that "one-and-only" perfect soul mate.

Well, life is not like that at all. The idea of "soul mates" can be considered a preposterous idea, where somewhere out there among the millions and billions of other human beings is our soul mate whom we have to search out and find before we die. It perpetuates the idea that the whole world spins around each one of us, and all people exist, or at least one such person exists, to fit our selfish needs. This perspective has unfortunately been widely perpetuated by popular songs, movies, romantic novels, and television shows.

We need a new perspective about life and love. We need to realise that the success of a marriage is not so much the result of marrying the right person, but is the result of choosing to do the right things regardless of one's feelings and emotions. It is about choosing to love someone, and less about choosing someone to meet our own needs.

According to Dr Rita DeMaria,[7] a distinguished professor, marriage and family therapist, author, researcher, and relationship educator, trust is what couples value the most in their marriages, as most marriages today are based on the expectations of lasting love and equal partnership, and trust is the foundation for creating a loving, passionate, cooperative, and healthy marriage.

Since trust is the foundation of a strong and lasting marriage, and Honour is the foundation of trust, couples need to ensure that they honour their marriages by fundamentally believing that marriage is good, and that the one whom they have married is good.[8]

We need to understand that love is not an emotion, but is a choice. Marriage is not a place always overflowing with happiness, but is a place where one learns how to love another person completely and unconditionally, even when the other person is not so loveable at times.

Liking vs Loving

Let us consider again the difference between "liking" and "loving". Liking is where there are things about the other person that pleases us—the centre or focus of liking is therefore ourselves. Loving is where we do what we can to satisfy or make the other person happy. In love, the focus is the other person.

What attracts, attacks.

We should get out of the mentality of hunting for "soul mates".

Marriage is a mirror. Marriage can empower our lives by helping us be better human beings if we are willing to reflect, change, and adjust.

We need to have the humility to see where we need to change.

Understanding that marriage has stages helps to relieve anxiety and stress when the marriage is no longer in the "lovey-dovey" stage.

A boy and a girl often get attracted to each other because of what they like in each other. This liking is often not about how similar they are but how different they are. They come together because they see each as complementing what the other lacks. They come together because they are different—a human manifestation of the magnet, where opposites attract. And, strangely or funnily or simply humanly enough, after they get together, they become annoyed and angry with each other because of their differences, wishing that each could be more like the other, and forgetting why they came together in the first place. As the saying goes: "What attracts, attacks!"

The solution to this conflict lies in love, a desire to give to each other and a capacity to receive from each other. So we should get out of the mentality of hunting for "soul mates" and switch to the perspective of finding someone whom we are happy to give to, who has the humility and graciousness to receive, who would similarly reciprocate the sentiment.

Marriage is a mirror

Marriage is a mirror that reflects our character flaws and weaknesses, and is a great sounding board for the areas of our lives that we need to change. This is why marriage can empower our lives by helping us be better human beings if we are willing to reflect, change, and adjust.

If we do not accept that marriage is a mirror that reveals both the good and the bad in our lives, we would be quick to conclude that our marriage is not good, that our spouse is not good, that our spouse has done something wrong to trigger bad feelings in us, and that our spouse is the one that needs the "fixing", not us.

We need to have the humility to see where we need to change, instead of blaming our spouses for bringing out the worst in us.

HONOUR THE SEVEN STAGES OF MARRIAGE

In her book, "The 7 Stages of Marriage" (The Reader's Digest Association, Inc. 2007), Dr Rita DeMaria expounds on the seven stages in marriage.

Understanding that marriage has stages helps to relieve anxiety and stress when the marriage is no longer in the "lovey-dovey" stage.

Honour the Seven Stages of Marriage:

- Stage 1: PASSION STAGE
- Stage 2: REALISATION STAGE
- Stage 3: REBELLION STAGE
- Stage 4: CO-OPERATION STAGE
- Stage 5: REUNION STAGE
- Stage 6: EXPLOSION STAGE
- Stage 7: COMPLETION STAGE

Knowledge about the stages of marriage enables one to better understand the dynamics in the relationship, and to take constructive action to strengthen the marriage according to the stage that it is in.

Knowledge about the stages of marriage also enables one to better understand the dynamics in the relationship, and to take constructive action to strengthen the marriage according to the stage that it is in.

The seven stages of marriage are:

Stage	Action
Stage 1: **PASSION STAGE** During the "Passion Stage", the relationship is all about the excitement, sex, and intimacy the couple is experiencing.	Couples can strengthen their relationship by conscientiously making time for each other and spending undivided quality time together.
Stage 2: **REALISATION STAGE** The couple gets to know each other's real strengths and weaknesses during this stage.	Couples should listen, confide, and speak each other's love languages to establish understanding and trust. Couples should also consider investing in communication classes for the long term stability and well-being of the marriage.
Stage 3: **REBELLION STAGE** The couple is in the "Rebellion Stage" when each party seeks to assert his or her own self-interests, and this results in a volatile relationship and power struggles. During this stage, individuals believe that they are right and that their partner is wrong, so drama is unavoidable. If rebellion is responded with frustration and anger, disasters such as infidelity might occur.	During this stage, couples must learn how to negotiate respectfully and how to build trust by honouring each other's word It is often the way that couples fight, and not the substance of the dispute that creates problems. Couples should identify areas of differences and start talking about them.

Couples should:

- Spend undivided quality time together
- Listen, confide, and speak each other's love languages
- Learn how to negotiate respectfully
- Build trust by honouring each other's word
- Identify areas of difference and talk about them
- Set up regular date nights
- Create special events
- Embark on special projects together

Keep yourself healthy and happy by surrounding yourself, your spouse, and your marriage with emotional, physical, mental, and spiritual support.

Stage	Action
Stage 4: **CO-OPERATION STAGE** In the "Co-operation Stage", couples start to feel more like business partners than lovers as they get more preoccupied with raising kids, paying mortgages, managing health, developing careers, and building homes.	During this stage, it is important for couples to prioritise their marriage by setting up regular date nights to de-stress and keep the passion alive.
Stage 5: **REUNION STAGE** During this stage, children have left the nest, and finances and careers are more established. With more time to spare, it is time for the couple to renew their relationship as lovers and friends. However, this is often hard to achieve as passion could have been depleted and disillusionment could have set in during the "Co-operation Stage", which usually lasts for 10–20 years.	Couples need to recalibrate their marriage and create special events that bring back good memories.
Stage 6: **EXPLOSION STAGE** The "Explosion Stage" can happen anytime in marriage. Major life-changing and/or life-shaking events such as financial issues, health concerns, job losses, etc., will affect the relationship. During this stage, marriage is either a source of comfort or an additional source of stress.	During this stage, keep yourself healthy and happy by surrounding yourself, your spouse, and your marriage with emotional, physical, mental, and spiritual support.

Study after study has shown that married people, particularly married men, live significantly longer than their single friends.

Women play a critical role in holding men up to relational standards to help men shoulder their role in society and live up to their full potential.

Win in marriage by:

- Honouring differences between husband and wife
- Learning how to fight to win

Stage	Action
Stage 7: **COMPLETION STAGE** Many surveys on marital happiness find that it often peaks after decades of being together. Couples enjoy stability and security as they enjoy each other and the life they have created.	Couples should seek to create a new sense of meaning and purpose for the marriage by embarking on a special project together.

Study after study has shown that married people, particularly married men, live significantly longer than their single friends. If marriage vows are honoured, marriage provides security, stability, fulfilment, and companionship for life. There are no better sentiments that undergird a traditional marriage vow than promising "to have and to hold from this day forward, for better or for worse, for richer, for poorer, in sickness and in health, to love and to cherish; from this day forward until death do us part."

Men often define themselves by their responsibilities—as a son, boss, husband, father, etc.—and women play a critical role in holding men up to relational standards to help men mature from being boys to men so that they can shoulder their role in society and live up to their full potential. If men are not held up to relational discipline and think that they are not needed, they will have no motivation to deny themselves frivolous pleasures and will likely neglect to fulfil their role in their family and society.

In the days of Queen Victoria (1819–1901), which is much of the 19th century, death parted husband and wife after about 15 years on average, since life expectancy was 41 years for a woman and 40 years for a man. Since life expectancy has doubled to about 80 years old, many couples can expect to be married not just 15 years, but more like 50 years. What formula can withstand such extended time together?

We would like to suggest that you can **win in marriage by**:

- **Honouring differences between husband and wife**
- **Learning how to fight to win**

Honour that husband and wife are different.

Men and women have differences that are relatively self-evident, but are complementarily important for one to live a fulfilling life.

Men and women generally have different needs.

HONOUR THAT HUSBAND AND WIFE ARE DIFFERENT

Before we can talk about a successful marriage, let us first recognise that there are fundamental differences between men and women. In his phenomenal New York Times bestseller "Men Are From Mars, Women Are From Venus" (HarperCollins 1992) that has sold more than 50 million copies, John Gray said that men and women have differences that are relatively self-evident, but are complementarily important for one to live a fulfilling life.

Men and women are structured differently and thus think and behave differently. For example, men have more gray matter than women, while women have proportionately more white matter. Gray matter areas of the brain are information and action-processing centres in a specific area of the brain. White matter connects the brain's gray matter and other processing centres with one another. This difference probably explains why women are good at multi-tasking, while men generally can only focus on one thing at a time.

Men and women generally have different needs:

Men need	Women need
• Trust	• Care
• Acceptance	• Understanding
• Appreciation	• Respect
• Admiration	• Devotion
• Approval	• Validation
• Encouragement	• Reassurance
Which explains their desires for	**Which explains their desires for**
• Sexual fulfilment	• Affection
• Recreational companionship	• Conversation
• An attractive spouse	• Honesty & Openness
• Domestic support	• Financial Support
	• Family Commitment

Men and women communicate differently.

Individuals in the relationship should feel that they are free to be their truest self without being judged as being wrong.

It is important for men and women to learn the thought process and code of conduct of the opposite sex in order to have effective communication and successful relationships.

During terse times in marriage:

- Realise that fighting is normal and important
- Fight honourably
- Fight fairly
- Speak honourably
- Practise forgiveness
- Choose to work it out
- Think win-win

Men and women communicate differently. For example, during times of stress, men feel better by thinking and figuring out the solution to their problems alone, while stressed women feel better by talking about problems.

While these are clearly generalisations that might not be always applicable to every single couple, a failure to acknowledge these differences will lead to a breakdown in communication and can result in misunderstandings, resentment, and bitterness if they are not dealt with swiftly and skilfully.

In order for a marriage to thrive, individuals in the relationship should feel that they are free to be their truest self without being judged as being wrong. Hence it is important for men and women to learn the thought process and code of conduct of the opposite sex in order to have effective communication and successful relationships—once individuals in a relationship know the "why" behind the behaviours of their partners, they are likely to be more understanding and loving towards their partners.

FIGHT TO WIN

There will always be tension in any human relationship, let alone the most intimate relationship in life—marriage. There are a few principles that one can perhaps note to **enhance communication during terse times in marriage**:

- Realise that fighting is normal and important
- Fight honourably
- Fight fairly
- Speak honourably
- Practise forgiveness
- Choose to work it out
- Think win-win

Fighting is Normal and Important

Arguments and disagreements between husband and wife are common and should be expected—after all, each grew up in a different family

If individuals want to get close, they should welcome conflict as it reveals how individuals feel about various situations, what perspective each one holds, what needs they have, etc.

There are solutions to conflict—all grounded upon overriding love and a willingness to honour each other.

Get to the root of the conflict, and gain mutual understanding by having a good heart-to-heart talk with your partner.

A good marriage is one based upon trust that both individuals want the best for the other, and Honour is the foundation of trust.

environment and has a different way of doing things. In fact, if individuals want to get close, they should welcome conflict as it reveals how individuals feel about various situations, what perspective each one holds, what needs they have, etc. Again, as the Chinese say, "不打不相识" (If you don't fight, you don't get to know each other) and "好事多磨" (The road to happiness is strewn with hardship).

Indeed, if there were no disagreements at all, it is more than likely that the couple has decided to ignore each other, or that one person is dominating the relationship, or worse, that the couple has decided in their hearts that their relationship is not worth fighting for. But there are solutions—all grounded upon overriding love and a willingness to honour each other.

Couples have to work out their own ways to fight and to declare "time outs". We know of one couple that handles tense moments by pronouncing blessing on the other each time an argument looks like it is about to blow up—when a disagreement sounds like it is getting nasty, one of them diffuses tension by saying "God bless you" to the other person, instead of saying harsh words that they might later regret—it is indeed difficult to argue with someone who keeps blessing you! Yet another couple has made it a rule that when they argue, the husband would commit to going outside of their house till he cooled down. Yet another couple has agreed to abide by the working principle that whoever speaks louder is wrong, even if he or she is factually right!

In times of conflict, instead of just minimising the symptom of tension, it is more important to get to the root of the conflict, and to gain mutual understanding by having a good heart-to-heart talk with your partner. One of the best ways to love someone is to consider their best interests, and this often involves the need to confront them with an issue that they have to deal with, even when these are things that you do not want to confront your partner about.

A good marriage is one based upon trust that both individuals want the best for the other, and Honour is the foundation of trust.

Fight Honourably

As mentioned earlier in the book, couples should note the following

When communicating during times of conflict:

- Honour the time and place
- Honour different beliefs and expectations
- Honour differences in style
- Honour commitment

To fight fairly:

- Clarify the issue at hand
- Address the issue when both parties are emotionally stable
- Pick the right time and place
- Espouse honesty, care, and vulnerability
- Affirm your commitment to your partner
- State the issue without placing blame
- Encourage dialogue

when communicating during times of conflict in order to understand their partner better:

- **Honour the time and place:** Take the time and make the effort to ascertain whether the moment is right for your spouse. Carve out a special time and quiet place for you to communicate with your spouse.

- **Honour different beliefs and expectations:** Be humble enough to be suspicious of our own biases and assumptions.

- **Honour differences in style:** Work hard to focus on the issue at hand, without stumbling over the style of your partner.

- **Honour commitment:** Start off the conversation by confirming your commitment to the relationship—this will communicate to your partner that you are focussed on solving the problem, and are not attacking or rejecting your partner.

Fight Fairly

As suggested in an earlier segment, these are a few steps that a couple can follow to fight fairly:

- Clarify the issue at hand
- Address the issue when both parties are emotionally stable
- Pick the right time and place
- Espouse honesty, care, and vulnerability
- Affirm your commitment to your partner
- State the issue without placing blame on anyone (Use "I feel" or "I think" statements rather than "you always" or "you never" statements)
- Encourage dialogue

Speak Honourably

Gungor also mentions in his book "Laugh Your Way to a Better Marriage" (Atria Books 2009) that it is important that couples speak honourably

Couples should speak honourably to each other by making positive verbal statements that help the couple move forward.

One of a couple's communication goals should be to reduce the negative statements they make to each other.

Marriage is about two imperfect people coming together to become one more complete self. Our spouses are not perfect... and more importantly, neither are we!

Choose to forgive and reset your marriage each time you argue with your spouse.

Conflicts are inevitable, but if you are willing to set aside self-centredness and focus on the needs of your partner, you can grow to be a better person, and these benefits will spill over into other areas of your life.

to each other by making positive verbal statements that help the couple move forward:

"Research supports the idea that it is not beneficial to share all of one's negative feelings.

One of a couple's communication goals should be to reduce the negative statements they make to each other. Researchers in social psychology have shown that making positive verbal statements helps you move toward deeper commitment in the relationship.

There are times when expressing a negative feeling is appropriate and necessary; however, you cannot allow the negative to overshadow the expression of positive and tender feelings you have or have had in the past.

It is important to recall fond memories and speak of the reasons you had for being drawn together in the first place. A positive trip down memory lane can bring great joy."

Practise Forgiveness

Forgiveness is paramount to keep a marriage going. Without forgiveness, a marriage is pretty much doomed. We need to remember that marriage is about two imperfect people coming together to become one more complete self. Our spouses are not perfect…and more importantly, neither are we! Hence, choose to forgive and reset your marriage each time you argue with your spouse. Refuse to let bitterness poison your mind, your marriage, and your future.

Choose to Work it Out

While marriage alleviates the problem of loneliness and can be extremely fulfilling and beneficial, it also creates the challenge and responsibility to work things out with one's spouse.

Conflicts are inevitable, but if you are willing to set aside self-centredness and focus on the needs of your partner, you can grow to be a better person, and these benefits will spill over into other areas of your life. It would be useful to remember that marriage is a reflection of your relational skills—if you learn how to get along with your spouse, you

Instead of solving problems by getting a divorce, we actually create other problems that we might not have anticipated.

When a couple gets divorced, the couple never return to their old single selves—they end up as two separate selves, each with some part of both their previous selves.

Two-thirds of unhappily married spouses who stayed married reported that their marriages were happy five years later.

Have faith that things do get better with time if you choose to work at it and stick with it!

also learn how to get along with your staff, family members, friends, etc.

It can always seem easier to run away from marital problems by getting a divorce, instead of tackling them head-on. However, it is also important to realise that instead of solving these problems by getting a divorce, we actually create other problems that we might not have anticipated.

When married couples get divorced, they think that they will be liberated once they leave their spouse, but they often do not realise that they still have to deal with the psychological and emotional pain of splitting or avoiding mutual friends, enduring awkward moments such as becoming grandparents together when their children have their children, etc.

When a couple gets married, two become one, so when a couple gets divorced, the couple never return to their old single selves—they end up as two separate selves, each with some part of both their previous selves.

For those who are considering getting a divorce and starting again with someone else, it would be useful to keep in mind that statistics reveal that second and later marriages are more likely to fail than the first marriage,[9] and often for the same reasons that caused the failure of the first marriage.

Hence if the individuals involved fail to make personal changes to address the issues that caused the rot of the first marriage, it is likely that the subsequent marriage will be unsuccessful. Remarriages with children also mean additional problems such as unwelcoming step-children, communication issues, disparate family cultures, discipline conflicts, the breakdown of parenting tasks, etc.

In his book, "Laugh Your Way to a Better Marriage", Mark Gungor cites a study by the University of Chicago that found that *"two-thirds of unhappily married spouses who stayed married reported that their marriages were happy five years later. In addition, the unhappiest marriages reported the most dramatic turnarounds: Among those who rated their marriage as very unhappy, almost eight out of ten who avoided divorce were happily married five years later."* Hence, do not run at the first sign of conflict! Have faith that things do get better with time if you choose to work at it and stick with it!

Think Win-Win. Marriage is a lifelong commitment of having two winners in a marriage.

Commit to always think of the other person, for your marriage is only as happy as your spouse is happy.

Celebrate your spouse constantly.

It is only when you make your spouse the happiest man or woman in the world that you will be the happiest woman or man in the world!

Start an honourable marriage with honourable dating by:

- Honouring singlehood
- Honouring dating objectives
- Honouring sex

Think Win-Win

Marriage should never be regarded as a contest to decide winners and losers, but as a lifelong commitment of having two winners in a marriage—each one looking out for the other, each one always wishing the best for the other. The commitment involves our total selves—body, soul, and spirit.

Commit to always think of the other person, for your marriage is only as happy as your spouse is happy. Think constantly of how to please, how to care, how to bring joy to your spouse…then only will you be happy! Husbands should be particularly aware of their wife's emotional needs—as the saying goes: "A happy wife makes a happy life!"

Listen to your conscience always as to what is good and what is bad, what is right and what is wrong. Do not put yourselves in the position of temptation to find pleasure in what you know is wrong, for we all reap what we sow.

Celebrate your spouse constantly—do not let him or her think that anyone else (including your children) or everyone else is more important than your spouse. It is only when you make your spouse the happiest man or woman in the world that you will be the happiest woman or man in the world!

HONOUR IN DATING

If you have not gotten married, this is the best time to **start an honourable marriage with honourable dating by:**

- **Honouring singlehood**
- **Honouring dating objectives**
- **Honouring sex**

Honouring Singlehood

First of all, it would be useful to understand that a successful marriage is not the result of two empty souls finding each other and completing each other—it is the result of two whole souls who choose to come together to help each other live a more fulfilling and satisfying life.

Two incomplete, miserable, and lonely souls who get married will

Learn how to be happy and learn what makes you happy before you get married!

Honour Dating Objectives:

- Develop Wholesome Interactions with the Opposite Sex
- Learn about the Person, Personality, and Philosophy
- See our Own Strengths and Weaknesses.
- Practise Serving Others
- Discover the Person you might Marry

just be a marriage of two incomplete, miserable, and lonely souls...and the disappointment that results when they realise that marriage does not bring wholeness leads to more emptiness, more misery, and more loneliness.

Hence if you are single and feel incomplete, miserable, and lonely, do yourself a favour by learning how to be happy and learning what makes you happy before you get married!

Honouring Dating Objectives

Next, one should be clear what the objectives of dating are. In his book, "The 5 Love Languages: Singles Edition" (Northfield 2014), Gary Chapman highlights that many singles fail in the dating game as they have never been clear about their objectives for dating. He suggests the following objectives:

- **Develop Wholesome Interactions with the Opposite Sex**. Learn how to relate with others without seeing them as a sex object or being treated as a sex object. You are a human being, "not an animal playing with his toys or allowing one's self to be a toy with which another animal plays."

- **Learn about the Person, Personality, and Philosophy**. *According to Chapman: "Dating provides an opportunity to break down the perceptions of each other that the world has built up, and to learn to see others as persons rather than objects. It is during dating that we learn names, personalities, and philosophies. These are the qualities of personhood. The name identifies us as a unique person. The personality reveals the nature of our uniqueness. And the philosophy reveals the values by which we live our lives."*

- **See our Own Strengths and Weaknesses**. Dating helps one to develop one's personality. As we become aware of our weaknesses and have the humility to acknowledge our weaknesses, we grow.

- **Practise Serving Others**. Dating provides us with the opportunity to serve others and to discover that "humanity's greatest contribution" is in the giving to others. Genuine service of others

Genuine service of others also "demands that we speak the truth in love."

Sex is meant to be special, and it is the highest physical, psychological, and emotional experience of love. Hence, it should be treated with Honour.

The process of imprinting happens to us not only sexually, but also filially.

also "demands that we speak the truth in love," and dating allows us to practise how to speak to our partner about their weaknesses in a loving way, without fearing that they will walk away.

- **Discover the Person you might Marry.** Dating helps us to develop a realistic idea of the kind of person we need as a spouse. It aids us to realise that while opposites might attract, similarities are more important for bigger issues of life, such as values, spirituality, morals, etc. Dating allows one to explore answers to the essential questions based on social, financial, or spiritual considerations.

Honouring Sex

Lastly, we should remember that sex is not just a physical activity. Sex is meant to be special, and it is the highest physical, psychological, and emotional experience of love. Hence, it should be treated with Honour.

First, we need to acknowledge that just like any other behaviour that is linked to a stimulus, there is a process called imprinting that occurs during one's first sexual experience. The phenomenon of imprinting has been well demonstrated by Austrian naturalist Konrad Lorenz (1903–1989), one of the founders of ethology, the study of animal behaviour, who was awarded the Nobel Prize for Medicine and Physiology in 1973.

Lorenz discovered that if Greylag geese were first reared by him after they are hatched, they would treat him as if he were their parental bird and follow him about—even in adulthood, they would prefer Lorenz over other Greylag geese!

In other experiments, Lorenz demonstrated that ducklings could not only be imprinted to other human beings, but also to inanimate objects such as balls if the ball was the first object that they interacted with after hatching.

While we are definitely more than geese, the process of imprinting still happens to us, not only sexually but also filially.

Sexual imprinting is a process whereby mate preferences are affected by experiences at a young age. Hence, for a guy, his first sexual experience often becomes his standard and his expectation for sex in his life in the years to come.

It is in a woman's best interest to offer her first sexual experience to the man who has demonstrated that he is prepared to make a commitment to her for life.

A man must be prepared to honour his partner by not asking for sex until he is prepared to make a life-time commitment to her.

If an 18-year-old boy is deemed to be mature enough to be a soldier to defend the nation with his life, surely he is old enough to make a commitment to protect, secure, and defend a girl for life. However, usually a young man's sexual appetite will not wait so if he cannot find the girl whom he is prepared to commit to and who is prepared to commit to him, his first sexual experience becomes casual sex, masturbation, or pornography.

Hence, if masturbation is his first definition of sex, there is a fair chance he will seek masturbation instead of sex with his wife in the later stages of marriage after the effects of lust have worn off. If pornography defines sex for him, there is a good chance he will seek pornography rather than sex with his wife. If it is casual sex, then it is the sex act, and not the girl, who defines sex for him.

What then happens is that sex with his wife, instead of the expression of love and the pinnacle of his sexual experience, becomes just another sex act… the beauty of something unique with his wife in later life is lost. In all these instances, the boy-man misses the intensity, intimacy, and sensation of the sexual expression of love with his wife.

Contrast this with the case where the boy's first sexual experience is with his wife in marriage. Here the imprinting is not with an act or an object, but with his wife for life. The girl defines love, intimacy, and comfort for him. She will be the object and focus of his sexual expression.

Sexual imprinting also occurs in girls too. However, due to the enhanced interconnectivity in a girl's brain, sex for the girl is an emotional experience of commitment, acceptance, and intimacy. If she indulges in sex outside of marriage, she will never get to this deep emotional sense of well-being and security, and thus sex will likely be reduced to a sex act; the result is a loss of self-respect that will stay with her through her whole life, despite any facade she may put up.

Women fundamentally require above all a sense of security. That security lies in one man who is prepared to give his life for her, and for the children that should result from their copulation. How can she be unique for that man? She needs to treat that man as unique, as the man should treat her as unique. It is in a woman's best interest to offer her first sexual experience to the man who has demonstrated that he is prepared to make a commitment to her for life. And a man must be prepared to

Honouring each other during the dating process is really for one's own well-being, and the well-being of one's partner.

Individuals should take the time to reflect whether the person they are dating is actually someone that would be suitable for them to marry.

In a strangely paradoxical way, early marriage with preservation of Honour reduces the chances of divorce.

honour his partner by not asking for sex until he is prepared to make a life-time commitment to her.

The failure to honour this commitment in marriage, either by the woman for her man, or by the man for his woman, leads to distrust and rebellion later in life. And distrust and rebellion are the very opposite of the love, commitment, security, and stability that couples seek. Honouring each other during the dating process is thus really for one's own well-being, and the well-being of one's partner.

Dating is a serious matter to be enjoyed but never casually, and always with an end of discovering who you would be prepared to give of yourself to. A true man will seek to preserve the Honour of the girl to whom he is prepared to make the commitment, instead of treating her as an object for his own enjoyment.

There used to be a wonderful word to describe the growing relationship between a boy and a girl—it is the word "courting" or "courtship". The word "dating" conveys no commitment—go out tonight, and forget about it the next day…as the date changes and you go out with someone else! If a boy and a girl begin to spend a considerable amount of time with each other, they should begin to stop thinking of it as "dating", but as "courtship" with the intention of marriage.

What this means is that individuals should take the time to reflect whether the person they are dating is actually someone that would be suitable for them to marry—if the person you are dating is not someone that you see yourself settling down with, it would be honourable to be honest with the other person and not waste their time just because you are in need of company, as they could be using the time spent with you to be with someone who truly loves them and who would be better for their long term well-being.

The point of commitment between a man and a woman can be made earlier rather than later. In a strangely paradoxical way, early marriage with the preservation of Honour reduces the chances of divorce, contrary to what a lot of people think, which is that dating should be an extended process of testing and discovery.

A recent study by the University of Utah[10] revealed that the best age range to get married is between 28 and 32 as divorce is less likely in the ensuing years—people in their late 20s and early 30s are mature and

It is in our best interest to honour courtship and not buy into non-committal dating or the romantic fluff of soulmates.

Honour our children. They are our best investment ... by far.

Parents need to realise that their children are separate beings from them and are merely "on loan" for the years leading up to their independence.

Parents have to understand that their child has a unique role in this world that no one else can fulfil.

The role of parents is to help their child find his/her special place in this world by providing a safe, loving, and non-judgmental environment, for them to build up their self-confidence and self-esteem.

responsible enough to understand if they are with someone out of love, not out of lust, and are not so old and set in their ways that they are not able to accommodate the myriad of adjustments in habits, lifestyle, goals, and personal hygiene that marriage requires. In addition, they probably do not have ex-spouses or children who will divert their time, resources, and loyalty.

Hence, it is time to honour courtship and not buy into non-committal dating or the romantic fluff of soulmates. It is after all in our own best interest to do so!

HONOURING OUR CHILDREN

Peter Lynch, the co-founder of Fidelity Investments, has said: "Children are our best investment…by far." His work is investing money, his time and experience are in investing money, yet his conclusion is that children are the best investment by far.

Besides honouring our parents and spouses, it is important to honour our children. There are many parents who see children as an extension of themselves; thus they impose many of their own dreams and expectations on their children. However, parents need to realise that their children are separate beings from them and are merely "on loan" for the years leading up to their independence.

Parents need to acknowledge that their children are unique creations with their own talents, strengths, and weaknesses. Parents have to understand that their child has a unique role in this world that no one else can fulfil. You might wish for your child to become a doctor, but his/her natural strengths might indicate that he/she would make a far better chef—your child would definitely be happier and more confident in a position where he/she can excel and feel self-assured, rather than be forced into a role that does not resonate with him/her instinctively and which he/she can do only just well enough.

The role of parents is to help their child find his/her special place in this world by providing a safe, loving, and non-judgmental environment for them to build up their self-confidence and self-esteem by exploring, experimenting, and experiencing life.

It is important for parents to establish a trusting relationship with their children by honouring them for who they are, and not what they do.

Parents should ensure that their children are equipped with a moral compass by keeping the following in mind:

- Honour that Honour starts from home
- Honour teachers
- Honour values first
- Honour that fathers and mothers have different roles
- Honour fatherhood
- Be the pride of your child/children

It is important for parents to establish a trusting relationship with their children by honouring them for who they are, and not what they do. When a child feels loved and trust that their parents sincerely want the best for them, and that they are not a prop that needs to "perform" in order to make their parents look good, the child would be more likely to make positive choices and display positive behaviour that will ensure their own success moving into the future. It is thus important for parents to learn the primary and secondary languages of love for their children so that each child knows that he/she is loved and wanted from an early age.

Above all, parents should ensure that their children are equipped with a moral compass that will help them make wise decisions, long after their parents are gone.

In order to equip their children with a strong moral compass, parents could keep the following in mind as they raise their children:

- **Honour that Honour starts from home**
- **Honour teachers**
- **Honour values first**
- **Honour that fathers and mothers have different roles**
- **Honour fatherhood**
- **Be the pride of your child/children**

Honour That Honour Starts From Home

One of our friends who is a taxi driver was lamenting about passengers cheating taxi drivers. He shared his many experiences of passengers reaching their destination, saying they did not have enough money to pay the fare, and asking the taxi driver to wait while they went on to get the money to pay, but never returning.

My friend was especially grieved about being cheated by a primary school kid—he grieved for the boy, not for himself. The boy had hopped into his taxi and asked politely whether he could accept payment for the fare by use of an electronic bank-issued card.

My friend replied, "Certainly!" He took the boy to his destination, whereupon the boy offered him his cash card for payment. After swiping the card into the card reader, my friend exclaimed: "There is no money in the card!"

"Give me a child till he is seven, and I will give you the man."

Values, morals, and ethics are basically "caught" from family rather than "taught" in school.

Parents and family are the first teachers of any child.

Crime is caused not so much by oppression, poverty, or environment, but by the lack of moral training in the morally formative years, which is from one to six years old.

It is very important that parents set a good example by displaying Honour right from the start through their words and actions.

Honouring others is definitely a very important life lesson that begins at home, not only for the benefit of the child but, in the long-term, for the parents as well.

The boy responded: "I only asked you whether you took payment by cash card; I did not say my card had money."

What has happened to Honour and honesty? Who are teaching our kids?

The Chinese have an ancient saying: "三岁看大，七岁看老[11]", which means that at three years old, one can see how a child would be like when grown, and at seven, one can see how the child would be like when old. It is interesting how the Jesuits also have a similar saying: *"Give me a child till he is seven, and I will give you the man."*

This ancient wisdom is affirmed by research that shows that a child's brain is about 80 percent formed at three years old, and is about 90 percent formed at six years old. What this means is that much of a child's attitude towards life is formed before he or she even begins formal education.

Values, morals, and ethics are basically "caught" from family rather than "taught" in school. Many mothers and fathers today "outsource" their parenting to either their domestic helpers or the teachers, but what they do not realise is that while a teacher has a significant influence on the development of the child's attitude for the rest of his or her life, parents and family are the first teachers of any child.

From zero till three years old, before they are able to completely express themselves, children are constantly moulded by their parents and their surroundings. While a young child does not understand all the influences around him or her, the child is constantly absorbing what is going on around him or her and is learning by imitating speech and behaviour—as the saying goes: "Monkey see, monkey do!"

In their definitive study on the causes of crime, "Crime and Human Nature", Harvard professors, Richard J Herrnstein and James Q Wilsons, found that crime is caused not so much by oppression, poverty, or environment, but by the lack of moral training in the morally formative years, which is from one to six years old.

Thus it is very important that parents set a good example by displaying Honour right from the start through their words and actions. Honouring others is definitely a very important life lesson that begins at home, not only for the benefit of the child but, in the long-term, for the parents as well.

Consider this: If parents are rude to their parents, do you not think that their child is probably going to be rude to them growing up and

Parents should invest the time and effort to build a trusting relationship and to instil the right values in the child during his morally formative years, which is from one to six years old.

Honour Teachers. While parents can delegate the role of teaching to the school, they must support what the school does—otherwise the school would be operating without legitimate authority over their children.

when they are old? If parents make their domestic helper serve and clean up after their child, chances are that children will grow up with a sense of entitlement and expect others, including their parents, to serve them and clean up their messes.

We know of many parents who choose to work during the early years of their child's life and then decide to stop working later on when their children start having problems closer to their teen years. We think that this is really a case of treating the fruit and not the root, and putting the cart before the horse. Such a scenario could have been avoided if parents had reversed their strategy and invested more time and effort to build a trusting relationship and to instil the right values in the child when he or she were young, instead of reacting only when the issues arose.

Since much of a child's attitude is instilled before he or she even goes to school, family involvement must be part of any values-driven education, and parents must honour that the education of every child begins at home.

Honour Teachers

Values, morals, and ethics are basically "caught" from family and school rather than "taught" in formal lessons and tests. Much research has shown that if parents are involved in their child's education, the child will learn more. And while parents can delegate the role of teaching to the school, they must support what the school does—otherwise the school would be operating without legitimate authority over their children.

We learnt at a meeting with leaders from the Singapore Teachers' Union and the Union of ITE Training Staff (UITS) that there are two particular challenges that teachers in Singapore have been facing in recent times:

- **Challenge Number One:** Unlike parents of previous generations, parents of children today tend to take the side of their children when any disputes occur rather than first listen to the teacher's version of events. Instead of leading their children, many parents today are being led by their children!

  Perhaps this is due to the guilt that working parents feel for not spending time with their children because they are busy working, or because parents today are more educated so they are less likely

Parents have to realise that by not co-operating with teachers in school and granting them legitimate authority over their children, their children are learning to dishonour authority and elders, including their own parents!

When parents challenge the authority of teachers, they undermine the ability of teachers to complement what the child has learnt or to make up for what the parents had failed to do right.

When parents interact with teachers in the presence of their children, they need to do so with due Honour and respect for the teachers.

to defer to teachers.

Parents however have to realise that by not co-operating with teachers in school and granting them legitimate authority over their children, their children are learning to dishonour authority and elders, including their own parents.

- **Challenge Number Two:** Parents are "outsourcing" the role of parenting to domestic helpers. Teachers have commented that instead of "Meet the Parents" session, it is now more aptly described as "Meet the Maids" session!

  Unlike the older generations who had outsourced their parenting to family members and/or domestic helpers who came from the same country, culture, or community, the domestic helpers of today are largely from different countries and cultures, and thus espouse diverse and often dissimilar values. In addition, due to the dynamics of the relationship, helpers are not able to discipline children the way children need to be guided. As the saying goes: "spare the rod and spoil the child"—children raised by helpers are likely to be "softer" and less self-reliant than those who have been raised by their parents. The well-known incident of the army recruit in Singapore who got his helper to carry his backpack to the army camp is an apt illustration of this problem.

It is important for parents to honour the authority of teachers over their children. By sowing seeds of dishonour in challenging teachers in front of their children, parents run the risk of reaping a harvest of dishonour upon themselves.

While it may be true that many parents today are more highly educated than the teachers, it is a narrow view to think that teachers are there just for knowledge transmission. Teachers have the task of developing the whole child, which means not just academically but also socially, emotionally, and morally. When parents challenge the authority of teachers, they undermine the ability of teachers to complement what the child has learnt or to make up for what the parents had failed to do right. Of course teachers are not perfect, but when parents interact with teachers in the presence of their children, they need to do so with due Honour and respect for the teachers.

Honour Values First.

"成人，成才，成功"–"Become a person, become a talent, become a success."

We all have a father and a mother, and whether they have been present or absent in our lives, we are all aware that their roles and their impact on our lives have been very different.

Most times, the mother is the protector and comforter, while the father is the encourager and adventurer.

Values, morals, and ethics are basically "caught" from family and school rather than "taught" in formal lessons and tests. Parents should thus be mindful and aware of the values that they are teaching their children who are constantly subconsciously learning through modelling. Remember, we all reap what we sow.

Honour Values First

Many parents focus on developing their children academically to ensure their future success, but very few families focus on developing their character first. These parents would do good to keep in mind the ancient Chinese saying that goes: "成人，成才，成功"—"Become a person, become a talent, become a success."

In order to be a success, one must first learn how to be a human being with a conscience and how to honour other human beings, and then only can one develop one's talents to become a success… a life without values is like a boat without a rudder.

Honour that Fathers and Mothers have Different Roles

Imagine a little boy running around gleefully, and suddenly he falls and hurts himself. The mother rushes to him, tells him everything is alright and there is no need to keep crying, cleans the wound, puts some ointment, sticks a plaster on his knee, and then is more than likely to say: "Next time, don't run."

If it were the father who gets to the child first, the father would probably tell the child that "boys don't cry," cleans the wound, puts some ointment, sticks a plaster on the knee, and finally be more than likely to say: "Now you can run again."

We all have a father and a mother, and whether they have been present or absent in our lives, we are all aware that their roles and their impact on our lives have been very different. Ask any child what he thinks, and he or she will tell you that their mother and father are different. As one saying goes: "The mother buys the toy; the father is the toy!"

No doubt there is a degree of stereotyping here, and sometimes the roles are reversed, but most times, the mother is the protector and

The role of the mother is to protect and comfort her children.

Honour Fatherhood.

Both the father and the mother of the child need to step up to the plate and play their complementary roles.

Researchers have found that the love or rejection of mothers and fathers equally affects the behaviour, self-esteem, emotional stability, and mental health of their children, but in some cases, "the withdrawal of a father's love seems to play a bigger role in kids' problems."

comforter, while the father is the encourager and adventurer. This is because men and women are largely different by nature and react differently instinctively when placed in the same situation.

We were once watching an award-winning short film about a puma going after a bear cub, with three children then aged five, eight, and eleven. The puma got so close that he scratched the face of the cub with his front paw, but at the end of the film, the puma unexpectedly simply slinked away and left the cub alone. The next shot showed a huge bear behind the cub, which of course was the reason for the puma giving up his prey.

We asked the children whether the huge bear was a mama bear or a papa bear. All three said it was a mama bear. The oldest said that in the animal world, the papa simply disappears and leaves the mama to take care of the babies. The middle child said that in the animal world, the mama is always the one fighting to protect her children. The youngest one said it was a mama bear, because she licked the blood off the wound on the face of the bear cub. The instincts of the three children were clear and immediate: The role of the mother is to protect and comfort her children.

Honour Fatherhood

Human fathers have to go beyond animal fathers and not simply disappear and leave the mothers to take care of the babies. Human beings are much more than animals; the human child needs to learn many more things and has to go beyond instincts to think rationally and act sensibly. Both the father and the mother of the child need to step up to the plate and play their complementary roles.

According to the Center for the Study of Parental Acceptance and Rejection at the University of Connecticut, researchers have found that the love or rejection of mothers and fathers equally affects the behaviour, self-esteem, emotional stability, and mental health of their children, but in some cases, "the withdrawal of a father's love seems to play a bigger role in kids' problems with personality and psychological adjustment, delinquency, and substance abuse."[12]

A study in the United States has found that children who grow up without a father are negatively impacted in many areas including poverty, health, incarceration, crime, teen pregnancy, child abuse, drug abuse, alcohol abuse, education, and childhood obesity.

Fathers have the special role of teaching life lessons and values, growing personal identity, and imbuing the child with self-confidence and courage.

In an urbanised society, fatherhood is less instinctive and runs the grave danger of being lost.

Fathers often think that their responsibility is merely to provide shelter and food for the body, but forget that they also need to cultivate the values, character, soul, and spirit of their child.

Too often we treat parenting as though it is as natural as making babies, but once we become parents, we know that this is not the case. Motherhood is probably more instinctive as the mother and child have a physical connection through the gestation of the child that lasts around 10 months—the need to feed and protect the child, respond to the child's cry, comfort the child in sickness, and attend to the child's health and hygiene, comes more or less naturally to the mother.

Fathers have the special role of teaching life lessons and values, growing personal identity, and imbuing the child with self-confidence and the courage to be different when necessary and appropriate. This need for father leadership is the same for both girls and boys. But fatherhood, especially in an urban setting, is arguably much less instinctive than motherhood.

In an agrarian society, fatherhood is more instinctive as children are taught the following life lessons by the father as he exercises his superior physical strength to plant, reap, and harvest:

- Honour seasons
- Sow in order to reap
- Exercise diligence
- Exercise discipline
- Honour your elders and learn from them
- Honour time
- Honour nature

In an urbanised society, fatherhood is less instinctive and runs the grave danger of being lost. In a society where many women choose to work while they raise a family, wives ask their husbands for help and fathers end up, if they are not conscious and deliberate about it, performing the role of mothers and forgetting their role as fathers.

Fatherhood is less instinctive because the need is less obvious—fathers often think that their responsibility is merely to provide shelter and food for the body, but forget that they also need to cultivate the values, character, soul, and spirit of their child.

In the early years, from nursery through kindergarten to primary school, the child needs most of all to feel protected and cared for—these

Fathers have the special role of leading their children through a world today that is seeing:

- A failure of leadership
- A shortage of ideas and of thinking
- The rise of relativism

These three challenges of leadership, thinking, and relativism have to be addressed by everyone having a clear set of values.

While the internet is a great source of knowledge and information, it is also a platform where readers, whether consciously or unconsciously, take the easy way out and stop thinking for themselves and stop questioning the veracity of what they are reading.

The responsibility for identity, self-confidence, and the courage to be different lies primarily with fathers.

needs are typically fulfilled by the mother. But as the child enters the teenage years, standing out from peers becomes awkward and it becomes much easier to follow the herd. These are the years where the child needs most of all to have a strong sense of identity, self-confidence, and courage to be different at times.

Fathers have the special role of leading their children through a world today that is seeing:

- **A failure of leadership**
- **A shortage of ideas and of thinking**
- **The rise of relativism**

It is a world where children, if not carefully grounded with self-confidence and self-respect, will end up simply following the crowd, only to discover later in life that most people are only looking out for their selfish wants, rather than caring about the well-being of others.

These three challenges of leadership, thinking, and relativism have to be addressed by everyone having a clear set of values for life, so as to:

- **Shape the way they think**
- **Guide what they think about**
- **Question why they think the way they think**

This is particularly important in the internet age. While the internet is a great source of knowledge and information, it is also a platform where readers, whether consciously or unconsciously, take the easy way out and stop thinking for themselves and stop questioning the veracity of what they are reading.

The responsibility for identity, self-confidence, and the courage to be different lies primarily with fathers. And these qualities are absolutely critical for children to succeed in a world that is increasingly volatile, uncertain, complex, and ambiguous.

Are You The Pride Of Your Child?

The book of Proverbs in the Bible (New International Version) states in Chapter 17 Verse 6: "Children's children are a crown to the aged, and parents are the pride of their children."

Children who are proud of their parents see that there is something honourable about how their parents behave and what their parents have done for them.

If you want to be able to be proud of your children, first ensure that you are behaving in a way that your children can be proud of you, and also ensure that you are treating your parents in a way that you would like your children to treat you.

Di Zi Gui (弟子规) is a useful standard teaching guide that has been used for thousands of years in China to highlight the basic requisites for being a good person and provides guidelines for living in harmony with others.

This is a very interesting statement.

The first part—that grandchildren are a prize for grandparents—is clear and intuitive. However, the second part—"parents are the pride of their children"—would be surprising to many people, because what we most often hear around us is children being the pride of their parents. Just think of how frequently you hear parents boasting about their children!

Parents work hard and sacrifice for their children, in hopes that their children would behave so well or achieve so much in life that they would boost the sense of pride or of achievement of their parents. Every achievement of their children, whether in school or university, in studies or athletics, is one more thing for the parents to be proud of.

What could "parents are the pride of their children" possibly mean?

It means that children are proud of how their parents act and behave on a daily basis, and are grateful to their parents for bringing them up. As children compare themselves with their peers, children who are proud of their parents see that there is something honourable about how their parents behave and what their parents have done for them. Their parents have taught them through their actions, reactions, responses, and attitudes towards others what it is to be an honourable human being.

So parents, if you want to be able to be proud of your children, first ensure that you are behaving in a way that your children can be proud of you, and also ensure that you are treating your parents in a way that you would like your children to treat you. Children should be learning primarily from their parents and family, rather than from their teachers, domestic helpers, or friends in school.

DI ZI GUI (弟子规)

Di Zi Gui (弟子规), roughly translated "Standards for Being a Good Pupil and Child—A Guide to a Happy Life", is a useful standard teaching guide that has been used for thousands of years in China to highlight the basic requisites for being a good person and provides guidelines for living in harmony with others.

Di Zi Gui comprises a collection of three character phrases, 1,080 characters in all, carefully selected to aid memory. Chinese students

While students of *Di Zi Gui* may not be perfect in all they think or do, *Di Zi Gui* provides a reference and serves as a benchmark that keeps them on and/or draws them back to a good path in life.

The ideas introduced in *Di Zi Gui* are useful for everyone, regardless of ethnicity or religion.

Basic moral values and virtues should be first taught to a child from birth:

- Honour elders
- Honour brothers and sisters
- Honour wife and husband
- Honour society
- Honour one's country

learn to recite the collection of wisdom at a young age, and even though they may not fully understand or appreciate the meaning, the concepts conveyed become their standard for life. While students of *Di Zi Gui* may not be perfect in all they think or do, *Di Zi Gui* provides a reference and serves as a benchmark that keeps them on and/or draws them back to a good path in life.

Based on the teachings of Confucius and the Chinese sages, the ideas introduced in *Di Zi Gui* are useful for everyone, regardless of ethnicity or religion. The moral precepts are universal in application, so all of us can profit from it.

An interesting comment on the wisdom of the Chinese ancients came from Pope Francis of the Catholic Church in an interview about China published on 2 February 2016 in the Asia Times, an online newspaper based in Hong Kong: *"For me, China has always been a reference point of greatness. A great country."* Pope Francis continued: *"But more than a country, a great culture, with an inexhaustible wisdom."*

According to *Di Zi Gui*, basic moral values and virtues should be first taught to a child from birth, otherwise all other learnings will be worthless. These values are:

- **Honour elders**
- **Honour brothers and sisters**
- **Honour wife and husband**
- **Honour society**
- **Honour one's country**

And this is reflected by the titles of the seven chapters in the book:

- **Chapter 1**: At Home, Be Dutiful to My Parents
- **Chapter 2**: Standards for Younger Brothers (and Juniors) when Away from Home
- **Chapter 3**: Be Cautious (or Reverent) in My Daily Life
- **Chapter 4**: Be Trustworthy
- **Chapter 5**: Love All Equally
- **Chapter 6**: Be Close to and Learn from People of Virtue and Compassion

The virtues mentioned in *Di Zi Gui* offer perspective against the selfishness, greed, and "win-at-all-cost" competitiveness that pervades so much of the world today.

Di Zi Gui starts by giving substance to the idea of honouring parents, then goes on to larger dimensions of attitudes towards others and the virtues that undergird identity, trustworthiness, and purposefulness, which would enhance one's ability to withstand the pressures of an ever changing world.

Di Zi Gui Chapter 1: At Home, Be Dutiful to My Parents

- **Chapter 7**: After All the Above are Accomplished, I Should Study Further and Learn Literature and Art to Improve My Cultural and Spiritual Life

While *Di Zi Gui* has often been denigrated as teaching blind obedience to parents, it needs to be understood in terms of its foundational precepts of honouring one's parents, trustworthiness, honesty, concern for others, and honourable conduct as more important than wealth or intellect. These are virtues that are still relevant to modern life. In fact, they are virtues that offer perspective against the selfishness, greed, and "win-at-all-cost" competitiveness that pervades so much of the world today.

Here are extracts from *Di Zi Gui* with English Translation.[13] They start by giving substance to the idea of honouring parents, then go on to larger dimensions of attitudes towards others and the virtues that undergird identity, trustworthiness, and purposefulness, which would enhance one's ability to withstand the pressures of an ever changing world.

Di Zi Gui Chapter 1: At Home, Be Dutiful to My Parents

父母呼，应勿缓，父母命，行勿懒
When parents call, when they ask me to do something, I will do it quickly.

父母教，须敬听，父母责，需我承
When my parents instruct me, I will listen respectfully.
When my parents reproach me, I will obey and accept their scolding. I will try hard to change and improve myself.

冬则温，夏则清，晨则省，昏则定
In the winter, I will keep my parents warm; in the summer, I will keep my parents cool.
I will always greet my parents in the morning to show them that I care.
At night, I will always make sure my parents rest well.

I will persist in whatever I do and will not change my aspirations at will.

A matter may be trivial, but if it is wrong to do it or unfair to another person, I must not do it thinking it will bear little or no consequence.

If my virtues are compromised, my parents will feel ashamed.

出必告，返必面，居有常，业无变

Before going out, I must tell my parents where I am going, for parents are always concerned about their children.

After returning home, I must go and see my parents to let them know I am back, so they do not worry about me.

I will maintain a permanent place to stay and live a routine in life.

I will persist in whatever I do and will not change my aspirations at will.

事虽小，勿擅为，苟擅为，子道亏

A matter may be trivial, but if it is wrong to do it or unfair to another person, I must not do it thinking it will bear little or no consequence.

If I do, I am not being a dutiful child because my parents would not want to see me doing things that are irrational or illegal.

物虽小，勿私藏，苟私藏，亲心伤

Even though a thing may be small, I will not keep it a secret from my parents.

If I keep it from my parents, I will hurt their feelings.

亲所好，力为具，亲所恶，谨为去

If whatever pleases my parents is fair and reasonable, I will try my best to attain it for them.

If something displeases my parents, within reason I will cautiously keep it away from them.

身有伤，贻亲忧，德有伤，贻亲羞

When my body is hurt, my parents will be worried.

If my virtues are compromised, my parents will feel ashamed.

If I can be dutiful to parents who hate me, only then will I meet the standards of the saints and sages for being a dutiful child.

When my parents do wrong, I will urge them to change.

Di Zi Gui Chapter 2: Standards for Younger Brothers (and Juniors) When Away from Home

When money and material things are taken lightly, how can resentment arise?

When I am careful with words and hold back hurtful comments, anger naturally dissipates.

亲爱我，孝何难，亲憎我，孝方贤

When I have loving parents, it is not difficult to be dutiful to them.

But if I can be dutiful to parents who hate me, only then will I meet the standards of the saints and sages for being a dutiful child.

亲有过，谏使更，怡吾色，柔吾声

When my parents do wrong, I will urge them to change.

I will do it with a kind facial expression and a warm gentle voice.

谏不入，悦复谏，号泣随，挞无怨

If they do not accept my advice, I will wait until they are in a happier mood before I attempt to dissuade them again, followed by crying, if necessary, to make them understand.

If they end up whipping me I will not hold a grudge against them.

Di Zi Gui Chapter 2: Standards for Younger Brothers (and Juniors) When Away from Home

兄道友，弟道恭，兄弟睦，孝在中

If I am the older sibling, I will befriend the younger ones.

If I am the younger sibling, I will respect and love the older ones.

Only when I can maintain harmonious relationships with my siblings am I being dutiful to my parents.

财物轻，怨何生，言语忍，愤自泯

When money and material things are taken lightly, how can resentment arise?

When I am careful with words and hold back hurtful comments, anger naturally dissipates.

Whether I am drinking, eating, walking, or sitting, I will let the elders go first; the junior ones should follow.

When answering a question, I will look at the person who is asking me the question.

Di Zi Gui Chapter 3: Be Cautious (or Reverent) in My Daily Life

When I realise that time is passing me by and cannot be turned back, and that I am getting older year by year, I will especially treasure the present moment.

或饮食，或坐走，长者先，幼者后

Whether I am drinking, eating, walking, or sitting, I will let the elders go first; the junior ones should follow.

长呼人，即代叫，人不在，己先到

When an elder is asking for someone, I will get that person for him right away.

If I cannot find that person, I will immediately report back and put myself at the elder's service instead.

称尊长，勿呼名，对尊长，勿见能

When I address an elder, I should not call him by his given name. This is in accord with ancient Chinese etiquette.

In front of an elder, I will never show off.

尊长前，声要低，低下闻，为非宜

Before an elder, I will speak softly.

But if my voice is too low and hard to hear, it is not appropriate.

进必趋，退必迟，问起对，视勿移

When meeting an elder, I will walk briskly towards him; when leaving, I will not exit in haste.

When answering a question, I will look at the person who is asking me the question.

Di Zi Gui Chapter 3: Be Cautious (or Reverent) in My Daily Life

朝起早，夜眠迟，老易至，惜此时

I will get up each morning before my parents; at night, I will go to bed only after my parents have gone to sleep.

When I realise that time is passing me by and cannot be turned back, and that I am getting older year by year, I will especially treasure the present moment.

I will avoid doing things in a hurry, as doing things in haste will lead to many mistakes.

I should not be afraid of difficult tasks, and I will not become careless when a job is too easy.

Before borrowing things from others, I must ask for permission. If I do not ask, it is stealing.

晨必盥，兼漱口，便溺回，辄净手

When I get up in the morning, I will wash my face and brush
my teeth.

After using the toilet, I will always wash my hands.

对饮食，勿拣选，食适可，勿过则

When it comes to eating and drinking, I will not pick and
choose my food.

I will only eat the right amount; I will not overeat.

年方少，勿饮酒，饮酒醉，最为丑

I am still young. I must not drink alcohol.

When I am drunk, my behaviour will turn ugly.

事勿忙，忙多错，勿畏难，勿轻略

I will avoid doing things in a hurry, as doing things in haste
will lead to many mistakes.

I should not be afraid of difficult tasks, and I will not become
careless when a job is too easy.

斗闹场，绝勿近，邪僻事，绝勿问

I will keep away from rowdy places.

I will not ask about things that are abnormal or unusual.

将入门，问谁存，将上堂，声必扬

When I am about to enter a main entrance, I must first ask if
someone is inside.

Before entering a room, I must first make myself heard, so that
those inside know someone is approaching.

人问谁，对以名，吾与我，不分明

If someone asks who I am, I must give my name.

To answer "It is me" or "Me" is not sufficient.

用人物，须明求，倘不问，即为偷

Before borrowing things from others, I must ask for permission.

If I do not ask, it is stealing.

Di Zi Gui Chapter 4: Be Trustworthy

When I speak, honesty is important.
Deceitful words and lies must not be tolerated.

Rather than talking too much, it is better to speak less. I will speak only the truth; I will not twist the facts.

Cunning words, foul language, and philistine habits must be avoided at all costs.

If I am asked to do something that is inappropriate or bad, I must not agree to it.
If I do, I will be doubly wrong.

凡出言，信为先，诈与妄，奚可焉
When I speak, honesty is important.
Deceitful words and lies must not be tolerated.

话说多，不如少，惟其是，勿佞巧
Rather than talking too much, it is better to speak less.
I will speak only the truth; I will not twist the facts.

刻薄词，秽污词，市井气，切戒之
Cunning words, foul language, and philistine habits must be
avoided at all costs.

事非宜，勿轻诺，苟轻诺，进退错
If I am asked to do something that is inappropriate or bad, I
must not agree to it.
If I do, I will be doubly wrong.

凡道字，重且舒，勿急疾，勿模糊
I must speak clearly and to the point.
I must not talk too fast or mumble.

彼说长，此说短，不关己，莫闲管
Some like to talk about the good points of others, while some
like to talk about the faults of others.
If it is none of my business, I will not get involved.

见人善，即思齐，纵去远，以渐跻
When I see others do good deeds, I must think about following
their example.
Even though my own achievements are still far behind those
of others, I am getting closer.

When I see others do wrong, I must immediately reflect upon myself.

If criticism makes me angry and compliments make me happy, bad company will come my way and good friends will shy away.

If any mistake I make is inadvertent, it is merely a mistake. If it is done on purpose, however, it is an evil act.

If I correct my mistake and do not repeat it, I no longer own the mistake. If I try to cover it up, I will be doubly wrong.

见人恶，即内省，有则改，无加警

When I see others do wrong, I must immediately reflect upon myself.

If I have made the same mistake, I will correct it.

If not, I will take extra care to not make the same mistake.

惟德学，惟才艺，不如人，当自励

When my morals, conduct, knowledge, and skills seem not as good as those of others, I will encourage myself to be better.

若衣服，若环食，不如人，勿生戚

If the clothes I wear, and the food I eat and drink are not as good as that of others, I should not be concerned.

闻过怒，闻誉乐，损友来，益友却

If criticism makes me angry and compliments make me happy, bad company will come my way and good friends will shy away.

闻誉恐，闻过欣，直谅士，渐相亲

If I am uneasy about compliments and appreciate criticism, then sincere, understanding, and virtuous people will gradually come close to me.

无心非，名为错，有心非，名为恶

If any mistake I make is inadvertent, it is merely a mistake.

If it is done on purpose, however, it is an evil act.

过能改，归于无，倘掩饰，增一辜

If I correct my mistake and do not repeat it, I no longer own the mistake.

If I try to cover it up, I will be doubly wrong.

Di Zi Gui Chapter 5: Love All Equally

Human beings, regardless of nationality, race, or religion—everyone—should be loved equally. We are all sheltered by the same sky and we all live on the same planet Earth.

A person of high ideals and morals is highly respected. What people value is not based on looks.

Admiration from others does not come from boasting or praising oneself.

If I am a very capable person, I should use my capabilities for the benefit of others.

I will not flatter the rich, or despise the poor.

凡是人，皆须爱，天同覆，地同载

Human beings, regardless of nationality, race, or religion—
   everyone—should be loved equally.
We are all sheltered by the same sky and we all live on the
   same planet Earth.

行高者，名自高，人所重，非貌高

A person of high ideals and morals is highly respected.
What people value is not based on looks.

才大者，望自大，人所服，非言大

A person's outstanding abilities will naturally endow him with
   a good reputation.
Admiration from others does not come from boasting or
   praising oneself.

己有能，勿自私，人有能，勿轻訾

If I am a very capable person, I should use my capabilities for
   the benefit of others.
Other people's competence should never be slandered.

勿谄富，勿骄贫，勿厌故，勿喜新

I will not flatter the rich, or despise the poor.
I will not ignore old friends, only taking delight in new ones.

人有短，切莫揭，人有私，切莫说

If a person has a shortcoming, I will not expose it.
If a person has a secret, I will not tell others.

道人善，即是善，人知之，愈思勉

Praising the goodness of others is a good deed in itself.
When people are being praised and approved of, they will be
   encouraged to try even harder.

Spreading rumours about the wrongdoings of others is a wrongdoing in itself.

When I encourage another to do good, both of our virtues are built up.

It is better to give more and take less.

When I ask others to do something, I must first ask myself if I would be willing to do it.

I must repay the kindness of others and let go of my resentments.

When I am directing maids and servants, I will act honourably and properly.

扬人短，即是恶，疾之甚，祸且作

Spreading rumours about the wrongdoings of others is a wrongdoing in itself.

When the harm done has reached the extreme, misfortunes will surely follow.

善相劝，德皆建，过不规，道两亏

When I encourage another to do good, both of our virtues are built up.

Not dissuading the other person from doing wrong damages both parties' character.

凡取与，贵分晓，与宜多，取宜少

Whether I take or give, I need to know the difference between the two.

It is better to give more and take less.

将加人，先问己，己不欲，即速已

When I ask others to do something, I must first ask myself if I would be willing to do it.

If it is not something I would be willing to do, I will not ask others to do it.

恩欲报，怨欲忘，报怨短，报恩长

I must repay the kindness of others and let go of my resentments.

I will spend less time holding grudges and more time paying back the kindness of others.

待婢仆，身贵端，虽贵端，慈而宽

When I am directing maids and servants, I will act honourably and properly.

I will also treat them kindly and generously.

Di Zi Gui Chapter 6: Be Close to and Learn From People of Virtue and Compassion

We are all human, but we are not all the same.

A truly virtuous person is greatly respected by others. He will not be afraid to speak the truth and he will not fawn on others.

势服人，心不然，理服人，方无言

If I use my influence to make them submissive, their hearts will not be with me.

If I can convince them with sound reasoning, they have nothing to object to.

Di Zi Gui Chapter 6: Be Close to and Learn From People of Virtue and Compassion

同是人，类不齐，流俗众，仁者希

We are all human, but we are not all the same.

Most of us are ordinary; only very few have great virtues and high moral principles.

果仁者，人多畏，言不讳，色不媚

A truly virtuous person is greatly respected by others.

He will not be afraid to speak the truth and he will not fawn on others.

能亲仁，无限好，德日进，过日少

If I can be close to and learn from people of great virtue and compassion, I will benefit immensely.

My virtues will grow daily and my wrongdoings will lessen day by day.

不亲仁，无限害，小人进，百事坏

If I choose not to be close to and learn from people of great virtue, I will suffer a great loss.

People without virtue will get close to me and nothing I attempt will succeed.

Di Zi Gui Chapter 7: After All the Above Are Accomplished, I Should Study Further and Learn Literature and Art to Improve My Cultural and Spiritual Life

If I do not actively practise what I have learned, but continue to study on the surface, even though my knowledge is increasing, it is only superficial.

If I do apply my knowledge diligently, but stop studying, I will only do things based on my own opinion, thinking it is correct. In fact, what I know is not the truth.

By honouring these unchangeable relationships with our father, mother, and relatives, we become more responsible in other areas of our life, and this maturity then helps us to fulfil our calling and lead more loving and meaningful lives.

Parents carry the primary burden in inculcating values and virtues. It is in the best interest of parents to honour teachers who share this journey with them.

Di Zi Gui Chapter 7: After All the Above Are Accomplished, I Should Study Further and Learn Literature and Art to Improve My Cultural and Spiritual Life

不力行，但学文，长浮华，成何人

If I do not actively practise what I have learned, but continue to study on the surface, even though my knowledge is increasing, it is only superficial. What kind of person will I be?

但力行，不学文，任己见，昧理真

If I do apply my knowledge diligently, but stop studying, I will only do things based on my own opinion, thinking it is correct. In fact, what I know is not the truth.

SUMMARY: HONOUR IN FAMILIES

We all have a father and a mother whom we did not choose. Whether we know who they are, or whether we like them, this parent-child relationship is unchangeable. And through this unchangeable relationship, we have other unchangeable relationships with other relatives.

Honour is what we give to others unconditionally, simply because they are fellow human beings. Because of the unchanging nature of these relationships with our parents and our relatives, instruction on Honour and the practice of Honour begins at home.

By honouring these unchangeable relationships with our father, mother, and relatives, we become more responsible in other areas of our life, and this maturity then helps us to fulfil our calling and lead more loving and meaningful lives.

Since values are "caught" and not taught, and the morally formative years are from one to six years old, parents carry the primary burden in inculcating values and virtues in their children. It is in the best interest of parents to honour teachers who share this journey with them.

The different roles of a father and a mother in a child's life unavoidably shapes the child. The degree to which fathers and mothers respect and support each other in their marriage, as well as how family members

The degree to which fathers and mothers respect and support each other in their marriage, as well as how family members honour each other, has enormous effect on the child's sense of security, assurance, and confidence in life.

As marriages are the foundations of families, it is in our best interest to build honourable marriages, and support the marriages in our lives to be honourable.

The first instruction for all children is to honour their mother and their father, simply because they are their parents.

Parents should take care to behave in a way that honours their children and causes their children to be proud of their father and their mother.

honour each other, has enormous effect on the child's sense of security, assurance, and confidence in life.

As marriages are the foundations of families, it is in our best interest to build honourable marriages, and support the marriages in our lives to be honourable. It is also in the best interest of those who are not yet married to date with Honour and also help every child in their spheres of influence live in a safe and loving environment.

The first instruction for all children is to honour their mother and their father, simply because they are their parents—not because they are perfect, but simply because they are the parents who had given life, and hopefully also love, to them. It is an unconditional relationship.

And aligned with the law of cause and effect, parents should also take care to behave in a way that honours their children and causes their children to be proud of their father and their mother.

It might be helpful to discuss as a family and agree on a set of simple family rules. And it would be useful to hang it on the living room wall to serve as a daily reminder. One example we have seen is as follows:

FAMILY RULES

Always tell the truth

Work hard

Keep your promises

Don't whine

Always say "I love you"

Use kind words

Do your best

Be thankful

Be kind

Share always

Help others

Clean up after yourself

Win in Family. Win with Honour.

WIN

WITH

HONOUR

IN YOUR

FAMILY

BY ASKING YOURSELF:

- Do I know the love language of my family members? If I know their love language, am I communicating in their love language?

- Am I honouring my father and my mother by showing them active regard and spending time with them?

- Am I honouring my marriage and/or supporting the marriages in my spheres of influence to be honourable?

- Am I living my life in such a way that my children and/or the children in my spheres of influence are proud of me?

- Am I helping my family members be the best that they can be?

PART VII

HONOUR IN COMMUNITIES
HONOURING OUR RESPONSIBILITY

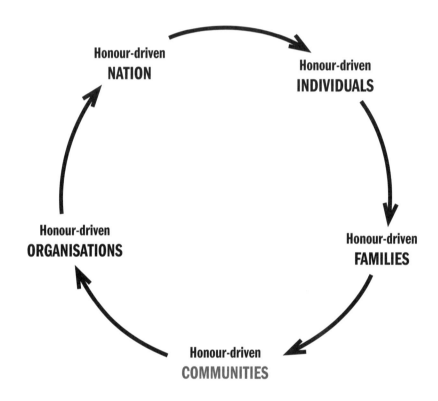

THE HONOUR CIRCLE

After the family, it is the community that defines life in a nation. Hence, it is important for us to think about contributing to our communities—for without strong communities, the chances for the survival and success of organisations, and of our nation will be compromised.

For communities to thrive, it is important for us to

- **Honour our Institutions**
- **Honour our Neighbours**
- **Honour Public Spaces**
- **Honour the Elderly**
- **Honour the Invisible People**
- **Honour the Forgotten People**
- **Honour Foreigners**
- **Honour Different Cultures and Religions**
- **Honour Collective Long-Term Well-Being**
- **Honour our Government**

HONOUR OUR INSTITUTIONS

There are two human institutions that give security and stability to our lives:

- **Marriage**—to provide security, stability, and protection for children and family in a society
- **Government**—to provide security, stability, and protection for people in the country

When either of these two institutions disintegrates or loses its influence and effectiveness, the survival and success of the country is endangered. It is thus important for us to honour these two institutions, even though we might not always agree with the parties or policies involved.

When considering the role of Honour in Community, it is natural to look first at the challenges in the immediate neighbourhood and then

Honour our Institutions. There are two human institutions that give security and stability to our lives:

- Marriage
- Government

Honour our Neighbours. Our neighbours are whoever we cannot avoid running into; they are anyone we see and whose paths we cross.

"Love your neighbour as yourself."

Living by the Golden Rule requires one to

- Empathise with one's neighbour
- Think of one's neighbour as oneself

Mutual social consideration acts as a "social grease".

go on to the broader framework of organisations, government policies and practices, and to the even larger global perspective such as our environment, climate change, and so on.

In so doing, we move from the immediate that we can act on, to the more distant that we can influence, to the global where we can only do our part and hope that others would do their part.

HONOUR OUR NEIGHBOURS

At the community level, the most important starting point is simply to think about our neighbours. As the Chinese saying goes: "远亲不如近邻"—"a distant relative is not as good as a near neighbour".

Who are our neighbours?

Our neighbours are whoever we cannot avoid running into—they are the people living next door to us; they are the people we mingle with at the market and malls; they are our fellow travellers on the buses and the trains; they are our schoolmates and work colleagues, etc. They are anyone we see and whose paths we cross.

The universal golden rule across religions and ethnic traditions to "love your neighbour as yourself" is an easy enough principle by which to live: treat others as one would like others to treat oneself, and be sure not to treat others in ways that one would not like to be treated.

Living by the Golden Rule requires one to

- Empathise with one's neighbour
- Think of one's neighbour as oneself

As we look out for the best interest of our neighbours, we initiate a positive cycle where we eventually reap the good that we sow.

HONOUR PUBLIC SPACES

Japanese cities are immensely crowded, but the Japanese have found a way to honour mutual social consideration that acts as a "social grease" that makes crowdedness imperceptible in daily interaction. It is about

Honour Public Spaces.

Honour others by thinking about how others are affected by your thoughts and actions.

Strike a reasonable balance between the "private space" of individuals and the "public space" necessary to keep peace and harmony in the community.

Discourse can lead to stable results only if:

- Parties involved honour each other, and concede the rights of others to hold their views.
- Parties involved honour the collective long-term well-being of the nation above their own preferences and desires, not just for the current generation but also for future generations.

honouring others by thinking about how others are affected by our thoughts and actions. It is about striking a reasonable balance between the "private space" of individuals and the "public space" necessary to keep peace and harmony in the community.

The **"private space"** is the space where the thoughts and actions of the individual do not impinge upon the freedoms of others to similarly enjoy their "private space". When one's thoughts and actions begin to restrict or affect what others can think and act, we have entered into the **"public space".**

For a large country, the conflict between the "private space" and the "public space" can be resolved by the individual moving somewhere else. For example, an American who does not like the way life is in New York can choose to go to California; similarly, a British national who does not like the public behaviour in London can choose to go to Manchester or Glasgow to find social norms that are more to his or her liking.

However, in a small place like Singapore where one can travel from east to west in under one hour, the individual cannot solve his discomfort with social standards or community mores in one part of Singapore by going to another part of Singapore. "Private space" in a small country such as Singapore runs quickly into the "public space", and ways must be found to conduct a public discourse to settle where a reasonable line between the "private space" and the "public space" may be set.

It is important to note that such discourse can lead to stable results only if:

- The parties involved **honour each other**, in that each has a right to his or her views, but also has to concede the rights of others to hold their views.

- The parties involved **honour the collective long-term well-being of the nation above their own preferences and desires, not just for the current generation but also for future generations**.

While geography may set the limits to physical space, it is demographics that will most of all challenge community harmony. An ageing population will hope that the youth of the country will care for the old and the infirm. A shrinking population will hope that the

Honour the Elderly. It is important to honour the elders in our society as one day, we will be old too.

It is essential that we build a society that honours the elderly regardless of kinship, race, religion, or culture, so that when we are old, we will be able to live in a society that honours their elders despite their failing physical capabilities.

It is important for us to be future ready and to actively build a culture of honouring the elderly in our society.

If we are intent to build a culture of Honour in our society, we should identify the teachable moment and take the opportunity to teach the young.

employed will be prepared to give more support, both financially and emotionally, to those who are not employed. A society where more women are giving birth later in life results in more children who are autistic,[14] and this requires society to be more willing to accept and accommodate children with special needs.

HONOUR THE ELDERLY

It is important to honour the elders in our society as one day, we will be old too. It is essential that we build a society that honours the elderly regardless of kinship, race, religion, or culture, so that when we are old, we will be able to live in a society that honours their elders despite their failing physical capabilities.

This is particularly important in Singapore as our population is rapidly aging. According to the United Nations World Population Prospects 2015, Singapore will become a super-aged society by 2026 when one in five persons will be aged 65 or older.[15] This trend will impact every sphere of the nation, not just economically, but also socially and psychologically. Hence, it is important for us to be future ready and to actively build a culture of honouring the elderly in our society.

A tradition of honouring one's elders has also been cited by the Japanese as one of the reasons why they have been able to build a culture of Honour—when an elder sees someone younger misbehaving in public, it is acceptable for the elder to publicly chide the youngster that his or her behaviour is incorrect and, in return, the youngster accepts the feedback provided by the elder and corrects his or her misstep.

Let us consider a situation that we often see during our train commute to work—an elderly person boards the train and is visibly unsteady as the train moves, but he is unable to take a seat as the priority seat is occupied by a youngster busy on his or her mobile device or pretending to sleep.

If we are intent to build a culture of Honour in our society, we should identify the teachable moment and take the opportunity to teach the younger person to give up his or her seat for the elderly by requesting him or her in a gentle voice to stand up in consideration for the elderly. I am sure that no youngster will complain if the request is conveyed in a

Honour the Invisible People.

Singapore is clean very much because there are "invisible people" working while Singaporeans are either fast asleep or not noticing.

It is important that we acknowledge these important "invisible people" either with our spirit and a grateful heart, or when it is possible, take the initiative to personally and publicly acknowledge the contributions of these "invisible people".

It is important that we learn to see beyond the seen to the unseen, and appreciate the efforts of others.

respectful manner that does not seek to shame or blame, but seeks to do what is right for the well-being of someone else.

HONOUR THE INVISIBLE PEOPLE

Ask most people what their impression of Singapore is, and the description "clean and green" often pops up. While Singapore is objectively relatively clean, are the habits of Singaporeans really that clean? One only needs to go to the stadium at the end of a football match or concert to see the mess left behind by the crowd to find out the answer!

Singapore is clean very much because there are "invisible people" working while Singaporeans are either fast asleep or not noticing. This is the same for our toilets, our workplaces, our schools, our trains, etc. It is important that we acknowledge these important "invisible people" either with our spirit and a grateful heart, or when it is possible, take the initiative to personally and publicly acknowledge the contributions of these "invisible people".

In the words of a Japanese person, there is a culture of Honour in Japan because the Japanese do not see with their eyes, but they feel with their "hearts" by actively acknowledging the contributions of "invisible people" in their daily lives. So when the Japanese see a clean room, they see beyond the clean room and appreciate the person and the effort that went into cleaning the room. Similarly, before a meal, the Japanese say "*ittadaki masu*" (meaning "I humbly receive") to acknowledge the farmers, the chefs, and all those who have contributed to every element of the meal.

It is important that we do the same and learn to see beyond the seen to the unseen, and appreciate the efforts of others. So take the time to thank the auntie in your office pantry today, or the bus driver who brings you to work every day. As we personally take the initiative to build a culture of appreciation, one day we will reap what we sow and will be appreciated for what we do for others.

HONOUR THE FORGOTTEN PEOPLE

Beyond honouring the invisible people, it is important for us to honour

Honour the Forgotten People.

When people are forgotten, they often spiral into psychological despair that results in actions that harm themselves and/or others—this affects the well-being of our society as hurt people hurt others, and we are all connected in one way or another.

It is thus important for us to remember the forgotten among us, and take the initiative to reach out to the forgotten by not only "giving him or her a fish, but also teaching him or her how to fish".

the forgotten people. The forgotten people are those whom we often forget because their suffering is hidden under the surface or the fear of rejection keeps them hidden in their homes.

Examples of forgotten people include:

- Children with special needs
- Lonely and isolated people
- The homeless
- The fatherless or motherless (physically, psychologically, and/or emotionally)
- Displaced people
- Depressed people

We all want to be remembered. We all want to be noticed. We all want to be chosen. We all want to matter. When we are forgotten or forsaken, we get hurt, and if we are forgotten on a continuous basis, our spirit might crumble.

When people are forgotten, they often spiral into psychological despair that results in actions that harm themselves and/or others—this affects the well-being of our society as hurt people hurt others, and we are all connected in one way or another. This is especially the case for a small country such as Singapore.

It is thus important for us to remember the forgotten among us, and take the initiative to reach out to the forgotten by not only "giving him or her a fish, but also teaching him or her how to fish" so that he or she can be a fully functioning member of society. We will all be much better off as a society if we choose to do so, as illustrated by the experiences of special education teachers.

The stories we have heard from special education teachers are truly inspirational and remind us of the importance of remembering the forgotten people for the well-being of our society. Special education teachers teach children born with special needs, such as autism, dyslexia, and ADHD (Attention Deficit Hyperactivity Disorder). Success to these teachers is when these children are able to take care of themselves.

While it is challenging to deal with children with special needs, the

The relationship between father, mother, and child is very important for the child's holistic development.

Caregivers are the ones who carry the heaviest burden in caring for the children with special needs. Hence, it is important to not only take care of the child in need, but also the caregivers.

impact of the work of special education teachers, while often under-appreciated and underpaid, is far reaching and directly affects the lives of their families.

One special education teacher shared how she brought 15 of her students on an overseas immersion programme without their parents. Extensive preparations had to be made to familiarise the children with the new situations they would experience, as these children function best when life is predictable and familiar. To prepare the children for their first experience flying in an aeroplane, the teacher arranged for the children to visit a simulated aircraft cabin at one of the polytechnics, and also arranged for a familiarisation experience on a grounded aircraft.

Remarkably, the trip proceeded without mishap. Indeed, while the children were enjoying their independence overseas, the teacher had a continuous stream of text messages from the parents back in Singapore who were worried about how their children were doing. The teacher was clear that it was important to show the children that they could manage themselves without their parents.

Another special education teacher described how her school raised funds to bring the children and their families on a trip to Melaka in Malaysia. These children were from low-income families—they and their parents would never have been able to experience a holiday trip without the support of the school. The school recognised that the relationship between father, mother, and child is very important for the child's holistic development, and also realised that the caregivers—mostly the parents and family at home—are the ones who carry the heaviest burden in caring for the children with special needs. Hence, it was important to not only take care of the child in need, but also the caregiver.

While the teachers of children with special needs do not have an easy time with the children, they are cognisant that they only have to spend five hours every weekday with the children, while the caregivers have to look after the children the rest of the time. Hence the teachers take care to think of time in perspective, and they constantly remind themselves of the good they are doing for parents and families, and not just the children. The teachers look at what they are doing not as a burden for themselves but as lifting the burden, if only for a few hours, for the caregivers.

Honour Foreigners.

You can't hate the roots of a tree and not hate the tree.

We need to honour the foreigners living in our land because without their contributions, our houses and schools will not be built, our toilets and houses will not be cleaned, our children will not be taught, our roads will not be maintained, and so on.

We need to be grateful for the "invisible" efforts of foreigners for we will not have the "visible" benefits that we enjoy without them.

HONOUR FOREIGNERS

More than a quarter of the people in Singapore are foreigners. Hence, it is also important for us to honour the foreigners in our midst, regardless of their economic and/or social status. This is particularly apt for Singaporeans as our ancestors too were immigrants and we must be a people who never forget our roots—as Malcolm X, the famous human rights activist, sagely commented: *"You can't hate the roots of a tree and not hate the tree."*

While there are many foreigners working in high positions for multinational corporations in Singapore, there are also many foreign workers on the opposite side of the economic spectrum who have come to Singapore to work for a fraction of what the average Singaporean earns in order to support their families back home. And for these less well-off foreign workers, there have been reports of Singaporeans abusing them by not giving them enough food, withholding their salaries, installing CCTVs to spy on their every action, not allowing them to have adequate rest, etc.

In addition, there have also been reports of clashes between foreigners and locals where physical blows and harsh words have been exchanged, with the incidents recorded and widely circulated on social media. Such tensions were extremely public during the "Little India Riot" in Singapore on 8 December 2013, involving about 300 migrant labourers from India and lasting for about two hours—it was the second riot in post-independence Singapore, and the first in over 40 years since the 1969 racial riot.

We need to honour the foreigners living in our land because without their contributions, our houses and schools will not be built, our toilets and houses will not be cleaned, our children will not be taught, our roads will not be maintained, and so on. We need to be grateful for their "invisible" efforts for we will not have the "visible" benefits that we enjoy without them.

Someone once commented that social behaviour has taken a turn for the worse in Singapore over the past few years because Singaporeans see foreigners getting away with "bad behaviour" (e.g. not waiting in line), and thus behave in a similar way so that they do not "lose out".

While this is plausible and while there are admittedly many foreigners

Singaporeans need to take responsibility for the social behaviour that they desire and educate foreigners when they act out of line.

The standard of Honour is something for us to set and for us to lose. It starts with us.

Honour Different Cultures and Religions.

A population with ethnic and religious diversity must continually work at seeing advantage and synergies in diversity, rather than conflict and disagreements.

Accepting differences while recognising strengths is the way forward if we want our nation to survive and our country to thrive.

who hold differing values, this is no excuse for Singaporeans to copy bad behaviour. Singaporeans need to take responsibility for the social behaviour that they desire and educate foreigners when they act out of line. This is seen in Japan where foreigners naturally become more polite and considerate because they know that this is the expected behaviour in Japan. Once we set a social benchmark, foreigners will naturally align themselves to this benchmark.

The standard of Honour is something for us to set and for us to lose. It starts with us.

HONOUR DIFFERENT CULTURES AND RELIGIONS

A population with ethnic and religious diversity must continually work at seeing advantage and synergies in diversity, rather than conflict and disagreements. It is better to have neighbours who interact, and even occasionally quarrel, than neighbours who do not talk to each other and let the annoyance accumulate till it blows up into irreconcilable dispute.

The idea that it is better not to interact with neighbours in order to keep the peace is false security. Identifying and honouring the good in other cultures and religions will ease the way for a win-win situation. New immigrants need to be integrated into the community, and it has to be the responsibility of long-standing residents to offer a helping hand and an open heart, and to teach the foreigner the expected standards and ways of doing things in our society. This will pave the way for sustained racial, religious, and community harmony. Accepting differences while recognising strengths is the way forward if we want our nation to survive and our country to thrive.

As Mohammad Alami Musa, Head of Studies on Inter-religious Relations in Plural Societies (SRP) Programme at the S. Rajaratnam School of International Studies (RSIS), Nanyang Technological University, wrote in a commentary[16]:

"Religious harmony built on scant knowledge and a non-inclusive attitude of the 'Religious Other' will not endure the severe tests on inter-religious relations in a world replete with religious-linked conflicts. A non-zero-sum mindset can develop sustainable religious peace."

The maintenance of religious harmony is too critical a matter to be left to chance.

One factor critics always miss is the strong selfless commitment of religious leaders in Singapore to protect religious harmony, arising from their sense of self-discipline and self-responsibility.

Alami Musa also made the following points in the same commentary published in 2015:

"Fifty years had passed since its independence and Singapore is still an oasis of harmony in a world of violent conflicts perpetuated by actors who use religious narratives to justify their actions.

"Critics of Singapore's political system are quick to attribute this success to their perception that Singapore is a quasi-authoritarian state characterised by the draconian use of a strict legislative framework, socially intrusive policies and uncompromising enforcement to 'nip in the bud' any tendencies causing disruptions to religious harmony.

Eradicating Feelings of Superiority and Arrogance

"Singapore offers no apology for adopting a very tough approach to maintain order inspite of the emergence of the 'new normal'—one that expects the state to be gentler in governing society, especially in the realm of religion. The maintenance of religious harmony is too critical a matter to be left to chance and because of this, the state will continue to play its custodial role in ensuring that religious peace is sustained in the coming years.

"Nevertheless, one factor critics always miss is the strong selfless commitment of religious leaders in Singapore to protect religious harmony, arising from their sense of self-discipline and self-responsibility. This is the uniquely Singapore factor that does not exist in many countries.

"Their influence on creating a positive inter-religious milieu is far greater than the available powerful instruments of the state and their significant contributions to social peace began even before the birth of the new Singaporean state.

"For example, leaders of the Inter Religious Organisation (IRO) were pro-active in mobilising faith leaders to put forth the peaceful nature of religion and played a major role in the reconciliation process within the population in the aftermath of the 1950 Maria Hertogh and the 1964 communal riots.

"Religious leaders continue to play a crucial role in building religious

The harmony now enjoyed by Singapore is largely dependent on goodwill as well as tolerance, and has been able to hold Singapore's religiously plural society together.

Religious communities should embrace a 'non-zero sum' mindset in religious life when encountering those from other communities.

The non-zero sum mindset calls for celebration of the joy of having others (neighbours, friends, and colleagues) as belonging to different religions and acceptance that these other religions are valuable.

Each religious community must put aside feelings of arrogance and claims of superiority.

harmony today. The harmony now enjoyed by Singapore is largely dependent on goodwill as well as tolerance, and has been able to hold Singapore's religiously plural society together even though it is built on less than adequate knowledge of each other's religious tradition and an attitude that lacks inclusivity of the 'Religious Other'.

"These shortcomings are a source of concern as Singapore enters the next 50 years of its existence in a world that is fraught with volatilities, uncertainties, complexities, and ambiguities in the realm of religious life due to rising fundamentalism, unprecedented religious diversity, and heightened intolerance towards the 'Religious Other'. These external threats may have spill-over effects and severely test inter-religious relations in Singapore.

Non-zero Sum Mindset

"The ties that bind religious communities and the harmony that exists amongst them in future need to be stronger, resilient, and sustainable. The harmony has to be well-founded on inter-religious literacy, a strong attitude of inclusivity of the 'Religious Other', and a feeling of mutual dependence on each other. A global scholar on religion, Paul Knitter, suggested that to achieve this state of relations, religious communities should embrace a 'non-zero sum' mindset in religious life when encountering those from other communities.

"A non-zero sum mindset discourages a religious community to feel superior over the other communities and to compete with, dominate, or even replace them. Rather, it promotes the virtue of humility as well as collaboration so that all religious communities will prosper and none will feel disadvantaged in their inter-religious encounters. This means that the non-zero sum mindset calls for celebration of the joy of having others (neighbours, friends, and colleagues) as belonging to different religions and acceptance that these other religions are valuable.

"To genuinely feel a part of the big Singapore family and collectively work towards stronger as well as resilient religious harmony that is sustainable in future years, each religious community must put aside feelings of arrogance and claims of superiority. These feelings may be

Humility is the hallmark of a gracious religious community seeking a genuine harmonious relationship with the other communities.

There can be a lot of 'cross-learning' amongst people of religion because goodness can be found in all religions.

The inter-religious learning can be so enriching and affirming that it strengthens one's appreciation and commitment to one's own religion.

There will be no harmony amongst communities without harmony amongst religions and there will be no harmony amongst religions without mutuality amongst religions.

difficult to eradicate but this is necessary. Humility is the hallmark of a gracious religious community seeking a genuine harmonious relationship with the other communities.

Prosper Together or Suffer Together

"It is with this feeling of humility that one can find 'gems' in religions other than one's own. These 'gems' are for keeps by those who find them. This is the same for the learning spirit wherever knowledge is found; it is waiting for the learner to acquire it. By the same token, there can be a lot of 'cross-learning' amongst people of religion because goodness can be found in all religions.

"Wherever they are found, they belong to all, regardless of the religion that they come from. In embracing such an ethos, one will discover how beautiful and inspirational other religions are. There is, however, a fear that the discovery of goodness and truths in other religions will weaken one's commitment to one's own religion. The fact may well be to the contrary. The inter-religious learning can be so enriching and affirming that it strengthens one's appreciation and commitment to one's own religion.

"The consequential benefit of such cross-learning is the consciousness that one does not need to hate all other religions, or denigrate, insult, or demonise other religions, to prove one's commitment to one's own religion and have deep faith in it. 'Those who know one religion knows none' according to a renowned scholar on religion, William Cantwell Smith.

"Another global scholar of religion, Hans Kung, wisely said that 'There will be no peace amongst nations without peace amongst religions.'

"Rephrasing Kung's dictum for the Singapore context, one could say: 'There will be no harmony amongst communities without harmony amongst religions and there will be no harmony amongst religions without mutuality amongst religions.'

"Mutuality means reciprocal relations between inter-dependent entities and this can be achieved when religious communities move away from 'zero sum-ness' where some prosper at the expense of others to 'non-zero sum-ness' where all may flourish and none will

Either all religious communities go forward with a non-zero sum mentality or all do not go forward because of the tight inter-dependent context that they are in.

The feeling of inter-dependence will be stronger when people mutually benefit from an inter-religious symbiotic relationship.

Honour Collective Long-Term Well-Being.

Apart from hard work, the Swiss are well-known for their strong sense of community, and their conviction that they themselves have to defend their land and their independence.

feel disadvantaged. Either all religious communities go forward with a non-zero sum mentality or all do not go forward because of the tight inter-dependent context that they are in.

"This feeling of inter-dependence will be stronger when people mutually benefit from an inter-religious symbiotic relationship. They realise how mutually nourishing and enriching the different religions can be on all communities, thus deepening the respect that they have for each other's religion and strengthening mutual trust. This religious harmony will then be resilient in the face of the severe tests on inter-religious relations arising from events within and outside Singapore."

HONOUR COLLECTIVE LONG-TERM WELL-BEING

Switzerland is a small mountainous central European country that is home to numerous lakes, villages, and the Alps. It is also home to a population of eight million, including two global economic centres: Zürich and Geneva. Despite its small size, Switzerland has been ranked as having one of the highest nominal wealth per capita figures in the world.[17]

Just like Singapore has four major languages, Switzerland comprises four main linguistic and cultural regions: German, French, Italian, and Romansh. The Swiss nation and its strong sense of identity and community is thus not founded on a common ethnicity or language, but on a common historical background, as well as shared values such as federalism, hard work, and direct democracy.

Apart from hard work, the Swiss are also well-known for their strong sense of community that is well displayed in their federalist system, where every Swiss citizen gets to vote on some national issue as frequently as once every three months in a referendum.

Several times the Swiss people have had to vote on whether to stop having national service; each time thus far, they have chosen to keep national service, and those who fail to perform their annual in-camp training of 21 days a year have to pay an extra tax amounting to three percent of their annual income—not a small sum! Such is the Swiss conviction that they themselves have to defend their land and their independence.

Think beyond one's own comfort and convenience, and for the long-term well-being of the entire community.

Honour our Government.

The job of the government is to provide the goods and services that people cannot provide for themselves effectively and efficiently.

People should first take the responsibility to provide for themselves to the greatest extent possible.

Where the people decide to hand the responsibility to the government, they have to accept that mass provision by the government can never be as responsive and individually-satisfying as if the people were to provide for themselves.

Even more interestingly, the Swiss have had recent referendums on whether to increase the number of vacation days a year, and to raise the minimum wage in certain sectors. Perhaps unsurprisingly for the Swiss but surprisingly for the rest of the world, the Swiss voted against both the changes! A Swiss limousine driver explained that both measures meant less work hours, so who is going to pay the extra taxes to make up for the loss in productivity?

The mentality of the Swiss to always think beyond one's own comfort and convenience, and for the long-term well-being of the entire community, is one that should be emulated by all of us—for ourselves, for our families, for our communities, for our organisations, and for our country's success.

HONOUR OUR GOVERNMENT

People get the government they deserve. The job of the government is to provide the goods and services that people cannot provide for themselves because they lack organisation and scale to get things done effectively and efficiently.

The fundamental idea should therefore be that people should first take the responsibility to provide for themselves to the greatest extent possible—this way they best exercise personal choice and are best able to satisfy themselves.

Where the people decide to hand the responsibility to the government, they have to accept that mass provision by the government can never be as responsive and individually-satisfying as if the people were to provide for themselves. The government can provide funding for social services, for example, but government can never provide the human touch and the human heart so necessary for many of the social services to be effectual.

The basics of defence and security, law and justice, clearly belong to government; what else the government should do is a matter of implicit or explicit agreement between the government and the people. But for the system to work ultimately to the benefit of the people, the people must be able to trust the government, as must the people honour the institutions

Citizens need the maturity to distinguish between the institutions that must be upheld to serve their need for security and justice, and the people whom they choose to lead the institutions.

The government of the day must provide for the generations to come and do what it believes to be right for the future, even though it may be unpopular for the current generation.

There is a demand for the government to have a superior ability to communicate, and there needs a maturity on the part of the citizenry to think beyond their immediate needs.

Short-sighted policies often result in "beggar thy neighbour" approaches.

of the state as existing for the good of the people. If the institutions are torn down or destroyed, what results is anarchy and confusion, the very antithesis of what is in the best interest of the people.

Citizens of course need the maturity to distinguish between the institutions that must be upheld to serve their need for security and justice, and the people whom they choose to lead the institutions.

In a democracy, the people choose at regular intervals whom they wish to have to lead their government. In this way, the citizens are able to give direct feedback on what they have been pleased or displeased with, and what they hope for the future. A government that is not responsive to the desires of the people will be taken down in due course.

Yet the government carries the responsibility to lead not just the current generation and also meet their needs, but also consider and plan for the needs of future generations to be met, so that they will leave a worthy legacy for the generations to come. It is a difficult call for the government of the day to provide for the generations to come and do what it believes to be right for the future, even though it may be unpopular for the current generation.

There is a demand for the government to have a superior ability to communicate, and there needs a maturity on the part of the citizenry to think beyond their immediate needs. A failure on both fronts will result in a government that is populist in policy and practice, to the detriment of the long-term interest of the people. The government will then be led by the people whom the government is supposed to lead. Such a failure is likely to result when the people do not honour the institution of government, and the government fails to honour the hopes and desires of the people.

Governments of countries, as opposed to local government, also have to be concerned about the global environment and the standing of their countries in the global community of nations. This pertains to peace, security, foreign policy, and diplomacy. It also pertains to cross-border issues such as the environment and illegal immigration.

Short-sighted policies often result in "beggar thy neighbour" approaches. The principle of honouring promises and honouring people in other countries applies here, just like the principle of honouring others applies in families, communities, and organisations. Looking after the

Must short-sighted self-interest prevail or can far-sighted enlightened self-interest hold sway instead? Can Honour rule the individual, the family, the community, the organisation, and the nation?

If we were to become a society where what is legal is right and what is illegal is wrong, we would have subjugated morality to the law, and the whole moral fibre of society would be left directionless.

The laws of the land are basically there to protect the weak and to assure fairness and justice for society as a whole; while congruent with the morals of society, they are not there to define morals.

environment, conserving forests and water resources, preserving flora and fauna as a heritage for future generations, are all cases in point.

Must short-sighted self-interest prevail or can far-sighted enlightened self-interest hold sway instead? Can Honour rule the individual, the family, the community, the organisation, and the nation?

As written in our previous book, "The Leader, The Teacher & You", if we were to become a society where what is legal is right and what is illegal is wrong, we would have subjugated morality to the law, and the whole moral fibre of society would be left directionless.

The law should be the expression of what the conscience of society and the intuition of the individual believe to be right and good. It should set the boundary beyond which the individual would be trespassing onto the rights of others or posing a danger to them.

However, when a society becomes one where the law defines what is right and what is good, the law must become tighter and tighter to tell the individual in greater and greater detail what he/she must do and what he/she must not do. The government will then become more and more autocratic and behave more and more like a god. Accordingly, society will weaken, as the conscience that resides in each one of us becomes silenced.

Where the conscience in the individual is strong and/or where people have the fear of God—which very often is a fear of divine retribution and of what may happen to them in this life or after they die—people will behave responsibly even when there is no one to catch them and punish them.

Think, for example, of the Golden Rule that Jesus Christ teaches: "Do unto others what you would have them do to you." The same rule can be found in various ancient cultures and religions. For example, Confucius taught: "Do not impose on others what you do not desire others to impose upon you"; the Hindu sacred literature *Mahabharata* states: "Let no man do to another that which would be repugnant to himself"; and the Buddhist sacred literature *Udanavarga* says: "Hurt not others in ways you yourself would find hurtful." The laws of the land are basically there to protect the weak and to assure fairness and justice for society as a whole; while congruent with the morals of society, they are not there to define morals.

Confucius said of government: *"If the people are governed by laws and punishment is used to maintain order, they will try to avoid the punishment but have no sense of shame. If they are governed by virtue*

Only Honour and religion can move people to act beyond self-interest and move society to a higher level of care and concern, as well as a deeper sense of community and social responsibility.

It is only when the entire community is committed to act honourably for the long-term well-being of the entire nation that society and community may truly thrive.

It is important that we conscientiously honour our humanity by making room in our lives and taking the time to touch the lives of those in our community who are vulnerable.

By honouring our community, we honour our humanity, and embrace what it means to be a human being.

and rules of propriety are used to maintain order, they will have a sense of shame and will become good as well."

Government cannot keep alive the conscience in each one of us and motivate people from within as to what is right and good. The law and the policeman are there to prevent people from doing what is irresponsible towards others. Only Honour and religion can move people to act beyond self-interest and move society to a higher level of care and concern, as well as a deeper sense of community and social responsibility.

And it is only when the entire community is committed to act honourably for the long-term well-being of the entire nation that society and community may truly thrive.

As Singapore's founding Prime Minister, Mr Lee Kuan Yew, once said: *"Your future really depends on what you make of it. The government can give you that framework and give expression to the will of a people. But the people must have that will. If you don't have it, there's nothing a government can do."*[18]

SUMMARY: HONOUR IN COMMUNITIES

In a broken world, it is important that we conscientiously honour our humanity by making room in our lives and taking the time to touch the lives of those in our community who are vulnerable.

We have to consciously fight the human tendency to form clusters with those who are like ourselves and avoid those who are different from us, as this creates segregation and relational disconnect. We have to consciously fight this natural consequence of abundance and embrace inclusiveness across racial, religious, social, and economic lines.

We should embrace the opportunity to celebrate our community and share with the vulnerable by not hoarding everything for ourselves, for those who are rich materially are often poor spiritually.

By honouring our community, we honour our humanity, and embrace what it means to be a human being.

WIN

WITH

HONOUR

IN YOUR

COMMUNITY

BY ASKING YOURSELF:

- Am I honouring my neighbours, public spaces, institutions, the elderly, the invisible people, the forgotten people, different cultures and religions, collective long-term well-being, and the Government?

- What good am I doing for the lives of others in my community?

- How am I helping the members of my community be the best that they can be?

PART VIII

HONOUR IN ORGANISATIONS
HONOURING OUR POTENTIAL

THE HONOUR CIRCLE

In this part, we discuss the role of Honour in organisations. By organisations, we mean all organisations other than government, be they businesses, corporations, not-for-profits, trusts, charities, societies, or any other corporate form.

As mentioned earlier in this book, there are **three key challenges facing the world today**:

- **The need for clear and strong leadership**
- **The need for individuals to think for themselves**
- **The rise of relativism**

All three challenges have a common solution, which is for goodness, moral behaviour, trustworthiness, and honesty to be honoured, and not compromised. There must be honourable intent and honourable purpose.

As mentioned at the beginning of this book, there are **two fundamental dimensions to Honour** that undergird the formation of trusting long term relationships:

- **Honouring Our Word**
- **Honouring Each Other**

But how many organisations honour their word and honour their customers, employees, etc.?

Many organisations state that they have values such as integrity, respect, honesty, etc. But how many company employees actually know what these values are, and how many employees actually live out these company values?

If a business is to succeed, it must honour its word, honour its values, and honour everyone involved in the business (e.g. customers, employees, stakeholders, etc.); otherwise its workers would be confused of how to act, while its customers will have to deal with a muddled and unfocussed brand.

The business that wants repeat customers must honour the customer in terms of honest, trustworthy service, even if it is a business competing on the basis of lowest cost. Growth of the business requires an ever expanding network of customers who trust the organisation.

In the age of the internet, good news travels fast and bad news travels

If we want a customer to come back again and bring his friends along, we have to ensure that we provide a product or service that honours the needs of others and delivers what has been promised.

We can only be successful if our customers and business partners are successful. Businesses in the 21st century must take responsibility to help solve the problems of society.

Win with Honour by:

- Honouring your Reputation
- Honouring your Customers
- Honouring Quality Business

even faster! The slick and smooth operator who partakes in shenanigans will not survive for long before his bad reputation catches up with him. The rise of the middle class means that customers are prepared to pay extra for a reputable brand that they can trust and be assured of quality. Honour is the name of the game.

Do we believe that Honour and integrity creates a brand that can bring good business? Do we believe we can do good business and have a good conscience at the same time?

If we think of how we choose friends, we know friendship is about trusting and honouring each other, for which honouring our word is critical and non-negotiable. So the same applies in running a business. If we want a customer to come back again and bring his friends along, we have to ensure that we provide a product or service that honours the needs of others and delivers what has been promised. We also need to look at the business as a matter of relationships and an expanding network of contacts, rather than seeing the business as a one-off transaction of a willing, and later possibly not so happy, buyer, and a willing and, for the moment, very happy seller.

As Jack Ma, the founder of Alibaba, wrote in an open letter to the company's investors after unveiling the largest tech IPO ever seen in 2014:

"We can only be successful if our customers and business partners are successful. We firmly believe that businesses in the 21st century must take responsibility to help solve the problems of society… 'customers first, employees second, and shareholders third'…Let me be clear: as fiduciaries of the company, we believe that the only way for Alibaba to create long-term value for shareholders is to create sustainable value for customers. So customers must come first." [19]

Mr Ma added: *"Today, making money is very simple. But making sustainable money while being responsible to the society and improving the world is very difficult."*

In this chapter, we discuss how organisations can Win with Honour by:

- **Honouring your Reputation**
- **Honouring your Customers**
- **Honouring Quality Business**

Honour Your Reputation.

We should be alarmed that corporate wrongdoing has come to be seen as such a routine occurrence.

Years after the global financial crisis rocked investors' confidence in the markets and financial services in general, a culture of integrity has failed to take hold.

HONOUR YOUR REPUTATION

In a New York Times article on 10 July 2012 headlined "The Spreading Scourge of Corporate Corruption", the opening line was: "Perhaps the most surprising aspect of the Libor[20] scandal is how familiar it seems."

And here are some other lines in the article:

- *"The misconduct of the financial industry no longer surprises most Americans.… And it's not just banks that are frowned upon. Trust in big business overall is declining."*

- *"Sixty-two percent of Americans believe corruption is widespread across corporate America. According to Transparency International, an anti-corruption watchdog, nearly three in four Americans believe that corruption has increased over the last three years."*

- *"We should be alarmed that corporate wrongdoing has come to be seen as such a routine occurrence. Capitalism cannot function without trust."*

The New York law firm, Labaton Sucharow LLP collaborated with the University of Notre Dame's Mendoza College of Business in a survey of more than 1,200 US-based and UK-based financial services professionals to examine views on workplace ethics. The results were published in May 2015 under the title "The Street, The Bull and The Crisis".[21]

The key findings were summarised as follows:

- *Nearly seven years after the global financial crisis rocked investors' confidence in the markets and financial services in general, the survey clearly shows that a culture of integrity has failed to take hold. Numerous individuals continue to believe that engaging in illegal or unethical activity is part and parcel of succeeding in the highly competitive field. With legal and regulatory sanctions coming out on almost a daily basis, the industry has a long way to go to regain the confidence of the public.*

- *47% of respondents find it likely that their competitors have engaged in unethical or illegal activity in order to gain an edge in the market. This represents a spike from the 39% who reported as such when*

More than one-third (34%) of those earning USD 500,000 or more annually have witnessed or have first-hand knowledge of wrongdoing in the workplace.

25% would likely use non-public information to make a guaranteed USD 10 million if there was no chance of getting arrested for insider trading.

Nearly one in five respondents feel financial services professionals must at least some-times engage in illegal or unethical activity to be successful.

surveyed in 2012. The figure jumps to 51% for individuals earning USD 500,000 or more per year.

- *More than one-third (34%) of those earning USD 500,000 or more annually have witnessed or have first-hand knowledge of wrongdoing in the workplace.*

- *23% of respondents believe it is likely that fellow employees have engaged in illegal or unethical activity in order to gain an edge, nearly double the 12% that reported as such in 2012.*

- *25% would likely use non-public information to make a guaranteed USD 10 million if there was no chance of getting arrested for insider trading. Employees with less than 10 years' experience are more than two times as likely as those with over 20 years' experience, reporting 32% and 14% respectively.*

- *In the UK, 32% of individuals said they would likely engage in insider trading to earn USD 10 million if there was no chance of getting arrested, compared to 24% of respondents from the US.*

- *Nearly one in five respondents feel financial services professionals must at least sometimes engage in illegal or unethical activity to be successful.*

- *27% of those surveyed disagree that the financial services industry puts the best interests of clients first. This figure rises to 38% for those earning USD 500,000 or more per year.*

- *Nearly one-third of respondents (32%) believe compensation structures or bonus plans in place at their company could incentivise employees to compromise ethics or violate the law.*

- *33% of financial services professionals feel the industry has not changed for the better since the financial crisis.*

- *While the majority of industry professional (89%) would report misconduct given the incentives and protections such as those offered by the SEC (US Securities and Exchange Commission) whistleblower programme, 37% of respondents are still not aware of the SEC's programme.*

- *28% of respondents earning USD 500,000 or more per year (16%*

The worst economic downturn since the 1930s wasn't a banking crisis, a credit crisis, or a mortgage crisis. It was a moral crisis, wilful negligence *in extremis*.

Capitalism is animated by self-interest, but when it's not tamed by moral self-discipline, it can easily become mendacious.

The "invisible hand" of the market is a wonderful thing, but when not guided by a deep sense of moral duty, it can wreak all sorts of havoc.

In the free market, honouring others by choosing to live out the values of integrity, honesty, dependability, and responsibility, is critical to the proper functioning of the market itself.

for all employees) say their company's confidentiality policies and procedures bar the reporting of potential illegal or unethical activities directly to law enforcement or regulatory authorities. In the UK, this rises to 21% for all employees.

- *25% of respondents earning USD 500,000 or more annually have signed or been asked to sign a confidentiality agreement that would prohibit reporting illegal or unethical activities to the authorities.*

- *19% of respondents find it likely that their employer would retaliate if they were to report wrongdoing in the workplace. This jumps to 24% for respondents from the UK.*

Gary Hamel, referring to the Global Financial Crisis in his book, "What Matters Now: How to Win in a World of Relentless Change, Ferocious Competition, and Unstoppable Innovation" (Jossey-Bass 2012), remarked: *"The worst economic downturn since the 1930s wasn't a banking crisis, a credit crisis, or a mortgage crisis. It was a moral crisis, wilful negligence in extremis."*

Hamel also observed in the book that: *"The moral superiority of capitalism rests on the fact that in a free market the only way to do well is to do well for others…Critically, though, the grocer doesn't feed us because he is concerned about our hunger—he feeds us because there is a profit in doing so."*

Hamel further stated: *"Capitalism is animated by self-interest, but when it's not tamed by moral self-discipline, it can easily become mendacious. … When that happens, the powerless get abused and the ignorant get duped, legislators get bought and safeguards get trampled… The 'invisible hand' of the market is a wonderful thing, but when not guided by a deep sense of moral duty, it can wreak all sorts of havoc."*

All the observations above speak of the need for Honour.

Indeed, in the free market, honouring others by choosing to live out the values of integrity, honesty, dependability, and responsibility, is critical to the proper functioning of the market itself. Businesses that seek long-term survival and success should pay heed to this critical foundation.

Businesses have to be concerned about a whole slew of risks, whether

The risk that the business is most in control of, that differentiates one company from another, and makes or breaks the company over the long-term, is reputation risk.

A reputation for professionalism, integrity, and trustworthiness draws customers and business opportunities of the kind that leads to stability and growth.

If it is fast and cheap, it cannot be good; if it is cheap and good, it cannot be fast; if it is good and fast, it cannot be cheap.

Businesses have to choose the reputation they want to build.

they be political risks, regulatory risks, operating risks, key man risks, etc. But the risk that the business is most in control of, which differentiates one company from another, and makes or breaks the company over the long-term, is reputation risk.

A reputation for professionalism, integrity, and trustworthiness draws customers and business opportunities of the kind that leads to stability and growth. A reputation for underhand dealings may yield quick, immediate results, but does not engender trust and confidence, and therefore undermines long-term growth. It is very hard to rebuild the superior image of a brand once it loses its reputation for consistency and reliability.

Reputation is a lot like information technology, which someone has aptly summarised as: "If it is fast and cheap, it cannot be good; if it is cheap and good, it cannot be fast; if it is good and fast, it cannot be cheap." It is an "impossible trilemma"!

Businesses have to choose the reputation they want to build.

There was this manager of a cleaning company whose business was to clean shopping malls and office complexes. She was eyeing the cleaning contract for a shopping mall when she was told that the general manager of the mall was expecting "something" from her. She told her boss that she refused to pay any bribes. She was told she would lose the contract, and indeed she lost the contract.

A few days later she received a phone call. It was from the staff at Citibank branch in the city, which said that they had heard she "did not do bribes", so they wanted her to clean their office. She subsequently got contacted by other companies who also wanted her to clean their offices because she "did not do bribes".

Would any of us have done what she did?

If we simply followed "the ways of the world", we might have decided it was not smart to not do what others were doing. But this would be not thinking for ourselves—it would be handing over our lives and allowing our beliefs to be determined by others.

On the other hand, it would require a measure of faith to do what the manager of the cleaning company did. The point is that she had her own convictions and would have lost her Honour if she simply agreed to do what was against her values and what she felt deep in her heart was wrong.

Choosing to be honourable may be perceived by some as not being street smart, but increasingly it will be seen to be wise and good for the soul and for one's reputation.

Honouring one's word and honouring one's customer makes for good business in the long run.

Honour Your Customers.

Expensive cities such as Zürich survive and manage to maintain high prices and high wages because their people honour themselves and their customers by providing value added customer-centric service, which results in long-term, trustworthy relationships.

This story makes the point that being known to be honest and trustworthy can be good for business. It draws a different range of customers to the business—these being customers who are willing to pay more for a product or a service on the assurance that what they would get is honest service, and who would be more likely to be honourable in payment since Honour is a criterion they use when choosing business partners!

Choosing to be honourable may be perceived by some as not being street smart, but increasingly it will be seen to be wise and good for the soul and for one's reputation. Honouring one's word and honouring one's customer makes for good business in the long run.

HONOUR YOUR CUSTOMERS

Switzerland is a wealthy high cost country that has a very high standard of living. What allows it to keep going strong and stay economically relevant despite its high cost?

If we took a walk through "Old Zürich", the historic part of the city of Zürich, we find many narrow, cobblestoned passageways lined with small, exclusive specialised shops that sell items that are not cheap.

How do these shops possibly succeed and survive?

The answer is not hard to find. These are shops with loyal, satisfied customers who keep coming back because they trust the integrity, honesty, quality, and reliability of the shop owners. These are shops that treat their customers with Honour, and for whom trusted, long-term relationships make for profit, survival, and security.

Expensive cities such as Zürich survive and manage to maintain high prices and high wages because their people honour themselves and their customers by providing value added customer-centric service, which results in long-term, trustworthy relationships that ensure the success and survival of their businesses.

Just think of how many superior brand names in the world have Swiss origins, and consider how they come from a variety of industries such as banks, watches, hotels, and chocolate.

Let us consider an example of an airport transfer. When a driver

The rise of internet transactions means that there is a growing need for trust, where orders are placed in the virtual world for products and services to be delivered in the real world.

Since trust is the life blood of any long-term relationship, and Honour is the foundation of trust, organisations need to continually choose and cultivate a culture of Honour by honouring their:

- Word
- Customers
- Employees
- Stakeholders
- Company values

Honour Quality Business.

in Switzerland picks up his client, he parks the car, finds the trolley, unloads the baggage, leads the client to the check-in counter, unloads the bags on the conveyor belt at the check-in counter, and even provides a commentary about the design of the airport! What the driver does is certainly more than what the average driver would do in Singapore, where such comprehensive service would have been regarded as several jobs. By providing superior customer service, the Swiss driver honoured his own talents and capabilities with his attitude towards his work and the knowledge he displayed.

The rise of the middle class in many countries in Asia represents a continuous growth in purchasing power. The middle class are the people with discretionary money. With the growth of e-commerce and discretionary money, people will be prepared to pay for quality products, as well as consistent and reliable services. The rise of internet transactions means that there is a growing need for trust, where orders are placed in the virtual world for products and services to be delivered in the real world.

Since trust is the life blood of any long-term relationship, and Honour is the foundation of trust, organisations need to continually choose and cultivate a culture of Honour by honouring their word, honouring their customers, honouring their employees, honouring their stakeholders, and honouring their company values.

HONOUR QUALITY BUSINESS

There is the story of the Chinese entrepreneur who had a religious conversion and was convicted that the way that he was conducting his business was wrong—his conscience had come alive and he decided that he had to change course.

The entrepreneur told his people that the company would no longer pay bribes to make its sales. He thought his people would welcome this switch to honesty. Instead his seniormost manager confronted him, saying his decision was most irresponsible, as it jeopardised the livelihood of all the workers, for whom bribes was the way by which they had generated business!

This was a most unexpected reaction, as the businessman thought it

If we are concerned about the survival and success of the business in the long-term, the fundamental driver of success has to be the right values.

Choosing to honour our values might mean losing some business in the short-term, but we will build a reputation of being honest and trustworthy in the long-term, and this will attract a different range of customers that will be willing to pay more for honourable service.

Honour is essential for organisations if the organisation wants to grow, to succeed, and to survive in the long-term.

would be plain that giving bribes was wrong. It obviously created a serious dilemma for the entrepreneur, who wanted to do right but found that his people did not agree that that would be doing good.

After thinking deeply over the matter, he called his people together and said that in the hotel business, the hotel owner could choose to run a five-star hotel business or to run a one-star business.

A five-star hotel would run on the basis of attracting customers who sought quality, reliability, dependability, and consistency of service. A one-star hotel would run on the basis of lowest cost, minimal service, and possibly bribes to win over customers. The entrepreneur then announced that he wanted to convert their business to a five-star business: a business based on honesty, quality, reliability, and excellence!

If we are concerned about the survival and success of the business in the long-term, the fundamental driver of success has to be the right values. Choosing to honour our values might mean losing some business in the short-term, but we will build a reputation of being honest and trustworthy in the long-term, and this will attract a different range of customers that will be willing to pay more for honourable service.

SUMMARY: HONOUR IN ORGANISATIONS

Trade, business, missions, and objectives can only be achieved and sustained in the long run if there is trust between two parties. Since Honour is living by the virtues, and Honour is the foundation of trust, Honour is essential for organisations if the organisation wants to grow, to succeed, and to survive in the long-term.

WIN

WITH

HONOUR

IN YOUR

ORGANISATION

BY ASKING YOURSELF:

- Am I honouring my word and honouring others (e.g. my customers, my boss, my colleagues, my peers, etc.)?

- Am I honouring myself by doing all I can to be skilled at my job?

- Am I using my heart (not only my hands and mind) and giving my best when I undertake any assignment?

- Am I helping my organisation and others (e.g. my customer, my boss, my peers, my subordinates, etc.) to be the best that they can be?

PART IX

HONOUR IN LEADERSHIP
HONOURING OUR PEOPLE

Regardless of your station in life, your life counts and you have the potential to be a thought leader and influencer to make a positive impact in your own spheres of influence, no matter how small these spheres might be.

Leadership is making good things happen that on their own would not happen.

The leader must ask himself what is good and right, as opposed to what is bad and wrong. He cannot escape making moral judgments if he is to do good for the lives of others.

Effective leadership has to be "other-centred".

You could be a CEO of a multinational corporation, a stay-at-home mother, an emergency room nurse, a primary school student, or the leader of a country. Regardless of your station in life, your life counts and you have the potential to be a thought leader and influencer to make a positive impact in your own spheres of influence, no matter how small these spheres might be.

This chapter discusses how we can win with Honour in leadership, be it with our families, communities, organisations, or nation.

DEFINITION OF LEADERSHIP

A leader makes things happen that on their own would not happen.

However, defining leadership as making things happen that on their own would not happen is not adequate, because the leader of a gang of robbers could also make things happen that on their own would not happen, but this would be at the unfair expense of other people. So we have to qualify the definition by saying: "Leadership is making good things happen that on their own would not happen."

But once we introduce the word "good", we have also introduced a moral dimension into leadership. And this is as it should be. The leader must ask himself/herself what is good and right, as opposed to what is bad and wrong. The leader cannot escape making moral judgments if he/she is to do good for the lives of others.

As the leader enters into the world of values and virtues, he/she has to decide what he/she needs to believe of his/her role as a leader if he/she wants to be a good leader.

Peter Drucker, the renowned management guru defined a leader as someone who has followers. What qualities would create followership?

The proposition here is that effective leadership has to be "other-centred", and Honour is a necessary virtue for the leader, his/her family, and his/her organisation.

GOOD vs RIGHT

Leadership is making good and right things happen that on their own

Leadership is fundamentally a matter of bringing about change that is useful for the present and essential for the future.

The moral dimension of "good and right" is a necessary demand on the leader.

It makes more sense to adopt the Goodness paradigm than to adopt the Rightness paradigm for various reasons.

Honour aligns with the Goodness paradigm as to honour is to seek to do good to increase collective long-term well-being.

would not happen. It is fundamentally a matter of bringing about change that is useful for the present and essential for the future. It is being clear about the change we want or need to bring about, and being smart about the way we bring about change that is beneficial, effective, and enduring. If the things would happen without us being around, the best thing we could possibly do is to get out of the way, rather than stick around and be an unnecessary burden or barrier to change.

The moral dimension of "good and right" is a necessary demand on the leader. A leader has to decide "good for what" and "right with respect to what". And what happens if what is good is not necessarily right, and what is right is not necessarily good? How does the leader choose between whether to put "good" above "right", or the other way round?

Dr William Meachem, an independent scholar in philosophy, discussed the approach to making the choice in his article "The Good and The Right".[22] After acknowledging that choosing between the good and the right is far from straightforward, he concluded:

"It is not impossible to make a choice, however. I believe it makes more sense to adopt the Goodness paradigm than to adopt the Rightness paradigm for the following reasons:

- *There is a way to determine which paradigm is better but not a way to determine which is right.*
- *It is easier to find out what is good than to find out what is right.*
- *The Goodness paradigm solves the 'is-ought' problem.*
- *It is methodologically easier to resolve conflicts among goods than conflicts among obligations.*
- *It is easier to justify obeying moral rules on the basis of consequences than to justify paying attention to consequences on the basis of moral rules.*
- *Excessive focus on being right promotes emotional distress.*
- *A Goodness paradigm promotes a recognition of the connectedness and unity of all things and as such is closer to reality."*

To honour is to seek to do good to increase the collective long-term well-being, so Honour aligns with the Goodness paradigm.

There are two aspects of leadership we have to master to be an outstanding leader:

- Position Leadership
- Personal Leadership

Position Leadership requires a leader to continually prepare and shape the company for the future.

The full depth of our leadership does not lie in the day-to-day decisions we make to keep the organisation going, but what continues in the organisation when we are no longer around.

Leaders must seek all the time to make sure that their organisations are "in time for the future".

TWO ASPECTS OF LEADERSHIP

There are two aspects of leadership we have to master to be an outstanding leader:

- **Position Leadership**, which describes what the leader in an organisation is expected to do well
- **Personal Leadership**, which makes the point that it is the quality of personal leadership that determines how successful you can be as a leader

POSITION LEADERSHIP

Position Leadership requires us to be clear about the purpose and direction for our organisation or company.

It expresses the mission of the organisation and our vision of what we would like it to become. It is also working out the strategy for the organisation and what needs to be done to effectively execute the plans. In addition, it is defining the culture and the values that we believe are essential for the sustained success of the company.

Above all, Position Leadership requires a leader to continually prepare and shape the company for the future, because the ultimate evidence of failed leadership is the failure of an organisation to meet the challenges of, and to sustain its success in, the ever-changing future. In a strange kind of way, the full depth of our leadership does not lie in the day-to-day decisions we make to keep the organisation going, but what continues in the organisation when we are no longer around.

To change in good time to position the organisation for the future is absolutely essential. In a highly globalised world, the winners are those who are alert, agile, innovative, responsive, and enterprising. They constantly look out for dangers and opportunities.

Leaders must seek all the time to make sure that their organisations are "in time for the future". This means being clear that performing well today is not good enough. Leaders must ensure that the company has the strategic perspective, the market awareness, equipment, technology, ambition, imagination, human skills, and capabilities to be sustainably

Resistance to change is normal.

There are two sets of impediments to change:

- People Barriers
- Resource Barriers

Change is an issue of hearts and minds, not simply an issue of clear intentions and detailed plans.

There are four kinds of People Barriers:

- Knowledge Barrier
- Beliefs Barrier
- Confidence Barrier
- Power Barrier

successful going into the future.

But anyone who has tried to drive change in any organisation knows that it is not straightforward. Resistance to change is normal. In fact, we should worry if we do not get resistance, because it means either the people are not taking the change seriously or they think we will give up easily and so there is no need for them to apply themselves.

Barriers to Change: People Barriers and Resource Barriers

While the decision may be made to proceed with change to accomplish good outcomes, it does not mean that the process will be easy or smooth.

There are **two sets of impediments to change:**

- **People Barriers**
- **Resource Barriers**

Between the two, People Barriers are often more difficult to deal with because issues of anxiety, mistrust, incompetence, and non-cooperation need to be overcome. The Resource Barriers are easier to overcome, either by allocation of funds or creative use of available resources, or both.

For the change process to succeed, ways have to be found to remove the barriers, to go over them, or to go around them. This requires imagination and determination, the forcefulness of will and, often more critically, the empathy of heart.

Leaders have to recognise that change is an issue of hearts and minds, not simply an issue of clear intentions and detailed plans.

People Barriers

There are **four kinds of People Barriers:**

- **Knowledge Barrier**
- **Beliefs Barrier**
- **Confidence Barrier**
- **Power Barrier**

Knowledge Barrier: this is where people do not support a change because, based on their knowledge and experience, they either do not see the

People who pose the Knowledge Barrier are basically objective and rational, and they can be won over by facts and reason.

People who raise the Beliefs Barrier have to be brought around to at least recognise a case for the proposed change, even if they may not instinctively or emotionally accept it.

People who raise the Confidence Barrier are not against the outcomes hoped for—they simply do not think the hopes would be realised.

necessity to change or the wisdom of changing in the way envisaged by their leader/s.

People who raise the Knowledge Barrier have to be brought around by helping them see that there are good and strong reasons to change. This may be done by showing them facts and data, having them visit competitor or peer organisations, or bringing them to the operating level to see for themselves that the identified problems are real and there is clear imperative to change.

People who pose the Knowledge Barrier are basically objective and rational, and they can be won over by facts and reason.

Beliefs Barrier: this is where people do not support a change because they perceive it as going against the values and beliefs they have about what the organisation is for and how the organisation should go about its business. In other words, they feel that the proposed change will undermine the purpose or the character of the organisation as they understand it.

People who raise the Beliefs Barrier have to be brought around to at least recognise a case for the proposed change, even if they may not instinctively or emotionally accept it, by being convinced that the change does not undermine the mission of the organisation, but is an attempt to keep the organisation up-to-date and relevant under evolving circumstances, arising from changes in demographics, technology and/ or the cultural or social environment.

Confidence Barrier: this is where people do not support a change because they do not have the confidence and conviction that the effort to change will be successful, and they therefore prefer not to attempt the change.

The reasons why they do not think the effort to change will work may be varied—for example, they may perceive that senior management is only paying lip service or is not fully committed, and therefore will not have the stamina or give the necessary time and resources for the effort to succeed. Alternatively, they may not think their colleagues will give genuine attention to, or support for, the change, or they may believe that the change will be too complex to be able to maintain the interest and attention of those affected for long enough.

People who raise the Confidence Barrier are not against the outcomes hoped for—they simply do not think the hopes would be realised, and they

The Power Barrier exists where Honour is missing — the objectors are less than fair, frank, and honest, and their selfish motivations jeopardise the lives and careers of their people.

There can be Resource Barriers that inhibit change due to the lack of:

- Time and attention from those in power
- Budget for capital expenditure
- Equipment and expertise

Resource Barriers exist when people believe that the resources will not be forthcoming to effectively execute the change, and they therefore prefer not to start.

Resource Barriers have to be addressed by way of persuasion, negotiation, and even "barter trading".

are uncomfortable with ambiguity and the uncertainty of success. They need to have their confidence to handle the proposed change built up by providing them with thorough training and involving them in the design of the change process, as well as strengthened by way of encouragement and explicit support of senior management.

Power Barrier: this is where people do not support a change because it will undermine their power and authority. It can be a particularly difficult barrier to identify because the people who are putting up the Power Barrier can hardly be expected to proclaim that they are objecting because they fear the change would undermine their position and standing in the organisation.

Instead, people who raise the Power Barrier will offer reasons that will make them sound, more honourably, as being caught by the Knowledge Barrier, or the Beliefs Barrier, or the Confidence Barrier, when in fact they are putting up the Power Barrier.

While every attempt should be made to bring them on board the change process by, for example, making them a sponsor of the change process, it has to be recognised that in many instances they will refuse to come on board. The Power Barrier exists where Honour is missing—the objectors are less than fair, frank, and honest, and their selfish motivations jeopardise the lives and careers of their people.

Resource Barriers

There can be Resource Barriers that inhibit change due to the lack of:

- Time and attention from those in power
- Budget for capital expenditure
- Equipment and expertise

Resource Barriers exist when people believe that the resources will not be forthcoming to effectively execute the change, and they therefore prefer not to start.

Resource Barriers have to be addressed by way of persuasion, negotiation, and even "barter trading". One common mistake is to ask for too much too early. There is nothing like small successes to give

Very often when people raise objections to a change, the tendency is to deal with every reluctance as though it were a case of the Knowledge Barrier. The fact is that not all objections are on account of the Knowledge Barrier.

People who are objecting may have to be asked to step aside, suspend their judgment, and allow the change to proceed; not proceeding with the change may simply be the wrong thing to do, and may even be fatal for the organisation.

Change is difficult, but change is the very essence of the function of leadership.

The failure to change may simply be catastrophe for the organisation or country, and may lead to the demise of organisation/country.

credibility to requests for more resources to build upon the success, so conduct experiments with the resources at hand to demonstrate the worthiness of investing in the new idea, and only then ask for more resources.

Very often when people raise objections to a change, the tendency is to deal with every reluctance as though it were a case of the Knowledge Barrier, and therefore more reasoning would help. If the organisational response to communicate and explain more does not work, the organisation must seriously think of pushing on with the change nonetheless.

The fact is that not all objections are on account of the Knowledge Barrier. There are times when objection on account of the Power Barrier, and sometimes also the Beliefs Barrier, simply cannot be reasoned off or overcome. In these instances, the people who are objecting may have to be asked to step aside, suspend their judgment, and allow the change to proceed; not proceeding with the change may simply be the wrong thing to do, and may even be fatal for the organisation.

While there will be occasions when deferring a change proposal and waiting for a more opportune time would be the wisest thing to do, there are also times when this would not be the most appropriate response. People may be objecting simply because they are not able to imagine what success will be like and why the pain of adjustment is worth the success that is sought.

Never forget that there is no change without disagreement. Machiavelli once remarked: *"It must be considered that there is nothing more difficult to carry out, nor more dangerous to handle, than to initiate a new order of things. For the reformer has enemies in all those who profit by the old order, and only lukewarm defenders in all those who would profit by the new order."*

It would not be unusual for organisations to reach a point where the situation has to be starkly put across to their people: *"The train is about to leave the station. You have the choice to get on the train or to get off the train, but don't get in front of the train."*

So change is difficult, but change is the very essence of the function of leadership, for which the failure to change may simply be catastrophe for the organisation or country, and may lead to its demise.

Before we embark on any change, we must be:

- Clear that our intentions are honourable and other-centred, and that we are not undertaking initiatives for our own glory or legacy.
- Have a long-term perspective that is in the long-term best interest of the organisation or the people affected, even though it might be painful for the organisation and/or people in the short- term.

There are three imperatives in Position Leadership:

- Be the Best You Can Be
- Harness the Creativity of Your People
- Be in Time for the Future

The barriers to change notwithstanding, if we are determined and smart in the way we go about doing things, we will be able to succeed in lowering the barriers or finding ways around the barriers. Nevertheless, there will be at times when we may have to remove a few people who simply keep resisting the change and instigating other people not to support the change.

Have Honourable Intentions

Before we embark on any change, we must first be clear that our intentions are honourable and other-centred, and that we are not undertaking initiatives for our own glory or legacy. It also means that we have a long-term perspective that is in the long-term best interest of the organisation or the people affected, even though it might be painful for the organisation and/or people in the short-term.

For example, if a staff member is a bad fit for the organisation or his/her current role despite having a good attitude and trying his/her best, while it might be painful for the person in the short-term to be asked to leave, it would be much better for the well-being of the person in the long run if you redirect him/her to a more suitable role and/or organisation, and help the person make the transition to the next position.

On the other hand, if the organisation is going through a hard time financially, unlike many organisations that will usually react by declaring redundancies, the wisest or most honourable choice could be to not sacrifice hardworking and experienced staff who create value for the organisation—instead, it might call upon the leadership of the leader to band the organisation together as a family, and institute pay cuts organisation-wide so that all are fed, even though all are not fed as much as before.

Three Imperatives in Position Leadership

There are three imperatives in position leadership:

- **Be the Best You Can Be**
- **Harness the Creativity of Your People**
- **Be in Time for the Future**

IMPERATIVE #1: "Be the Best You Can Be" is a call to the individual to do his/her best and to be all he/she can be.

IMPERATIVE #2: "Harness the Creativity of Your People" is a call to leaders to honour their people by allowing them to exercise their talents and abilities the best way possible.

IMPERATIVE #3: "Be in Time for the Future" is a rallying call to be alert, never to be complacent, and to always be actively preparing for an uncertain future.

The first two pertain to the stewardship of talents and abilities that every individual has.

IMPERATIVE #1: "Be the Best You Can Be" is a call to the individual to do his/her best and to be all he/she can be. It is a matter of motivation, attitude, and humility to learn and to serve.

In order for the organisation to be the best that it can be, six factors have to be addressed.

- **Morale and Motivation:** are your people doing the best they can?
- **Capacity and Capability**: are your people being the best they can be?
- **Symbiosis and Synergy**: are efforts being coordinated and integrated to maximum effect?

IMPERATIVE #2: "Harness the Creativity of Your People" is a call to leaders to honour their people by allowing them to exercise their talents and abilities the best way possible, to discover themselves, to build up their self-confidence, and to enhance their ability to contribute.

To harness the creativity of our people, we must start with the belief that everyone has talents and abilities, and that our challenge is how to create a work environment and promote a culture that allows people to express their ideas and pursue their convictions for the betterment of the organisation—to believe otherwise is to forgo all the latent capabilities in the organisation, which represents a loss of engagement on the part of the individual, and a loss of the hearts and minds of the people on the part of the organisation.

IMPERATIVE #3: "Be in Time for the Future" is a rallying call to be alert, never to be complacent, and to always be actively preparing for an uncertain future.

There is an old African saying: *"Every day the gazelle wakes up knowing that if it can't outrun the fastest lion, it's going to be somebody's breakfast. Every day the lion wakes up knowing that if it can't outrun the slowest gazelle it will go hungry."*

Often when this proverb is quoted to urge people to make sure their organisations are always fit to run, they go into a discussion as to whether

Are You a Multiplier?

These three imperatives are fundamentally about responsible stewardship of the talents and abilities in the organisation of both the individual and the leader for not only the current, but also future generations.

- Call to the INDIVIDUAL:
  "Be the Best You Can Be"

- Call to the LEADER:
  "Harness the Creativity of Your People"

- Call to both the INDIVIDUAL and LEADER:
  "Be in Time for the Future"

their company is the lion or the gazelle.

Actually it does not matter whether your organisation is the lion or the gazelle—when morning comes, you had better be running. However, it matters a lot as to whether you are running as No.2 or as No. 1!

Are You a Multiplier?

The three imperatives are fundamentally about responsible stewardship of the talents and abilities in the organisation of both the individual and the leader for not only the current, but also future generations.

- **Call to the INDIVIDUAL: "Be the Best You Can Be"**
  Are you honouring yourself by doing and being all that you can do and be? This is a matter of motivation, attitude, and humility to learn and to serve.

- **Call to the LEADER: "Harness the Creativity of Your People"**
  Are you honouring your people by allowing them to exercise their talents and abilities in the best way possible, to discover themselves, to build up their self-confidence, and to enhance their ability to contribute?

  Let us ask ourselves: "How many major tasks can we handle at any one time?" Three would be nice, four would be quite good, and five would be outstanding. So if all we want from our people is to undertake tasks directly and immediately related to our personal task list, the most we can hope for our department to accomplish by the end of the year is just the three, four, or five things.

  But consider the case when we can engage our people and give them the leeway to exercise their initiative to improve things under their sphere: Even if our people were less capable than we and can therefore handle just two important tasks each, and if there were ten persons under our charge in the department, by the end of the year, our department would have more than 20 improvements, and not just three or four or five!

  This is the multiplier principle that comes about through honouring our people for their talents and their desire to do good for others and feel good about themselves.

A winning organisation thinks ahead and acts in good time. Future-focussed leadership is what sets apart the superior organisation from the mediocre one.

Organisations suffer fatal failure for three reasons:

- A failure to learn from the past
- A failure to adapt to the present
- A failure to anticipate the future

- **Call to both the INDIVIDUAL and LEADER: "Be in Time for the Future"**

Are you honouring the current and future generations by preparing yourself and your organisation to be ready for future needs of your customers? Are you honouring future generations by running your business in an environmentally sustainable way by reducing, reusing, and recycling, as well as choosing to work with responsible contractors who do the same, even if it might be more expensive to do so?

A winning organisation thinks ahead and acts in good time. Future-focussed leadership is what sets apart the superior organisation from the mediocre one. To "Be in Time for the Future" offers strong motivation for continuous improvement and creative innovation. This call to action demands an organisation to be always questioning, always open to new ideas, and always willing to learn from anywhere. It requires a confident, courageous, and humble leadership that is able to engage in a debate over ideas without sinking into a battle of personalities.

THREE REASONS WHY ORGANISATIONS FAIL

Organisations suffer fatal failure for three reasons:

- A failure to **learn from the past**
- A failure to **adapt to the present**
- A failure to **anticipate the future**

Failure to learn from the past: The failure to learn from the past, either from past mistakes within the organisation itself or, even better, the mistakes of other organisations, is to ignore valuable lessons and learning opportunities!

Failure to adapt to the present: The failure to adapt to the present is the failure to recognise or admit that every policy or practice, when first adopted, is the best possible or practicable at that point. But as the external environment and customers change, the policies and practices

The failure to anticipate the future is probably the most common reason for the demise of successful organisations.

The failure to change in good time and in good times is the consequence of complacency or the absence of courage.

become less and less relevant and more and more inappropriate for the time. The failure to adapt to the present is the surrender to bureaucracy or the triumph of indifference.

Failure to anticipate the future: The failure to change in good time and in good times is the consequence of complacency or the absence of courage. It is probably the most common reason for the demise of successful organisations.

THE LESSON OF THE FROG

How to Boil a Frog: Cooking Instructions

To boil a frog, do not put it in boiling water. It will jump out immediately.

Put the live frog in cold water in a pan. Put the pan over a low fire. Let the water heat up slowly. As it gets to boiling point, you will notice the frog is no longer moving. It is dead. You have successfully cooked the frog.

Explanation

The above instructions work because frogs are cold-blooded—this means their body temperature is the same as the surroundings, unlike us human beings. We are warm-blooded, meaning our body temperature remains more or less constant and does not follow that of our surroundings. We shiver in cold weather to keep our body temperature up. We sweat in warm weather to cool ourselves down.

The frog's body temperature follows its surroundings. If you put the frog directly in boiling water, it will sense the heat immediately and jump out. But when you heat the water slowly, the frog keeps adjusting to the rising temperature. When the heat is too much for the frog to take, it is too late. The frog collapses and dies.

Fatal Failures

All fatal failures in organisations are the result of failure to learn from the past, or failure to adapt to the present, or failure to anticipate the future.

Look at the history of nations and companies. Study wars and battles, crises and bankruptcies. Isn't it so?

Look around. Be alert. Imagine the future. Do not be complacent.

Do not allow the comforts of today lull you into thinking tomorrow will always be the same or only a little different.

Honourable leadership has to be future-oriented and anticipative.

The most common causes in the demise of successful organisations are the failure to:

- Change in good time<u>s</u>
- Change in good time

Think again about the frog mentioned above. Its body temperature keeps adapting to the slow change in the surrounding temperature. The frog does not realise the temperature can rise so high that it will collapse under the heat. It feels nice and comfortable at every point on the road to death.

The lesson of the frog for us is this: Look around. Be alert. Imagine the future. Do not be complacent. Take precautions. Prepare for danger. Make use of the opportunities. The future will surprise you only if you do not bother to think about it. Do not allow the comforts of today lull you into thinking tomorrow will always be the same or only a little different.

WHY SUCCESSFUL ORGANISATIONS FAIL

Honourable leadership has to be future-oriented and anticipative. The lives and livelihoods of your people depend on it. The most common causes in the demise of successful organisations are the failure to:

- **Change in good time_s**
- **Change in good time**

When things are going well for the organisation, costs are neglected and people who are not up to the job are kept on the payroll. However, when the business goes down, tough measures have to be taken in a hurry, and people may have to be retrenched when it is the worst of times for them—the worst of times for getting alternative employment and at the same time meet the demands of life and family.

An equally bad situation is neglecting people who are adequate for the present but do not have the potential for higher degrees of responsibility in the years to come. Leaders fail if these people are not helped or advised early to seek a better place that can offer them growth possibilities in the future.

Thus, when a worker who is considered to be performing just satisfactorily is not advised to build his capability or advised to move elsewhere for a better job fit when he/she is 30, and then is later found to be unsatisfactory in his/her 40s and has to be asked to leave then, it would be a really bad event for him/her, for at that point he/she may well

If leaders have taken the effort to build honourable relationships of trust and respect with their subordinates so that they know that the leader always has their long-term well-being at heart, leaders will naturally:

- Commend the good
- Advise the weak to improve or to go somewhere else where they can succeed better

An organisation where trust and respect is absent is usually one where the virtue of honouring each other is missing.

There are grave disadvantages when change is undertaken only when there is a crisis.

be bogged down with a mortgage or young children to support, or both.

Here is where the virtue of honouring our peers and our subordinates becomes particularly important. The reason why so many supervisors cannot bring themselves to advise their sub-performing, or even just-performing, subordinates to leave for another job is because they had never bothered to develop a relationship with them, which is based on trust and concern for their long-term well-being.

Leaders also often do not differentiate between the performance of those who are very good and those who are mediocre, the result of which is to demoralise the former and mislead the latter. They end up with staff who do not exert themselves to do their best or contribute their most, with their best people complaining and finally leaving, while their average staff think they are doing fine. In due course, the enterprise fills up with sagging energy and limited imagination, and it loses its future even if it appears to be alright today.

If leaders have taken the effort to build honourable relationships of trust and respect with their subordinates so that they know that the leader always has their long-term best interests at heart, leaders will naturally commend the good and advise the weak to improve or to go somewhere else where they can succeed better.

Leaders will also be moved to help the weak to move on with a good conscience of having honoured them as individuals who deserve the opportunity to build upon their strengths and find a place that brings out the best in them, so that they can experience the best that life can offer them.

If supervisors fail to build trusting relationships with their people, they will fear to confront them with the truth about sub-par performance, because they fear their people will accuse them of selfish intentions, even victimisation, in asking them to go. An organisation where trust and respect is absent is usually one where the virtue of honouring each other is missing.

There are two grave disadvantages when change is undertaken only when there is a crisis:

- An organisation in crisis is usually in a state of low morale and high anxiety, especially since the people within the organisation

It is always best to change in good times in order to change in good time.

It is important to honour people as human beings with their own responsibilities and obligations, doubts and fears.

To change without a crisis demands top management with foresight, insight, and a refined capacity for communication.

Personal Leadership is what makes Position Leadership succeed.

Effective leadership depends above all on effective personal leadership.

often know that a crisis is looming before the public outside, or sometimes even the board of directors, know about it.

- Some of the best staff would have left the organisation, as they know things are in bad shape and reckon someplace else would be better able and willing to recognise their capabilities and welcome their contributions.

Dealing with an organisation of people with low morale and lesser capability unnecessarily adds to the challenges faced during the change process. Thus, it is always best to change in good times in order to change in good time.

There is also another critical advantage for changing when an organisation is not in crisis: should the staff have to leave or decide to leave, the best welfare they can be given is to leave when alternative jobs are much more readily available, and they have the time to seek such alternative jobs rather than have to leave in a hurry and face an uncertain future. This is honouring people as human beings with their own responsibilities and obligations, doubts and fears.

On the other hand, to change without a crisis demands top management with foresight, insight, and a refined capacity for communication. People need to see a need for change, so if the need is not obvious, unlike in a crisis, that need has to be effectively communicated so that the people may visualise the challenges and perceive the opportunities.

PERSONAL LEADERSHIP

Personal Leadership is what makes Position Leadership succeed. Effective leadership depends above all on effective Personal Leadership. This is a matter of the heart and the mind. It makes people want to follow you because there is something worthy about your abilities, about your concern, and about your example that moves them to be the best they can be and to aspire to be a leader themselves.

If we do not have followers, we are not leaders. We may be called Chairman or CEO or Director or Commander; but we are not leaders. A leader must have willing followers. As succinctly expressed by

The Essence of Leadership is:

- Not Position but Followers
- Not Popularity but Results
- Not Preaching but Examples
- Not Privileges but Responsibility

People will often follow leaders who are very tough and demanding, but with a quality about them that makes them worthy of followership.

Leaders must be people of integrity, where honouring their word and honouring their people are a natural part of their daily behaviour.

Peter Drucker in "The Leader of the Future" (Jossey-Bass Publishers 1996), **the essence of leadership is:**

- **Not Position but Followers**
- **Not Popularity but Results**
- **Not Preaching but Examples**
- **Not Privileges but Responsibility**

This is not to say that a good leader has to be a soft-hearted, affable, gregarious, and jovial person who never wields the stick, and who leaves his or her people to do as much as they want of whatever they wish to do. People will often follow leaders who are very tough and demanding, but with a quality about them that makes them worthy of followership.

People very often ask: "What do I need to do to be a good leader?" The answer is simple, although doing it may not be easy. It lies in each one of us acting on our own answer to the question: "What would make me personally want to follow someone?"

Leaders must be people of integrity, where honouring their word and honouring their people are a natural part of their daily behaviour. This is authentic leadership, worthy of followership. No one wants a boss who is dishonest or disingenuous—someone whose word cannot be trusted, who is seen as manipulative, and whose intentions we are always suspicious of. The lack of Honour is written in the boss's expressions and demeanour; the absence of Honour speaks out from the heart, and while there may be efforts at camouflage and deception, the truth will come out in moments of stress and crisis, if not earlier.

A follower may believe he is better off having a person as his/her leader either out of fear for his/her livelihood or well-being, or out of respect for what the leader is doing for the follower's life. If followership is the critical factor in leadership, it is obviously necessary to understand leadership from the perspective of the prospective follower.

What we are assuming here is that all of us desire to unlock the total capability of our people, and that we are not simply satisfied with getting one task or another done.

Getting the immediate job done can very much be just a matter of training, direction, and perhaps threat—but getting the job done with

Every person comprises three parts:

- Body
- Soul
- Spirit

If supervisors expect full engagement and full realisation of the potential of the organisation, they need to activate the spirits of their people.

Five essential things people want their supervisors to do:

- **G**uide
- **E**mpathise
- **E**nergise
- **S**ynergise
- **E**mbolden

pride, with attention to detail, with cheerful delivery, with an eye always on quality and reliability, with a desire for continual improvement, with a passion to constantly innovate, and a desire for excellence, requires the total harnessing of the hearts and minds of our people.

As introduced earlier in this book, **every person comprises three parts:**

- **Body**
- **Soul**
- **Spirit**

The effective leader has to see his or her task as not simply giving directives and demanding compliance (which is operating at the "body level" of his people) but has to recognise the ideal as connecting with the spirit of the people to motivate them to seek and do what they know in the innermost part of their being to be the best and correct thing. Hence, if supervisors expect full engagement and full realisation of the potential of the organisation, they need to activate the spirits of their people and "release" their people to be the best they can be.

G.E.E.S.E Leadership

What do people look for in their supervisors? Integrity is of course not enough for superior personal leadership. In a study that asked what people would like of their supervisors, the conclusion was very interesting. There are just five essential things people want their supervisors to do: Guide, Empathise, Energise, Synergise, Embolden (**G.E.E.S.E**).

- **Guide**: Leaders must be knowledgeable and capable, while at the same time have the desire to help their people learn and improve.
- **Empathise:** Leaders must be able to feel for others, and must be genuinely interested in the well-being of their people by being willing to listen and to care.
- **Energise:** Leaders must somehow be able to make their people feel engaged and interested in their work. There is no way supervisors can have people who are full of energy and drive if they are not keen about their work.

Personal leadership is first and foremost a matter of the heart—skills can be taught and learnt, but helping others is a matter of the heart and the mind.

It is what is inside us that drives us to do whatever we can that is good and right.

The most important question for honourable leadership: "How can I help YOU do your job better?"

Honour your Boss by:

- Always trying to help your boss succeed
- Never trying to undermine his or her position

- **Synergise:** Leaders must be able to synergise to help people and departments work together so that the result of their work is more than what they can accomplish working individually on their own. Leaders must be able to persuade and communicate well in order to manage relationships and traverse organisational boundaries.

- **Embolden:** Leaders must help their people have the courage to speak out when they are unclear or in disagreement, and to try new things. This will only happen if supervisors create work environments where it is safe to offer different ideas, to innovate, and to make mistakes and learn from them.

If you put the first letters of **G**uide, **E**mpathise, **E**nergise, **S**ynergise and **E**mbolden together, they make up the word "GEESE". The idea is simple, the execution perhaps not so easy. It demands a desire to help our people be the best they can be, both as individuals and as a team. It is treating our people with Honour, believing in each one of them, and sincerely wishing the best for everyone.

Personal leadership is first and foremost a matter of the heart—skills can be taught and learnt, but helping others is a matter of the heart and the mind. It is what is inside us that drives us to do whatever we can that is good and right, and inspires us to do whatever we can to help our people grow and blossom.

How can I Help You?

Everything in G.E.E.S.E leadership revolves around what is the most important question for honourable leadership: **"How can I help YOU do your job better?"**

Who does the "you" refer to?

Honour your Boss: First and foremost, "you" refers to your own boss. Honour your boss by always trying to help your boss succeed and never trying to undermine his or her position. You want your boss to have no doubt that you are always willing to do what you can to help him or her succeed. When you gain your boss' trust by proving your credibility and competence, he or she is then much more likely to grant you the freedom to decide and act. You will receive the empowerment so many people

Honour your Peers by helping them be the best that they can be.

Honour your People by having a heart for them.

Honour Yourself by taking steps to improve yourself on a daily basis so that you are a better person today than you were yesterday.

The most critical requirement for energised workers is for leaders themselves to be energised.

crave for but do not get because they do not take the effort to establish a relationship of Honour and trust with their bosses.

Honour your Peers: The next "you" refers to your peers. Honour your peers by helping them be the best that they can be. We know this may sound odd because too many people regard their peers as competitors rather than helpmates. But in today's world of complexity, there are very few instances where we can get a proposal through or a job done all on our own, so having the goodwill of your peers is an excellent proposition. If they will not go out of the way to help you, they will at least be less likely to go out of the way to undermine you.

Honour your People: The next "you" refers to the people who report to you. Nothing will boost their willingness to follow you more than them knowing that you sincerely want the best for them and are prepared to help them succeed. Honour your followers by having a heart for them. Bear in mind they will very easily read you if you are not sincere about it. Your authentic self must be a self that cares.

Honour Yourself: The final "you" is yourself. How are you honouring yourself by helping yourself be the best that you can be? Are you giving your best in everything that you do and undertaking everything with excellence? Are you continuously learning and innovating in all that you do? Are you taking steps to improve yourself on a daily basis so that you are a better person today than you were yesterday?

Energise Yourself

Leaders must somehow be able to have their people engaged and interested in their work so that they are full of energy and drive. If people are not energised about their work, it will show in their faces and their actions—this will certainly impact the customer and business either directly or indirectly.

The most critical requirement for energised workers is for leaders themselves to be energised. When people are not energised at work, almost invariably we will find that their immediate bosses are not energised, though the opposite may not hold, in that energised supervisors may not necessarily result in energised staff.

Energy levels are heavily influenced by the drive and passion of the supervisors themselves who may create a work environment that bubbles with energy or who may burst whatever bubbles of energy there may be in the environment.

There are four kinds of energy:

- Physical energy
- Emotional energy
- Mental energy
- Spiritual energy

Since energy is one of those things that is caught, rather than taught, energy levels cannot simply be directed or prescribed by supervisors; more often than not, they are heavily influenced by the drive and passion of the supervisors themselves who may create a work environment that bubbles with energy or who may burst whatever bubbles of energy there may be in the environment.

Before we can think about how to energise those around us, it would be useful to know that there are four kinds of energy:

- **Physical Energy**
- **Emotional Energy**
- **Mental Energy**
- **Spiritual Energy**

Physical Energy is the quantity of our energy, and refers to the physical fitness of the individual. It is the basic source of fuel in one's life. If we are not physically fit, it will affect our mental energy, emotional energy, and spiritual energy. Think of the times we are sick even if it were just a slight cough—it immediately impacts our sense of well-being, reduces our capacity to concentrate, and perhaps gives us a shortness of temper, if not an unwillingness to interact with others.

Emotional Energy is the quality of our energy. Jim Loehr and Tony Schwartz posit in their book, "The Power of Full Engagement" (Free Press 2005), that in order to perform at our best, we must access pleasant and positive emotions to experience enjoyment, challenge, adventure, and opportunity.

Mental Energy is the focus of our energy, and is what we use to organise our lives; it reflects our capacity to withstand mental pressures and emotional strains.

Spiritual energy is the purpose to which we put our energy, and provides the force for action in all dimensions of our lives. It derives its strength from the depths of a person's being—namely, deeply held values and a purpose beyond one's self-interest (e.g. a legacy one wants to leave behind, a to-do list of what one wants to accomplish in life, or a drive to please the god of one's beliefs). The courage and conviction to honour our deepest

Spiritual energy can directly impact a person's mental energy and emotional energy, even more than his or her physical energy.

It is of paramount importance for all of us to cultivate our spiritual selves and energy, and spiritualise everything that we do.

师傅 (Shīfù): A teacher who imparts "technical skills".

师父 (Shīfù): A teacher with a paternal heart who teaches "fundamental skills" and imparts life lessons.

If a leader is first and foremost a 师父 who wants the best for his or her followers' lives, he or she should find it a lot easier to impart technical skills as a 师傅.

values by living them out, supported by passion, commitment, integrity, and honesty, are the key muscles that fire spiritual energy.

As spiritual energy may grip a person's mind and heart, and fuel his passion in life, spiritual energy can directly impact a person's mental energy and emotional energy, even more than his or her physical energy. It is thus of paramount importance for all of us to cultivate our spiritual selves and energy, and spiritualise everything that we do.

The nature of the four kinds of energy has been succinctly summarised by The Energy Project as:

- **Physical Energy** — the <u>**quantity**</u> of our energy
- **Emotional Energy** — the <u>**quality**</u> of our energy
- **Mental Energy** — the <u>**focus**</u> of our energy, and
- **Spiritual Energy** — the <u>**purpose**</u> to which we put our energy

师傅 vs 师父: TEACHER vs FATHER FIGURE

In our previous book, "The Leader, The Teacher & You", we pointed out that the heart of the teacher is different, as the true mark of success for a teacher is the immense sense of achievement when the student surpasses the teacher in realising his or her full potential. We opined that the heart of a leader should be no different.

But what should a teacher be like?

In the Chinese language, the word for teacher or master, *Shi Fu*, has two different forms that reflect two different aspects:

- **师傅 (Shīfù)**: A teacher who imparts "technical skills", such as arts, skills, and knowledge.
- **师父 (Shīfù)**: A teacher with a paternal heart who teaches "fundamental skills" and imparts life lessons on how one should live and plan one's life.

While it is important for a leader to be both types of *shifu-s*, if a leader is first and foremost a 师父 who wants the best for his or her followers' lives, he or she should find it a lot easier to impart technical skills as a 师傅.

"太上，不知有之；
其次，亲而誉之；
其次，畏之；
其次，侮之；
信不足焉，有不信焉。
悠兮其贵言。
功成、事遂，
百姓皆谓：我自然。"

老子

"As for the best leaders,
the people do not notice their existence.
The next best,
the people honour and praise.
The next, the people fear;
and the next, the people hate.
When the best leader's work is done,
his aim fulfilled,
the people will say,
'We did it ourselves!'"

Laozi

Have a heart of Honour for your people, and everything else should fall in place!

SUMMARY: HONOUR IN LEADERSHIP

Let us summarise what is essential for effective leadership of organisations in a highly globalised world.

There are two aspects:

- **Position Leadership**
- **Personal Leadership**

Position Leadership requires us to lead the way into the future and initiate change, even if the company is going well at the current time. If the company is in trouble today, of course the most critical thing is to deal with the crisis. But once the crisis is over, we must get back to thinking about how to make the company alert, agile, innovative, responsive, enterprising, and future-oriented.

Personal leadership requires us to do whatever is necessary for our people to naturally want to follow us because they respect us and believe that we want the best for their lives and livelihoods. Remember that people desire **G.E.E.S.E. leadership**—Guide, Empathise, Energise, Synergise, and Embolden. Choose to be a 师父 (shīfù), whose emphasis is on the lives of your people, before being a 师傅 (shīfù), who just imparts technical skills and knowledge.

Leadership is about making good things happen that on their own would not happen. And the three most critical ends that leaders of organisations should pursue by combining position leadership with personal leadership are:

- **Be the Best You and Your Organisation Can Be**
- **Harness the Creativity and Capabilities of Your People**
- **Be in Time for the Future**

Laozi, the ancient Chinese sage, expressed it best about leadership when he said: *"As for the best leaders, the people do not notice their*

Leadership is a deep privilege and a wonderful opportunity to extend the heritage, enlarge the influence, and establish the success of your organisation.

It is an Honour to be in a position of leadership as you are in a seat of influence to make a difference in the lives of your people.

When people do not give all of themselves in their work, the organisation fails to reach its highest potential.

The starting point for success in leadership is to honour people as individuals.

existence. The next best, the people honour and praise. The next, the people fear; and the next, the people hate... When the best leader's work is done, his aim fulfilled, the people will say, 'We did it ourselves!' "

Leadership is a deep privilege and a wonderful opportunity to extend the heritage, enlarge the influence, and establish the success of your organisation. But above all, it is an Honour to be in a position of leadership as you are in a seat of influence to make a difference in the lives of your people. While you will be inevitably assessed on your Position Leadership, please do not forget that it is invariably Personal Leadership that will determine how successful you can be.

Leaders can get the desired responses from their people by threat or persuasion, but the approach they choose will make an enormous difference to how much their people will commit their minds and hearts to achieve the desired outcomes. People may be doing just enough to satisfy their bosses by doing just what they are told—this is like hiring hands and feet, without winning hearts and minds. When people do not give all of themselves in their work, the organisation fails to reach its highest potential.

The starting point for success in leadership is to honour people as individuals—each with his or her own gifts, talents, hopes, and dreams, and everyone wanting to be respected, trusted, recognised, and appreciated. Everyone wants to taste success and realise his or her potential.

WIN

WITH

HONOUR

IN

LEADERSHIP

BY ASKING YOURSELF:

- Am I doing all that I can to help others in the organisation (e.g. my boss, my subordinates, my peers, etc.) be the best that they can be?

- Am I doing all that I can to help myself be the best that I can be?

- What good am I doing in the lives of those who I seek to lead?

PART X

A STUDY OF SINGAPORE, A STUDY OF HONOUR

SMALL CITY, SMALL STATE

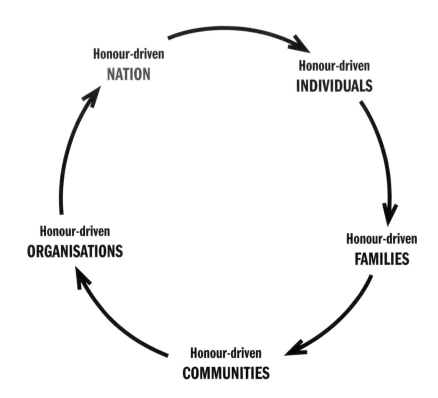

THE HONOUR CIRCLE

According to *Brand Finance*, the world's leading independent brand valuation and strategy consultancy, headquartered in London, Singapore was the world's strongest nation brand in 2015.[23] As the CEO of *Brand Finance* said in his foreword: "*In a global marketplace, a nation brand is one of the most important assets of any state, encouraging inward investment, adding value to exports, and attracting tourists.*"

In the Executive Summary of Brand Strength (as distinct from Brand Value) came the statement:

"**Singapore is the world's strongest nation brand in 2015**. *Nation brand value is reliant upon GDP, i.e. revenues associated with the brand. Singapore's small size means it will never be able to challenge for the top spot in brand value terms, because its brand simply cannot be applied extensively enough to generate the same economic uplift as 'brand USA' for example. However in terms of its underlying nation brand strength, Singapore comes out on top.*

"*As the city-state celebrates its 50th anniversary its citizens can be rightly proud of the nation they have created. ... The chief architect was of course Lee Kuan Yew. The vision, pragmatism, longevity, intolerance of corruption, and relative benevolence of the country's first prime minister and elder statesman are widely seen as the key reasons for its success.*

"*Unfortunately for nations looking to replicate Singapore's success, finding the next Lee Kuan Yew is no easy task and may be a foolhardy one.* **Long term leaders are often correctly regarded as more concerned about their own power than the interests of the nation**, *with Lee Kuan Yew being the exception that proves the rule. ... Singapore's international reputation has spread by word of mouth as much as it has by active promotion.*

"**Though the passing of Lee Kuan Yew in March this year is a sad loss, he leaves a legacy that few can hope to better**. *Singapore is now seen as modern, innovative, industrious, welcoming to outsiders, and increasingly culturally rich, and has left its neighbours (including Malaysia) far behind it.*"

We believe that Honour is the essential quality that has enabled Singapore to come so far since its independence in 1965, and it has

• SINGAPORE

SINGAPORE IN THE WORLD

distinguished Singapore from many nations in the world to become the world's strongest nation brand in 2015.

In this part, we:

- **Describe the important role that Honour has played in the Singapore story** since its independence in 1965.

- **Describe how Singapore's history in the 50 years since its independence in 1965 has illustrated what is possible if imagination and human enterprise are coupled with Honour,** even if there is a lack of resources.

- **Review the current state of values in Singapore.**

- **Consider the possible scenarios that might occur should Honour not be honoured.**

O, SINGAPORE

If you look at a map of the world, the little island of Singapore fits quite nicely into the letter "o" of the name of the country. Indeed, in most atlases, they have to make a special point of enlarging the dot or including an arrow so that Singapore can be noticed!

That is how small Singapore is. Unlike most countries in the world whose names fit into their boundaries in the atlas, Singapore's name is much longer than its size. It is basically a diamond-shaped island in Southeast Asia with Malaysia lying to the north and east of Singapore, and Indonesia lying to its west, south, and east.

Singapore, with a population of around 5.5 million as of June 2014 and a land area of 718 square kilometres (278 square miles), is even smaller as an entire country than cities such as:

- **New York City**, with an estimated population of 8.5 million people and a land area of 789 square kilometres (305 square miles)

- **London**, with an estimated population of 8.6 million and land area of 1,572 square kilometres (607 square miles)

- **Tokyo,** with an estimated population of 13.4 million and land area of 2,188 square kilometres (845 square miles)

For a small state such as Singapore, survival and success are two sides of the same coin.

Singaporeans must never forget that no one owes Singapore a living and no one else is responsible for our security.

The drive to be exceptional in the way Singaporeans think and act is not an option; it is destiny for Singapore and Singaporeans.

IMPLICATIONS OF BEING SMALL

What are the implications for survival, security, and success for a small state such as Singapore?

As mentioned in our first book, "The Leader, the Teacher & You" (Imperial College Press 2014), two of Singapore's founding fathers, Mr Lee Kuan Yew (Singapore's founding Prime Minister) and Dr Goh Keng Swee (Singapore's First Deputy Prime Minister), strongly believed that survival and success are two sides of the same coin for Singapore.

While Singapore seeks to be friends with all who would be friends with Singapore, Singaporeans must never forget that no one owes Singapore a living and no one else is responsible for our security. The drive to be exceptional in the way Singaporeans think and act is not an option; it is destiny for Singapore and Singaporeans.

SINGAPORE, THE LITTLE RED DOT

If you look again at the world map, Singapore is separated from Peninsular Malaysia to the north by the Straits of Johor and from Indonesia's Riau Islands to the south by the Singapore Strait.

In 1998, then Indonesian President B J Habibie referred to Singapore as a "little red dot"—he could have meant it as a disparaging remark. Little would Mr Habibie have expected that Singaporeans would take it up as a badge of Honour and as a symbol of success despite the odds!

When Singapore was unexpectedly booted out of Malaysia on 9 August 1965, it had to find its own way while facing racial tensions internally and unfriendly forces externally, with little by way of an army to defend herself. Singapore was extremely vulnerable as the merger with Malaysia was broken. Malay ultranationalists were denouncing Singapore, and Indonesia was still conducting *konfrontasi*[24] (military confrontation) because Indonesia had deemed the formation of Malaysia in the merger of the Federation of Malaya, Sabah, Sarawak, and Singapore in 1963 as a neo-colonialist plot.

Following its sudden and unexpected independence, Singapore reached out beyond its surroundings and "leap frogged" the countries in the region by embracing the whole world as its economic hinterland, a

Singapore's seemingly miraculous rise from the ashes of a failed merger with Malaysia is a testimony of what visionary leadership and effective governance coupled with the spirit of Honour can achieve.

The real legacy of Mr Lee Kuan Yew is the indomitable spirit of Honour that drove him and our founding fathers to do all that they could to secure the survival and well-being of the nation and its people.

veritable source of capital, investment, management capability, research, technology, and, most of all, markets.

Later, as its reputation for efficiency and its firm stand against corruption became widely established, Singapore grew to be a global financial centre, with the potential to be *the* global financial centre in Asia. From 1965 to 2015, Singapore's per capita Gross Domestic Product at Current Market Prices (GDP)[25] increased a hundred fold, from US$516 to US$52,888.

With no natural resources and only human capital to rely on, Singapore's economic growth since its independence has been the result of human imagination and human enterprise, with a good dose of providence. Singapore's seemingly miraculous rise from the ashes of a failed merger with Malaysia is a testimony of what visionary leadership and effective governance coupled with the spirit of Honour can achieve.

THE LEGACY OF LEE KUAN YEW

In 2015, Singapore marked its 50th year of independence with much celebration, and commemorated its Golden Jubilee with stirring pride. It was also a year stained with national mourning for the demise of its iconic founding father, Mr Lee Kuan Yew, on 23 March 2015.

In the days following Mr Lee's passing, there were many comments on Mr Lee's legacy—quite a few equated Singapore's transformation into a modern metropolis and imaginative developments, such as the Marina Barrage, as Mr Lee's legacy.

However, this would be the wrong way to think of Mr Lee's legacy. The material accomplishments of Singapore are but evidence that what Mr Lee and the founding generation of leaders dared to do was right. The real legacy of Mr Lee Kuan Yew is the indomitable spirit of Honour that drove him and our founding fathers to do all that they could to secure the survival and well-being of the nation and its people.

A people living upon the values of meritocracy, justice, and equality has made Singapore a model multi-cultural nation, and one of the most religiously diverse societies in the world. Many have commented that

There is an urgent need to reflect on what has made Singapore succeed in the past and, even more critically, what would be important for the continued survival and success of Singapore moving forward into the future.

Singapore is a unique and special nation, where every race, language, and religion has its equal place in yielding peace and security, as well as a social harmony that is the envy of many around the globe.

While there is much to celebrate with its attainment of social harmony across religions and races, and its attainment of First World economic status in 50 years, there is also an urgent need to reflect on what has made Singapore succeed in the past and, even more critically, what would be important for the continued survival and success of Singapore moving forward into the future.

Over the past 50 years, Singapore has become a model for many nations. Often when foreign dignitaries come to Singapore, they are briefed about the agencies and systems in Singapore that are the envy of so many developed and developing countries in the world. These agencies and systems include:

- **Housing and Development Board (HDB):** HDB is the planner and developer of public housing that solved poor and overcrowded housing conditions many years ago, and has made possible home ownership for more than 80 percent of Singaporeans today.

- **Central Provident Fund Board (CPF):** CPF is Singapore's comprehensive social security system that has enabled many Singaporeans to own their own homes, and actively save for their healthcare, home ownership, family protection, and asset enhancement.

- **Urban Redevelopment Authority (URA):** URA has enabled sound urban planning as Singapore made the transition from a "grimy and dirty" city to a "clean and green" metropolis.

- **Bilingual Education System:** The bilingual system in which students are taught subject-matter curriculum with English as the medium of instruction, while also having to study their "mother tongue" (such as Mandarin Chinese for the ethnic Chinese, Malay for the ethnic Malays, and Tamil for the ethnic Tamil Indians) to connect them with their cultural roots, has placed Singaporeans in a unique position to connect the world to Asia and Asia to the world.

Successful systems and schemes in Singapore have been the result of careful thought and methodical execution under sound and determined political leadership, backed by a competent and efficient public service, and a hardworking populace willing to forgo the immediate rewards today for a better tomorrow.

There is a deeper cultural reason that explains Singapore's success since independence.

The most obvious, important realities are often the ones that are hardest to see and talk about.

- **Healthcare System:** Singapore's healthcare system was ranked the most efficient in the world by Bloomberg in 2014.[26]

No doubt these successful systems and schemes have been the result of careful thought and methodical execution under sound and determined political leadership, backed by a competent and efficient public service, and a hardworking populace willing to forgo the immediate rewards today for a better tomorrow.

While these are critical factors in ensuring that plans are well-conceived and effectively executed, there is a deeper cultural reason that explains Singapore's success since independence.

HONOUR, SINGAPORE'S WATER[27]

The late American author David Foster Wallace began his commencement address to the graduates of Kenyon College in 2005 with this story:

"There are these two young fish swimming along and they happen to meet an older fish swimming the other way, who nods at them and says 'Morning, boys. How's the water?'

"And the two young fish swim on for a bit, and then eventually one of them looks over at the other and goes, 'What the hell is water?'"

The point of Wallace's fish story is merely that the most obvious, important realities are often the ones that are hardest to see and talk about.

When Mr Lee Kuan Yew came into power in 1959, Singapore was facing serious water challenges. Extreme droughts in the 1960s led to severe water shortages and painful bouts of water rationing.

When Singapore separated from Malaysia in 1965, two water agreements allowed the island to continue obtaining water from the state of Johor, just north of Singapore, until 2011 for one agreement signed in 1961 and 2061 for the other agreement signed in 1962.

Mr Lee constantly worried about Singapore's water self-sufficiency even though the water agreements were enshrined in Malaysia's constitution in the 1965 separation. Malaysia's first prime minister Tungku Abdul Rahman is said to have remarked to a British diplomat

Mr Lee not only cleaned up Singapore's physical water, he also cleansed the "spiritual dirt" in the governance system by adopting a "zero tolerance" approach to corruption.

Mr Lee also established a culture of Honour by ensuring that the Singapore Government delivered on all the promises that it had made to the MNCs.

We often forget that Singapore is an artificial construct—the city state is the result of human effort and imagination, built upon a foundation of Honour, which manifested in integrity, reliability, incorruptibility, and hard work.

at Singapore's parting from Malaysia that he would "turn off the water supply" if Singapore behaved in a way inimical to Malaysia's interest.

In Singapore's early years of independence, Mr Lee made it a priority to make Singapore as self-sufficient in water as possible. He drove the country's civil servants and engineers to clean up polluted waterways and increase the country's catchment areas first to half and now to two-thirds of the island. The Public Utilities Board (PUB) also added to Singapore's water supply new novel sources of water, namely, recycled wastewater (referred to as "Newater") and desalinated seawater.

Mr Lee not only cleaned up Singapore's physical water. He also cleansed the "spiritual dirt" in the governance system by adopting a "zero tolerance" approach to corruption, thus creating a strategic comparative advantage for Singapore that helped to attract the investments of multinational corporations (MNCs) to a region, which was ingrained with a culture of bribery, kickbacks, and fixers.

In addition, Mr Lee also established a culture of Honour by ensuring that the Singapore Government delivered on all the promises that it had made to the MNCs, whether it be tax incentives, land allocation, or labour and social harmony.

We often forget that Singapore is an artificial construct—the city state is the result of human effort and imagination, built upon a foundation of Honour, which manifested in integrity, reliability, incorruptibility, and hard work. The fact that Singapore is the product of Honour, human ingenuity, and trustworthiness can be easily lost if current and future generations of Singaporeans do not understand its significance and are not committed to sustain it.

As with Wallace's story at the beginning of this section, it could well be the situation with Singaporeans that Honour may be such a prevalent culture that newer generations of Singaporeans may not be aware of it, and therefore run the danger of saying, as the fish at the beginning of this story, "What the hell is water?" without recognising that "Singapore's water" is Honour and trustworthiness built up over many years through consistent behaviour, predictable policy, social stability, and national unity.

The "secret sauce" that explains Singapore's success since its independence in 1965 lies in answering questions such as:

Companies invest billions of dollars in Singapore each year knowing they would need tens of years to recover their investments because they have found the people and government of Singapore to be trustworthy, who can be relied on to work hard, to strive for excellence, and to deliver on their promises.

Singapore is trusted to offer integrity, incorruptibility, reliability, quality, as well as the assurance to deliver on its promises.

Trust is the most important currency for long term relationships, and it is the lifeblood that determines the quality of relationships that undergird every nation.

- Why has Singapore been able to successfully and consistently draw billions of dollars' worth of investments every year from all over the world, with companies investing in Singapore being prepared to wait 10, 15, or 20 years to recover their investment?

- Why have businesses in which the protection of intellectual property is the name of the game, chosen to locate their research and development centres in Singapore?

- Why are many foreigners choosing to manage their assets and store their wealth in Singapore?

Companies invest billions of dollars in Singapore each year knowing they would need tens of years to recover their investments because they have found the people and government of Singapore to be trustworthy, who can be relied on to work hard, to strive for excellence, and to deliver on their promises. The investors are able and willing to trust that the government and people of Singapore would:

- Honour their Word
- Honour the Rule of Law
- Honour Justice
- Honour Intellectual Property Rights
- Honour Meritocracy
- Honour Government Policies

Singapore is trusted to offer integrity, incorruptibility, reliability, quality, as well as the assurance to deliver on its promises even though it may involve lots of hard work and overcoming unexpected difficulties.

Trust is the most important currency for long-term relationships and it is the lifeblood that determines the quality of relationships that undergird every nation, such as:

- Parents and family
- Friends and relatives
- Bosses, colleagues, and subordinates
- Business partners and customers

Honour is the foundation of trust.

Singaporeans carry the Singapore brand of Honour and trustworthiness overseas.

To ensure that Singapore will continue to be a **HOME** offering **HO**pe and **ME**mory to Singaporeans today and the generations to come, it is important to honour these two dimensions of Honour:

- Honouring Our Word
- Honouring Each Other

- Government and community

And Honour is essentially the foundation of trust—it is only when the virtue of trust is initiated and mutually honoured that long term relationships of success can be forged and formed.

HONOUR, THE SINGAPORE BRAND

Singaporeans carry the Singapore brand of Honour and trustworthiness overseas.

A business leader who had spent many years in China once made the observation that the Chinese still find it very difficult to trust each other; this is a legacy of the Cultural Revolution in China, even though it had happened almost 50 years ago, from 1966 to 1976.

The Cultural Revolution sowed seeds of distrust as children had turned their parents in, parents had turned their children in, and siblings had turned each other in, not to mention friends, relatives, work colleagues, and acquaintances. This leader observed that somehow many Chinese in China were finding themselves able to trust Singaporeans more than they could trust their fellow Chinese nationals. It is no coincidence that a good number of companies in China hire Singaporeans to be their financial controllers, auditors, accountants, and their manufacturing and production managers.

Singapore's perspective has been that of long-term business and personal relationships—the type of relationship that can only survive where trust and credibility are never in doubt. These attributes have certainly made Singapore unique among the many developing countries of the world. The challenge is whether Singapore will sustain its uniqueness in this.

HONOUR OUR HOME

While there are arguably many dimensions to Honour, there are two dimensions that are particularly important for the continued survival and success of Singapore to ensure that Singapore will continue to be a **HOME**, offering **HO**pe and **ME**mory to Singaporeans today and the

Honour is the blueprint for Singapore's success and survival.

Honour is an enabler for constructive, respectful debate.

In order to maintain peace, harmony, and stability even in times of debate and individual actions, there must be a national consensus that all things are done with a view to ensure the survival and success of the nation, not only for today, but also, for the generations to come.

To achieve this, there must be:

- A culture of Honour
- A common mission to positively enhance the long-term collective well-being of the nation

generations to come. These two dimensions of Honour are:

- **Honouring Our Word**
- **Honouring Each Other**

Honour as the explanation of Singapore's success as a country since independence and its criticality for Singapore's continued success, reflects two perspectives on Singapore:

- **Honour as Singapore's Blueprint for Success:** Singapore's success in the last 50 years is the result of human imagination and hard work, as well as the courage to be different and unique.

  The investment in Singapore by Singaporeans and foreigners is founded on the belief that the government and people of Singapore will choose to not only do good, but more importantly to do what is right in the long-term for themselves, their families, their society, and the generations to come.

  It is a matter of "enlightened self-interest", where Honour makes good sense for living and livelihood—for without the survival and stability of the country, individuals and families will not have the place and the opportunity to thrive.

- **Honour as an Enabler for Constructive, Respectful Debate**: As we look into the future, we can expect an increasing desire by citizens to speak out on a widening array of national issues, to hold an increasing diversity of views, and to be able to act on their own initiatives.

In order to maintain peace, harmony, and stability even in times of debate and individual actions, there must be a national consensus that all things are done with a view to ensure the survival and success of the nation, not only for today, but also, more importantly, for the generations to come.

To achieve this, there must be:

- **A culture of Honour** and mutual respect between individuals, even when there may be sharp differences in views over particular issues.

- **A common mission to positively enhance the long-term**

While each generation must decide its own way according to its own circumstances, it is imperative that the culture of Honour be embraced by people as a fundamental virtue for the country's success in the years to come.

Honour needs to be espoused and embraced by schools, parents, leaders, workers, and community groups, so that there is an understood code of conduct for working towards a common end.

Being a small island with no physical or economic hinterland means that we have to accept that our private space, where we can think and do as we wish without trespassing into someone else's private space, will necessarily be smaller than in most other countries.

For communal and personal well-being, Singaporeans need to make up for the limited physical space by honouring each other.

collective well-being of the nation for current and future generations of Singaporeans.

While each generation must decide its own way according to its own circumstances, it is imperative that the culture of Honour be embraced by people as a fundamental virtue for the country's success in the years to come. Honour needs to be espoused and embraced by schools, parents, leaders, workers, and community groups, so that there is an understood code of conduct for working towards a common end. It is a virtue that has to be renewed with every generation of Singaporeans, and should be honoured by all Singaporeans in their daily lives.

PUBLIC SPACE vs PRIVATE SPACE

Being a small island with no physical or economic hinterland means that space is an inescapable issue—while we enjoy the convenience and connectivity of living in a small place, we also have to accept that our private space, where we can think and do as we wish without trespassing into someone else's private space, will necessarily be smaller than in most other countries.

The reality simply is that we cannot have it all: our geography dictates our destiny. Our smallness is a physical limitation we cannot escape from. And as the space per person matrix decreases, the pressure and stress of close-living increases.

Hence for communal and personal well-being, Singaporeans need to make up for the limited physical space by honouring each other by:

- Conscientiously making more mental and emotional space for each other through allowing for differences
- Consciously seeking common ground for the greater good
- Recognising that each person has his or her particular talents and abilities
- Welcoming contributions from everyone
- Acknowledging that the world does not revolve around our selfish needs

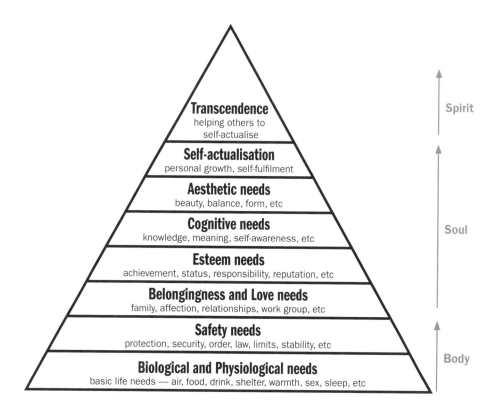

Maslow's Hierarchy of Needs Extended

We need to act, decide, and behave in ways that maximise our long-term well-being as a whole, and not just as individuals.

MASLOW'S HIERARCHY AND THE DEVELOPMENT OF SINGAPORE

When Lee Kuan Yew and the founding leaders came into power, the needs of the people were those largely found at the bottom of Maslow's Hierarchy of Needs (please refer to diagram on the left) namely, **Biological and Physiological needs** (e.g. food, water, housing), as well as **Safety needs** (e.g. security, stability, law, jobs).

These needs were wisely prioritised by the government, and then efficiently executed by institutions such as the Housing and Development Board, the Central Provident Fund Board, the Public Utilities Board, the Singapore Armed Forces, the Singapore Judiciary, and the Economic Development Board of Singapore.

Love needs (e.g. family, friends, sense of belonging, etc.) were reinforced by a strong community spirit, fondly referred to as the "Kampung Spirit".

Esteem needs (e.g. status, reputation, achievement) and **Self-actualisation needs** (e.g. the realisation of one's potential) were also met as the country's economy grew with the growing investments of the Multi-National Corporations (MNCs) and jobs created in the public sector as well as a growing private sector.

With a largely uneducated population, the governance and policy development of Lee's time was a "top-down" approach where the relatively uneducated person deferred to the wisdom of the more educated person, in faith that the better educated in government knew best what to do for the survival and success of the nation.

We need to recognise that this "top-down" approach to governance no longer works well with a well-educated and self-aware population who have their own opinions and the means to do most things for themselves.

Cognitive needs: Going forward, there needs to be a mindset shift to meet the cognitive needs of the people who are now more highly educated and have more access to information due to the internet revolution. The "top-down" approach will no longer work as people have a greater need to

Growing aesthetic needs means that there is a need to make a mindset shift from quantity to quality, and to pay greater attention to little details.

The need for Transcendence has been ranked as the highest of all needs in the human psyche.

There is a need to honour oneself by honouring others—to serve others beyond the individual self and acknowledge one's oneness with all beings and every creation.

understand and be understood; this is evident from the growing discussion and criticism on social media over the bases of government policies, as well as the less than perfect delivery of some public services.

Aesthetic needs: When our lower needs are met, we look increasingly to our aesthetic needs, a sense of balance in our lives, a reduction in stress, a desire for peace, beauty, and inner joy. There is a need to make a mindset shift from quantity to quality, to demonstrate greater thoughtfulness and mindfulness, and to pay greater attention to little details such as position, form, design, taste, smell, and sound.

We must also be cognisant of the need to refresh ourselves with the beauty of nature, the joy in dance and music, and the peacefulness of the environment.

The need to honour the aesthetic needs is particularly important for Singapore as it is a city state that is highly urbanised. According to a study by the American Chemical Society (ACS) journal *Environmental Science & Technology*, exposure to nature directly improves mental health. The study, which was conducted in the United Kingdom, compared the mental health of 100 people who moved from urban to greener, more natural settings and those who relocated in the reverse direction. The results of the study showed that the participants who relocated to natural settings were found to be overall happier during the three years that their mental health was recorded.[28]

Transcendence needs: It is very interesting that the need for Transcendence—that is, helping others reach their personal growth and fulfilment—has been ranked as the highest of all needs in the human psyche. This is the need to honour oneself by honouring others—to serve others beyond the individual self and acknowledge one's oneness with all beings and every creation.

NATIONAL VALUES IN SINGAPORE

From March to June 2015, a survey of national values in Singapore was conducted by A-advantage Consulting based in Singapore, in conjunction with the Barrett Values Centre based in the United Kingdom. The survey

From March to June 2015, a survey of national values in Singapore was conducted. The survey took into consideration Maslow's Hierarchy of Needs.

In this survey, 2,000 Singapore residents were asked to pick 10 words from a common list of values, beliefs, and behaviours that they felt would:

- Best reflect their own personal values

- Best reflect the current Singapore society

- Best reflect the Singapore society they desired to be part of took into consideration Maslow's Hierarchy of Needs. Similar surveys have been conducted in other countries such as Australia, Canada, Finland, Sweden, Switzerland, the United Kingdom, and the United States of America. A previous survey was conducted in Singapore in 2012.

In this survey, 2,000 Singapore residents were chosen through stratified quota sampling to ensure the sample matched the distribution of the resident population on the basis of age, gender, and housing-type. Respondents were asked to pick 10 words from a common list of values, beliefs, and behaviours that they felt would:

- **Best reflect their own personal values**
- **Best reflect the current Singapore society**
- **Best reflect the Singapore society they desired to be part of**

The top 10 choices for each of these categories came out as follows (with the ranking in the 2012 survey indicated in brackets):

PERSONAL VALUES OF SINGAPOREANS	WHAT SINGAPORE SOCIETY IS TODAY	WHAT THEY WOULD LIKE TO SEE IN SINGAPORE SOCIETY
1 (1) Family	1 (1) *Kiasu* (afraid to lose)	1 (1) Affordable housing
2 (7) Responsibility	2 (2) Competitive	2 (2) Caring for the elderly
3 (2) Friendship	3 (4) Materialistic	3 (3) Effective healthcare
4 (4) Happiness	4 (3) Self-centred	4 (5) Compassion
5 (3) Health	5 (5) *Kiasi* (afraid to die)	5 (7) Quality of life
6 (5) Caring	6 (8) Blame	6 (4) Caring for disadvantaged
7 (6) Honesty	7 (10) Security	7 (*) Peace
8 (*) Compassion	8 (*) Education opportunities	8 (10) Employment opportunities
9 (*) Positive attitude	9 (*) Effective healthcare	9 (*) Caring for environment
10 (9) Respect	10 (*) Peace	10 (6) Concern for future generations
*The new items replace "well-being" (8) and "work-life balance" (10) in the 2012 list.	* The new items replace "deteriorating values" (6), "elitism" (7) and "uncertainty about the future" (9) in the 2012 list.	*The new items replace "equal opportunities" (8) and "social responsibility" (9) in the 2012 list.

Overall, the results of the 2015 National Values Assessment for Singapore were very encouraging.

While Singaporeans have not arrived at the ideal society and considerable work still needed to be done, the starting point was good, with the top three highest personal values listed by the respondents being other-centred.

Nine out of 10 of the highest ranked personal values are for the individual to work out in his/her life.

Overall, the results of the 2015 National Values Assessment for Singapore were very encouraging. While Singaporeans have not arrived at the ideal society and considerable work still needed to be done, the starting point was good, with the top three highest personal values listed by the respondents being other-centred:

1. Family
2. Responsibility
3. Friendship
4. Happiness
5. Health
6. Caring
7. Honesty
8. Compassion
9. Positive attitude
10. Respect

Looking at these 10 highest ranked personal values, Health seemed like the one thing that would be a joint responsibility between the individual and the government. All the other nine values would be for the individual to work out in his or her life. In addition, out of the 10 values:

- **Five pertained to the individual attitudes and behaviours in life and work**—namely, Responsibility, Happiness, Health, Honesty, and Positive Attitude.

- **Five pertained to relationships**—namely, Family, Friendship, Caring, Compassion, and Respect.

PERCEPTION OF SINGAPORE SOCIETY

In contrast, the top 10 values and behaviours that best described the Singapore society as currently perceived were quite different:

1. *Kiasu* (afraid to lose)
2. Competitive
3. Materialistic

The difference between how the individual saw himself or herself and how the individual perceived society to be was profound—practically everything appeared to be the fault of others!

Personal values should be lived out in such a way that they positively influence the well-being of those around.

4. Self-centred

5. *Kiasi* (afraid to die)

6. Blame

7. Security

8. Education opportunities

9. Effective healthcare

10. Peace

Kiasu, or "afraid to lose" (with 1,134 votes) came way ahead of the next value, which was Competitive (with 696 votes). The difference between how the individual saw himself or herself and how the individual perceived society to be was profound—practically everything appeared to be the fault of others!

The disconnect between the two sets of results would appear to be confusing—how could the description of oneself and the description of others in society be so different?

There could be only one of two explanations:

- One is that while people professed to esteem certain values, they did not honour them by living them out.

- The second is that the values have been lived out in such a way as to result in negative manifestations that did not increase the well-being of society. For example, one might think that valuing and providing for the family meant that one had to play politics at office in order to get ahead or one had to undermine others to help family members win. If valuing family were activated at the expense of all other considerations, it would be socially negative, even disruptive.

Whichever be the explanation, what is clear is that personal values should be lived out in such a way that they positively influence the well-being of those around.

Of the 10 items, the lowest four would mainly be for the government to deliver (namely: Security, Education Opportunities, Effective Healthcare, and Peace), while the top six would be for the individual to work out (namely: *Kiasu*, Competitive, Materialistic, Self-centred, *Kiasi*, and Blame).

Many critics of Singapore society base their point of reference as the West. However, are Singaporeans really prepared for a similar perception of the current state of Singapore's society in another 20, 50, or 100 years as the US and the UK have today?

DO WE REALLY WANT SINGAPORE TO BE LIKE THE WEST?

In the country comparison, the top 10 values and behaviours listed in the United Kingdom (UK) as describing the current state of UK society in 2012 were:

- Bureaucracy
- Crime/violence
- Uncertainty about the future
- Corruption
- Blame
- Wasted resources
- Media influence
- Conflict/aggression
- Drugs/alcohol
- Apathy

The list describing the current state of US society in 2011 were:

- Blame
- Bureaucracy
- Wasted resources
- Corruption
- Materialistic
- Uncertainty about the future
- Conflict/aggression
- Crime/violence
- Unemployment
- Short term focus

It is interesting how similar the list is between the UK and US, and how different the lists are from Singapore's.

Many critics of Singapore society base their point of reference as the West. However, are Singaporeans really prepared for a similar perception of the current state of Singapore's society in another 20, 50, or 100 years as the US and the UK have today?

Our values determine our thoughts that in turn determine our actions, which ultimately determine our destiny.

What kind of society do we wish for ourselves and our future generations?

The sense of self-responsibility in Singapore society appears low. Like a typical teenager, Singaporeans seem to want the freedom to do their own thing but at the same time want the Government (their "parents") to still provide for their needs.

Singaporeans have to make sure that the governing political party is one that listens well and understands their concerns, and at the same time has the competence to think out solutions and deliver them effectively.

Our values determine our thoughts that in turn determine our actions, which ultimately determine our destiny. What kind of society do we wish for ourselves and our future generations?

DESIRED SINGAPORE SOCIETY

Next, the top 10 values and behaviours which those surveyed said would be, for them, the desired Singapore society, were:

1. Affordable housing
2. Caring for the elderly
3. Effective healthcare
4. Compassion
5. Quality of life
6. Caring for the disadvantaged
7. Peace
8. Employment opportunities
9. Caring for the environment
10. Concern for future generations

What is striking about the list is how many of the desired items would be for the government to deliver—almost all!

This has two implications:

- Judging from the list, the sense of self-responsibility would appear to be low. Like a typical teenager, Singaporeans seem to want the freedom to do their own thing but at the same time want the Government (their "parents") to still provide for their needs.

- Singaporeans have to make sure that the governing political party is one that listens well and understands their concerns, and at the same time has the competence to think out solutions and deliver them effectively.

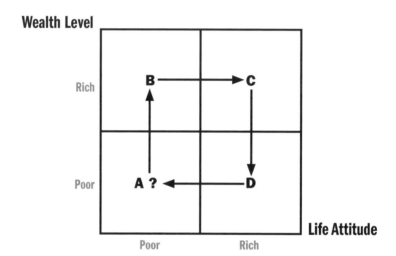

WEALTH ATTITUDE GRID

WEALTH ATTITUDE GRID

There would seem to be a certain disconnect today between the expectations of Singaporeans and the policies of the government.

If Singaporeans start with the premise that the government is always wrong, does not want the best for them, and is stupid or heartless, communication between the government and the people would be difficult because such basic distrust would not engender empathy or understanding. **But if Singaporeans and the government could each start by honouring the good intentions of the other, with a common mission to increase the collective well-being of the nation in the long-term positively, there would be much hope for fruitful discourse.**

Appreciating each other's mental model is a necessary starting point. A good way to understand the current situation could be by way of the diagram on the left, which we have called the Wealth Attitude Grid.

The Wealth Attitude Grid is a simple 2 x 2 matrix, with "Life Attitude" as the x-axis and "Wealth Level" as the y-axis.

In the early years, Singapore was poor, and the life attitude of both the people and the government was that of a "poor man"—life is uncertain, earn what you can, save what you can, spend only on what you need for you can never know what tomorrow will bring, so be prepared and save for a rainy day. Thus Singapore was at Point A of the Wealth Attitude Grid—the country was poor, and the life attitude of the people was that of a "poor man".

Over time, Singapore became rich, but many people still perceived the Government as having the attitude of the "poor man". So the people reckon the Singapore government to be at Point B of the Grid. However, what some people think is: "If we are really rich, shouldn't we be at Point C of the Grid, where the country is rich and the government provides for the people for a life attitude of that of a 'rich man'?"

And that, to our minds, is the fundamental reason for much of the angst between the people and the government: the people reckon we should be at Point C, while the government is perceived as sticking closer to Point B.

The government, understandably, has the particular concern that if Singapore were to progress to Point C, it could be setting itself up to fall

A democracy is always temporary in nature; it simply cannot exist as a permanent form of government.

A democracy will continue to exist up until the time that voters discover that they can vote themselves generous gifts from the public treasury.

From that moment on, the majority always votes for the candidates who promise the most benefits from the public treasury, with the result that every democracy will finally collapse due to loose fiscal policy, which is always followed by a dictatorship.

into Point D of the Grid. Point D is where the country is in fact poor, but the government provides for the people a lifestyle as though they were rich, whether this is by way of free education, free healthcare, free transport, or "cradle to grave" welfare.

The interesting question is: Are there countries at Point D of the Grid?

Many observers reckon there are indeed many countries at Point D—countries named include Greece, Europe, Japan, and the United States. At point D, people have been used to having their governments adopt policies and provide benefits like a "rich man", but in fact these governments no longer have the revenues to support such policies, so they are forced to borrow to be able to continue to extend these benefits to the people.

The "poverty" of these governments is often "invisible" because of their "pay-as-you-go" pension and social security schemes, where the pension and social benefits for the retirees are paid for by collections from the working population. The sustainability of these schemes is however threatened by dwindling populations coupled with low birth rates, while the retiree populations balloon with increased life expectancies arising from advances in medicine and healthcare.

Why are these governments unable to "correct" the schemes by lowering the pension and social benefits, or increasing the contributions from the working public, or raising the retirement ages to more or less keep constant the number of years between retirement and life expectancy?

Perhaps at least part of the answer can be gleaned from an interesting point by Alexander Tyler, a Scottish history professor at the University of Edinburgh, who said in 1787:

"A democracy is always temporary in nature; it simply cannot exist as a permanent form of government. A democracy will continue to exist up until the time that voters discover that they can vote themselves generous gifts from the public treasury. From that moment on, the majority always votes for the candidates who promise the most benefits from the public treasury, with the result that every democracy will finally collapse due to loose fiscal policy, which is always followed by a dictatorship."

Apparently, the dictatorship at that point is not necessarily unwelcome, because the collapse of democracy leads to riots and civil disorder, and people then begin to value order and public security more.

Singaporeans should debate these three questions:

- What kind of Singapore do we want in the next 10, 20, 50, 100 years?
- What economic policies would Singapore need to keep the wealth level up?
- What social policies do we need to keep government spending expectations within sustainable limits?

In the end, it is the kind of society we want to be and the sustainability of such a society that are the crucial issues.

The dimensions are not just economic, but are also about values, culture, and life attitudes.

It is not about rights *per se*, because there will be times where right and rights clash.

The interesting question is: Can Singapore recover from Point D should it fall from Point C to Point D? Because if Singapore can recover from Point D to Point C, rather than inexorably go from Point D to Point A, perhaps the risk of getting to Point C may be worth taking.

Singapore had made it from Point A to Point B by astute national leadership and a trusting public; its honourable and wise leadership made good use of opportunities arising from a confluence of geostrategic factors, whether it was the withdrawal of British military forces east of Suez, the Vietnam War, or the Plaza Accord.

The situation is different today, so that the chances of recovering from Point D to go back to Point C, rather than fall into Point A, are far from assured. Why risk it? Perhaps the government thinks the chances of avoiding Point D are best assured by staying closer to Point B, possibly nudging towards Point C but never quite getting there.

The real discussion that is necessary should begin with a recognition of the disconnect between the public perception of the government being at Point B, while the public desire is most likely to be at Point C, and to have a good national debate on how to keep staying at Point C, if Singapore were to move there.

This national debate has to be centred on three questions:

- What kind of Singapore do we want in the next 10, 20, 50, 100 years?

- What economic policies would we need to keep the wealth level up?

- What social policies do Singapore need to keep government spending expectations within sustainable limits?

In the end, it is the kind of society we want to be and the sustainability of such a society that are the crucial issues. The dimensions are not just economic, but are also about values, culture, and life attitudes.

The debate has to be about what would be right for Singapore and Singaporeans, not just for the current generation but for the generations to come. It is not about rights *per se*, because there will be times where right and rights clash, in which case it makes a lot more sense to do what is right for the sake of the long-term well-being of Singaporeans as a whole, regardless of how the rest of the world may be choosing, for if the nation does not survive and thrive, the individual has no chance

It makes a lot more sense to do what is right for the sake of the long-term well-being of Singaporeans as a whole, regardless of how the rest of the world may be choosing—if the nation does not survive and thrive, the individual has no chance to survive and thrive.

Singaporeans need the courage to be selflessly different, forward thinking, and innovative because Singapore's smallness and lack of natural resources makes it more vulnerable than other countries.

The next phase of Singapore development should be what we may call "values-driven".

to survive and thrive.

Singaporeans need the courage to be selflessly different, forward thinking, and innovative because Singapore's smallness and lack of natural resources makes it more vulnerable than other countries.

VALUES DRIVEN SOCIETY

Another point we had mentioned in our previous book, "The Leader, The Teacher & You" is that the next phase of Singapore development should be what we may call "values-driven".

By values, we mean something much wider than personal and social values, and even wider than the National Values that had been approved by Parliament in 1991, namely:

- Nation before community and society above self
- Family as the basic unit of society
- Community support and respect for the individual
- Consensus not conflict
- Racial and religious harmony

Neither do we mean values about national independence and sovereignty borne in the five aspects of Total Defence:

- Military Defence
- Civil Defence
- Economic Defence
- Social Defence
- Psychological Defence

Nor are we only referring to the values expressed in the six National Education Messages:

- Belongingness
- Harmony
- Integrity
- Resilience

We must bring national values to life by honouring these values and living a life driven by Honour every day.

"Values-Driven" Approach:

- Values of Identity
- Values of Community
- Values of Discovery

VALUES OF IDENTITY: We need a strong sense of identity and this can only be achieved if we honour ourselves.

VALUES OF COMMUNITY: We need a strong sense of community and this can only be achieved if we honour our word and honour each other.

- Responsibility
- Confidence

While all these values are essential and critical, we have to build on them and go beyond them. We must bring them to life by honouring these values and living a life driven by Honour every day. This "values-driven" development would encourage each of us to be the best that we can be.

When we speak of a "values-driven" approach, we are thinking of what it is in our beliefs, attitudes, and fundamental motivations that would empower us to be the best that we can be—not only for ourselves, but for our families, our communities, our nation, and for future generations.

As shared in our previous book, we would list these as:

- **Values of Identity**
- **Values of Community**
- **Values of Discovery**

VALUES OF IDENTITY: First, we need a strong sense of identity and this can only be achieved if we honour ourselves. We need to feel comfortable with ourselves and have a sense of belonging to our family, to our community, and to our country. "Values of Identity" basically answer the question: "Who am I?" This is grounded in one's character, personality, morals, and ethics, and is also derived from family, religion, language, culture, and country.

VALUES OF COMMUNITY: Next, we need a strong sense of community and this can only be achieved if we honour our word and honour each other. If "Values of Identity" address the question: "Who am I?", "Values of Community" address the question: "What can I do?"

We need to have "Values of Community" so that we can get along with each other and have a strong sense of social and moral responsibility. We need to honour the values of integrity, other-centeredness, harmony, and trustworthiness.

We also need to understand what is good for the public at large and commit to place society over self, not only for the short term, but also for the long term. We need to keep the government accountable to ensure

We need to do our part for others and for our country, if not driven by "love", then by "enlightened self-interest".

There is a need to continually think and debate how Singapore is to continually survive and succeed in the real world.

VALUES OF DISCOVERY: We need to have "Values of Discovery", which can only thrive after a culture of Honour and honouring has been established.

We need to have the maturity to:

- Think through things for ourselves
- Think through the implications of our thoughts and actions on other people and future generations

that it fulfils its role of assuring justice, security, stability, and the rule of law, as well as establishing and maintaining the supporting social and legal institutions to assure the public good.

Above all, it is about us doing our part for others and for our country, if not driven by "love", then at least by what Dr Goh Keng Swee often referred to as "enlightened self-interest".

The majority of Singaporeans today are a generation of children and teachers who have grown up without living through the struggle, doubts, and fears of the early years of independence. There is a need to continually think and debate how Singapore is to continually survive and succeed in the real world.

As succinctly described by Lord Henry Palmerston, the English statesman of the 19th century (1784–1865): *"Nations have no permanent friends or allies; they only have permanent interests."*

VALUES OF DISCOVERY: Lastly, we need to have "Values of Discovery", which can only thrive after a culture of Honour and honouring has been established, so that instead of being told facts and conclusions, we have the maturity to think things through for ourselves, and think through the implications of our thoughts and actions on other people and future generations.

"Values of Discovery" would lead one to be constantly curious, and to take the initiative to learn by doing. "Values of Discovery" would also give one the courage to be different, be willing to try and to learn from mistakes, and have a sense of adventure, dedication, persistence, and determination. "Values of Discovery" is undergirded by a relentless drive for excellence.

We often lament a lack of innovative spirit among Singaporeans, and we accept too easily the analysis of outside commentators who say that this situation has arisen because Singaporeans are brought up to conform and are too scared to question. We think the reason Singaporeans simply go along with the herd and keep to the tried and tested path is because they think that it is the smart and efficient thing to do. Instead of thinking through things and considering why they are doing what they do, they choose the easier way and go with the crowd. We have to change this.

Being different is not the same as being contrarian: it is knowing why

Being different is not the same as being contrarian: it is knowing why you believe what you are believing and why you are doing what you are doing.

This idea that the focus should be on others and not ourselves runs directly into the face of self-focussed materialism that marks every first-world country.

Success and purpose comes about when we make others our focus.

Honouring others is not always easy, not always fun, and not always nice.

Honour is the path that gives purpose and meaning to our lives.

you believe what you are believing and why you are doing what you are doing.

As we contemplate the future for Singapore, we think one of the greatest threats to continuing success and national well-being is the lack of entrepreneurs, innovators, researchers, and leaders. Entrepreneurs build businesses that would never exist without them; innovators do things differently from how they have always been done; researchers discover things never known before; and leaders make good things happen that would otherwise not happen on their own.

In every instance, the driving force of energy and imagination is to bring about something new and something different, whether this be in the public or the private sector, for the well-being of society, and to serve others, not themselves.

This idea that the focus should be on others and not ourselves runs directly into the face of self-focussed materialism that marks every first-world country, an insight aptly noted by Jack Ma, Executive Chairman of Alibaba, which had the largest IPO ever in 2014.

In a speech he delivered in South Korea, Ma said:

"I'm lucky to know a lot of famous people…Bill Gates, Warren Buffett, Jack Welch…the difference between those people and other people is that they are always optimistic about the future. They never complain. They always try to solve the problems of others…opportunity always lies in the place where others complain…If you really want to work for yourself, make sure that you help others…because only when other people are a success and when other people are happy, you will be successful…you will be happy."

As noted by Ma, success and purpose comes about when we make others our focus. Honouring others is not always easy, not always fun, and not always nice. But Honour is the path that gives purpose and meaning to our lives.

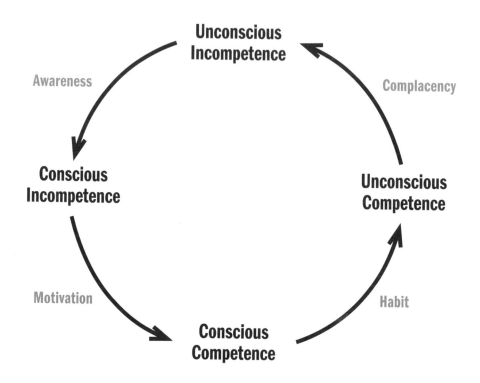

CIRCLE OF IMPROVEMENT

IS SINGAPORE IN A STATE OF UNCONSCIOUS COMPETENCE?

We had also introduced in our previous book, "The Leader, The Teacher & You", the "Circle of Improvement", which illustrates the challenge for organisations to remain "consciously competent" and highlights the dangers of slipping into being "unconsciously incompetent".

Unconscious Incompetence: Many organisations start in a state of "unconscious incompetence", as the entire organisation or parts of the organisation are unaware of their inadequacies.

Conscious Incompetence: There comes a day when management becomes aware of the organisation's inadequacies and brings the organisation into a state of "conscious incompetence". This awareness may arise through peer comparison, visiting other organisations, reading literature, etc.

Conscious Competence: If there is the desire to improve, the organisation will conduct studies, send its staff for training programmes, review its processes, and so on; as a result, the organisation will enter into a state of "conscious competence". Almost invariably, what happens at this point is that someone will produce a series of work rules, or standard operating procedures, for others to follow.

Unconscious Competence: When the people in the organisation observe the standard operating procedures but do not understand why they are doing what they are doing, the organisation enters into a state of "unconscious competence", where its customers, at least for a time, will still reckon they are getting good service despite the service provider not fully knowing why it is competent.

The state of "unconscious competence" is the danger zone, because, being "unconscious", the organisation will easily slip into a state of "unconscious incompetence" without knowing how or when it got there. This will happen over time because the environment changes whether for reasons of demographics or technology or geography, and what was once sound and appropriate will become incongruent and irrelevant.

Organisations that do not continually question what they are doing and how they are doing it run the danger of being caught in "unconsciousness"; the complacency may well be fatal, resulting in the

Organisations that do not continually question what they are doing and how they are doing it run the danger of being caught in "unconsciousness"; the complacency may well be fatal, resulting in the demise of the organisation.

Extrapolate this to the national level, and one can see the danger that Singapore is in if its government and its people fail to reflect enough on how we have gotten to where we are, and neglect to make timely choices that take into consideration the consequences of what we choose today on the generations to come.

Most great nations do not last longer than 250 years, and many last much shorter periods of time.

demise of the organisation.

Extrapolate this to the national level, and one can see the danger that Singapore is in if its government and its people fail to reflect enough on how we have gotten to where we are, and neglect to make timely choices that take into consideration the consequences of what we choose today on the generations to come.

WILL SINGAPORE FALL?

While Singapore proudly celebrated its Golden Jubilee in 2015, we must be humble and not forget that nations rise, and nations fall.

The Chinese have a saying: "富不过三代" or "Wealth does not last beyond three generations". After celebrating its 50th year, Singapore is moving into its third generation. Will Singapore's wealth and stability last?

Sir John Bagot Glubb (1897–1986) was a British soldier, scholar, and author, who led and trained Transjordan's Arab Legion between 1939 and 1956. Glubb wrote a profound essay, "The Fate of Empires and Search for Survival", which analyses the lifespan of great nations from their genesis to their decline.

In "The Fate of Empires and Search for Survival", Glubb notes that over the last 3,000 years, the "periods of duration of different empires at varied epochs show a remarkable similarity". Glubb explores the facts and notes that most great nations do not last longer than 250 years (or 10 generations), and many last much shorter periods of time.

Here is his summary:

The nation	Dates of rise and fall	Duration in years
Assyria	859–612 B.C.	247
Persia (Cyrus and his descendants)	538–330 B.C.	208
Greece (Alexander and his successors)	331–100 B.C.	231
Roman Republic	260–27 B.C.	233
Roman Empire	27 B.C.–A.D. 180	207

According to Glubb, the stages of the rise and fall of great nations seem to be as follows:

- Age of Pioneers
- Age of Conquests
- Age of Commerce
- Age of Affluence
- Age of Intellect
- Age of Decadence

Age of PIONEERS: The first stage of the life of a great nation is a period of amazing initiative, enterprise, courage, and hardihood. These qualities produce a new and formidable nation.

The nation	Dates of rise and fall	Duration in years
Arab Empire	A.D. 634–880	246
Mameluke Empire	1250–1517	267
Ottoman Empire	1320–1570	250
Spain	1500–1750	250
Romanov Russia	1682–1916	234
Britain	1700–1950	250

Glubb also observes that "immense changes in the technology of transport or in methods of warfare do not seem to affect the life-expectation of an empire"—it merely changes the "shape of the empire".

In his essay, Glubb describes many of the stages of empire and many of the reasons why they break down and eventually disappear.

According to Glubb, the stages of the rise and fall of great nations seem to be as follows:

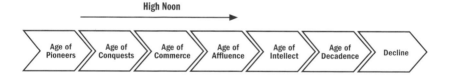

Age of PIONEERS

A small nation, treated as insignificant by its contemporaries, suddenly emerges and conquers the world.

This age is characterised by an extraordinary display of energy and courage.

Pioneers are ready to improvise and experiment: *"Untrammelled*

Age of CONQUESTS: The principal objects of ambition are glory and Honour for the nation.

Age of COMMERCE: This is the period of time when values start shifting from the self-sacrifice to self-interest. The acquisition of wealth soon takes precedence over everything else.

by traditions, they will turn anything available to their purpose. If one method fails, they try something else. Uninhibited by textbooks or book learning, action is their solution to every problem."

The first stage of the life of a great nation is a period of amazing initiative, enterprise, courage, and hardihood. These qualities produce a new and formidable nation.

The second stage of expansion consists of more organised, disciplined, and professional campaigns. Methods employed tend to be practical and experimental.

Age of CONQUESTS

The nation acquires the "sophisticated weapons of old empires" and a great period of expansion ensues. The principal objects of ambition are glory and Honour for the nation.

The conquests result in the "acquisition of vast territories under one government", thereby birthing commercial prosperity.

Age of COMMERCE

The main purpose of this era is to create more wealth.

The first half of this age seems to be splendid: *"The ancient virtues of courage, patriotism, and devotion to duty are still in evidence."*

The nation is proud and united, and boys are still required to be manly. In addition, courageous initiative is displayed in the quest for profitable enterprises all around the world.

Age of AFFLUENCE: "Money replaces Honour and adventure as the objective of the best young men. The object of the young and ambitious is no longer fame, Honour, or service, but cash."

HIGH NOON: The period of the transition from the Age of Conquests to the Age of Affluence.

Characteristics of "High Noon":

- The change from service to selfishness
- Defensiveness

But the acquisition of wealth soon takes precedence over everything else. The previous objectives of "glory" and "Honour" are but "empty words, which add nothing to the bank balance" for the people.

This is the period of time when values start shifting from the self-sacrifice of the initial pioneers to self-interest.

Age of AFFLUENCE

Money causes the people to gradually decline in terms of courage and enterprise.

Wealth first hurts the nation morally: "Money replaces Honour and adventure as the objective of the best young men...the object of the young and ambitious is no longer fame, Honour, or service, but cash."

Instead of seeking wealth for their nation or community, men seek wealth for their own personal benefit.

Education is also affected negatively. Instead of seeking learning, virtues, and qualifications that serve the nation, parents and students seek qualifications that enable them to grow rich.

The divide between the rich and poor increases and the wealth of the rich is flaunted for people to see. People enjoy high standards of living and consume in excess of what they need.

HIGH NOON

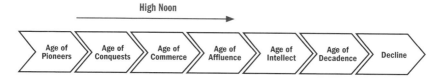

Between the period of the transition from the Age of Conquests to the Age of Affluence is a period that Glubb entitles "High Noon".

History indicates that nations decline not because its people do not have a conscience, but decline because of:

- A weakening sense of duty
- An increase in selfishness and the desire for wealth and ease

Age of INTELLECT: Business people that made their wealth in the age of commerce seek fame and the praise of others by:

- Endowing works of art
- Patronising music and literature
- Founding/endowing institutions of higher education

While the immense wealth of the nation impresses other nations, this period reveals the same characteristics:

- **The change from service to selfishness**
- **Defensiveness**

CHANGE FROM SERVICE TO SELFISHNESS: During this period, *"enough of the ancient virtues of courage, energy, and patriotism survive to enable the state successfully to defend its frontiers. But beneath the surface, greed for money is gradually replacing duty and public service."*

DEFENSIVENESS: The rich nation is no longer interested in glory or duty, but is preoccupied with the conservation and maintenance of its wealth and luxury. Money replaces courage, and subsidies are used to "buy off" enemies.

History indicates that nations decline not because its people do not have a conscience, but decline because of:

- A weakening sense of duty
- An increase in selfishness and the desire for wealth and ease

Age of INTELLECT

During this stage, wealth is no longer needed for necessities or the luxuries, and there are also abundant funds for the pursuit of knowledge.

Business people that made their wealth in the age of commerce seek fame and the praise of others by:

- Endowing works of art
- Patronising music and literature
- Founding/endowing institutions of higher education

It is ironic that while civilisations make advancements in science,

Constant dedication to discussion seems to destroy the power of action.

For a nation to thrive and survive, its citizens must display:

- Loyalty
- Self-sacrifice

The Age of Decadence comes about due to the following factors:

- Extended period of wealth and power
- Selfishness
- Love of money
- Loss of a sense of duty

philosophy, the arts, and literature, and the spread of knowledge seems to be one of the most beneficial of human activities, yet history shows us that every period of the decline is characterised by the expansion of intellectual activity.

Why is this so?

The answer is NATO.

NO ACTION, TALK ONLY (NATO): Intellectualism leads to discussion, debate, and argument, which is often seen in Western nations today. But this "constant dedication to discussion seems to destroy the power of action."

Inadequacy of Intellect: The most dangerous by-product of this age is the birth and growth of the notion that human intellect can solve all the problems of the world, when in fact the survival of the nation really depends on its citizens.

In particular, in order for that nation to thrive and survive, its citizens must display:

- Loyalty
- Self-sacrifice

Intellectualism, selfishness, and the lack of a sense of duty to one's family, community, and nation, all appear simultaneously in the nation.

Age of DECADENCE AND DECLINE

Decadence is a mental, moral, and spiritual disease that disempowers its people to the extent that they do not make an effort to save themselves or their nation because they do not think that anything in life is worth saving.

The Age of Decadence comes about due to the following factors:

- Extended period of wealth and power

The Age of Decadence is marked by:

- Defensiveness
- Pessimism
- Materialism
- Frivolity
- An influx of foreigners
- The welfare state
- Weakening of religion

- Selfishness
- Love of money
- Loss of a sense of duty

The Age of Decadence is marked by:

- Defensiveness
- Pessimism
- Materialism
- Frivolity
- An influx of foreigners
- The welfare state
- Weakening of religion

Defensiveness: People are so consumed with defending their wealth and possessions that they fail to fulfil their duty to their family, community, and nation. Glubb also notes another remarkable and unexpected sign of national decline is civil dissension and intensification of internal political hatreds. Various political factions hate each other so much that instead of sacrificing rivalries to save the nation, internal differences are not reconciled, leading to a weaker nation.

Pessimism: As the nation declines in power and wealth, universal pessimism invades its people and accelerates its decline.

Materialism: People enjoy high standards of living and consume in excess of what they need.

Frivolity: As the pessimism invades its people, people start to think: "Let us eat, drink and be merry, for tomorrow we die." The people forget that material success is the result of courage, endurance, and hard work, and spend an increasing part of their time indulging in sex, leisure, amusement, or sport. The heroes in declining nations are the athlete, the singer, or the actor, not the statesman, general, or literary genius.

Influx of Foreigners: In his essay, Glubb also shares that one frequent phenomenon in the decline of cities is the influx of foreigners.
Glubb opines that the problem does not consist in any inferiority

THE WELFARE STATE: History shows that the decline of a nation is often preceded by a tendency for philanthropy and sympathy.

The impression that it will always be automatically rich causes the declining empire to spend lavishly on its own benevolence, until such a time as the economy collapses, the universities are closed, and the hospitals fall into ruin.

WEAKENING OF RELIGION: Without religion, men are more likely to snatch than serve, and the spirit of self-sacrifice is weak.

of one race compared to another, but simply the differences between them. While second or third generation immigrants may seem to have assimilated outwardly, they are weak links in the society for various reasons such as:

- Immigrants will be less willing to sacrifice their lives and property for the nation.

- Immigrants form communities of their own that protect their own interests above that of the nation.

Glubb states clearly that he is not saying that immigrants are inferior in any way—they are just different, and thus they tend to introduce cracks and divisions in the society.

The Welfare State: As history shows, the decline of a nation is often preceded by a tendency for philanthropy and sympathy. State assistance to the young and the poor are generous, free medical treatment to the poor is provided, and university students receive grants to cover their expenses.

As stated by Glubb: *"The impression that it will always be automatically rich causes the declining empire to spend lavishly on its own benevolence, until such a time as the economy collapses, the universities are closed, and the hospitals fall into ruin."*

The welfare state is just another milestone in the life-story of an ageing empire in decline.

Weakening of Religion: Glubb defines religion as *"the human feeling that there is something, some invisible Power, apart from material objects, which controls human life and the natural world."*

Without religion, men are more likely to snatch than serve, and the spirit of self-sacrifice is weak.

The nation is characterised by defensive minded militaries, decaying morals, loss of religion, frivolous consumption of food, entertainment, sex, and the complete focus on individual interests.

Is Sir John Glubb's essay, "The Fate of Empires", applicable to Singapore?

While other nations have acquired "sophisticated weapons of old empires" in the military sense, Singapore has managed to acquire "sophisticated weapons of old empires" in the commercial sense by attracting MNCs to invest in Singapore with promises to support their investments and operations in Singapore.

"THE FATE OF EMPIRES" AND SINGAPORE

You may be wondering at this point: Glubb's essay is about empires, how is it even applicable to a small nation like Singapore?

Glubb mentions in his essay that "if the small country has not shared in the wealth and power, it will not share in the decadence."

Singapore has definitely had its share of wealth. According to data provided by the International Monetary Fund and compiled by the Global Finance Magazine in July 2015, Singapore is the third richest country in the world.[29]

Singapore has also had its share of power. When Lee Kuan Yew passed away in March 2015, US President Barack Obama commented that Lee's *"views and insights on Asian dynamics and economic management were respected by many around the world, and no small number of this and past generations of world leaders have sought his advice on governance and development… He was a true giant of history who will be remembered for generations to come as the father of modern Singapore and as one of the great strategists of Asian affairs."*

Dignitaries who flew in specially to attend Lee's funeral in 2015 included: Brunei's Sultan Hassanal Bolkiah, China's Vice-President Li Yuanchao, India's Prime Minister Narendra Modi, Indonesia's President Joko Widodo, Japan's Prime Minister Shinzo Abe, Malaysia's Prime Minister Najib Razak, former US President, Mr Bill Clinton, and former US Secretary of State, Dr Henry Kissinger.

You may also argue that Glubb's essay does not apply to Singapore because it did not have an age of military conquest. But if we were to look back at the time of Singapore since World War II, the conquests in the world have mostly not been of a military nature, but have been those of trade and investment.

While other nations have acquired "sophisticated weapons of old empires" in the military sense, Singapore has managed to acquire "sophisticated weapons of old empires" in the commercial sense by attracting MNCs to invest in Singapore with promises to support their investments and operations in Singapore. By honouring its word to support the MNCs, the Singapore Government gained the trust of the MNCs, which led to further investment accompanied by commercial success.

Based upon social observations of increased materialism and consumerism, Singapore has experienced the "High Noon" and is somewhere between the Ages of Affluence and Decadence.

Of the seven characteristics of the Age of Decadence, we note that there are already signs of five of them in Singapore, namely:

1. Defensiveness
2. Pessimism
3. Materialism
4. Frivolity
5. An influx of foreigners

WHICH AGE IS SINGAPORE IN?

So, if we accept that Glubb's essay is possibly applicable to Singapore, which age is Singapore in?

Based upon social observations of increased materialism and consumerism, Singapore has experienced the "High Noon" and is somewhere between the Ages of Affluence and Decadence. While the immense wealth and growth of our nation has "dazzled other nations", we are sure that most Singaporeans would have observed that there has been a decreased sense of public duty with a change from service to selfishness; there is a growing defensiveness and desire to grow and retain individual wealth.

As Glubb described in his essay, the Age of Affluence is one where *"the object of the young and ambitious is no longer fame, Honour or service, but cash."* We see many Singaporeans seeking wealth for themselves and not for their nation or community, and we see many parents and students in Singapore seeking an education that enables them to grow rich, instead of *"seeking learning, virtues, and qualifications that serve the needs of the nation."* In addition, we also note that the divide between the rich and poor has increased.

Singapore also registers certain markers of the Age of Intellect, which is a stage where wealth is no longer needed for necessities or luxuries, and there are also abundant funds for the pursuit of knowledge.

Aligned with the history of other nations, we note that people who have invested in the Age of Commerce are now increasingly founding and endowing institutions of higher education, as well as patronising arts, music, and literature.

Another sign that Singapore has reached the Age of Intellect, is the increase in discussions, debates, and arguments, especially on online social media.

Of the seven characteristics of the Age of Decadence, we note that there are already signs of five of them in Singapore, namely:

1. Defensiveness
2. Pessimism
3. Materialism

While the government has been quick to emphasise that the shift to collective responsibility does not mean self-reliance is less important, this shift would be a slippery slope if the people and government were to let their guard down.

While diversity has increased, the Singapore Census, which is taken once every 10 years, reflected that the number of citizens who do not profess to have a religion has increased.

4. Frivolity
5. An influx of foreigners

Of the remaining two characteristics, "welfare state" and "weakening of religion", we note that:

WELFARE STATE: In Singapore's early years of nation-building, the emphasis in its social policies was self-reliance, but in recent times, there has been a shift to collective responsibility. While the government has been quick to emphasise that this shift to collective responsibility does not mean self-reliance is less important, this shift would be a slippery slope if the people and government were to let their guard down.

WEAKENING OF RELIGION: A 2014 analysis by the Pew Research Center commented that Singapore is the world's most religiously diverse nation. However, while diversity has increased, the Singapore Census, which is taken once every 10 years, reflected that the number of citizens who do not profess to have a religion has increased.

Figures for major religions in Singapore for the past three decades are as follows:

Major Religions in Singapore	Year	Adherences*	Change
Buddhism	1990	31.2%	
	2000	42.5%	+11.3%
	2010	33.3%	-9.2%
Christianity	1990	12.7%	
	2000	14.6%	+1.9%
	2010	18.3%	+3.7%
Catholicism	1990	-%	
	2000	4.8%	-
	2010	7.1%	+2.3%
Protestantism	1990	-%	
	2000	9.8%	-
	2010	11.3%	+1.5%
Hinduism	1990	3.7%	
	2000	4.0%	+0.3%
	2010	5.1%	+1.1%

Glubb's observations are, of course, by no means predictive. But we can benefit at least by being reflective over it.

"Athens was more and more looked on as a co-operative business possessed of great wealth in which all citizens had a right to share. The larger and larger funds demanded made heavier and heavier taxation necessary, but that troubled only the well-to-do, always a minority, and no one gave a thought to the possibility that the source might be taxed out of existence. Politics was now closely connected with money, quite as much as with voting. Indeed, the one meant the other. Votes were for sale as well as officials."

Major Religions in Singapore	Year	Adherences*	Change
Islam	1990	15.3%	
	2000	14.9%	-0.4%
	2010	14.7%	-0.2%
Taoism	1990	22.4%	
	2000	8.5%	-13.9%
	2010	10.9%	+2.4%
Other religions	1990	0.6%	
	2000	0.6%	+0.0%
	2010	0.7%	+0.1%
No Religion	1990	14.1%	
	2000	14.8%	+0.7%
	2010	17.0%	+2.2%

*Adherences amongst total resident population aged 15 years and above

Glubb's observations are, of course, by no means predictive. But we can benefit at least by being reflective over it.

Just another quote from history to lend us perspective. Ancient Greece was the pioneer of democracy 2,500 years ago. How did democracy in ancient Greece come to an end?

One of the experts on the history of the period was Edith Hamilton (1867–1963). In her book "The Echo of Greece" (W.W. Norton 1957) on Athen's Failure, she wrote:

"What the people wanted was a government that would provide a comfortable life for them, and with this as the foremost object, ideas of freedom and self-reliance and service to the community were obscured to the point of disappearing.

"Athens was more and more looked on as a co-operative business possessed of great wealth in which all citizens had a right to share. The larger and larger funds demanded made heavier and heavier taxation necessary, but that troubled only the well-to-do, always a minority, and no one gave a thought to the possibility that the source might be taxed out of existence. Politics was now closely connected with money, quite as much as with voting. Indeed, the one meant the other. Votes were for sale as well as officials.

"Athens had reached the point of rejecting independence, and the freedom she now wanted was freedom from responsibility. There could be only one result. 'The excess of liberty in states or individuals,' [Plato] said, 'seems to pass into excess of slavery.' If men insisted on being free from the burden of a life that was self-dependent and also responsible for the common good, they would cease to be free at all."

"Those that fail to learn from history, are doomed to repeat it."

"There are enduring values of great civilisations and great religions, which individuals and societies can ignore and discard at their own peril."

"The whole process was clear to Plato. Athens had reached the point of rejecting independence, and the freedom she now wanted was freedom from responsibility. There could be only one result. 'The excess of liberty in states or individuals,' he said, 'seems to pass into excess of slavery.' If men insisted on being free from the burden of a life that was self-dependent and also responsible for the common good, they would cease to be free at all.

"Responsibility was the price every man must pay for freedom. It was to be had on no other terms. (…)

"But, by the time, Athens had reached the end of freedom and was never to have it again."

As Winston Churchill, the former Prime Minister of the United Kingdom said: "*Those that fail to learn from history, are doomed to repeat it.*"

THE IMPORTANCE OF HONOUR FOR SINGAPORE

Dr Goh Keng Swee, when he was First Deputy Prime Minister and Minister of Education, made some highly notable observations in an interview published in *The Straits Times* over three days from 28 to 30 December 1982 that are aligned with Glubb's observations:

- *"There are enduring values of great civilisations and great religions, which individuals and societies can ignore and discard at their own peril. This I have learnt through years and years of experience. I can put it this way—the effect on individuals.*

  "I have noticed people who have succeeded and become rich. And those who have moral values, whether religious or non-religious, have conducted their lives in a satisfactory way. That is to say, they raised and brought up their children properly, they are not obsessed with acquiring money for the sake of acquiring money, although the rich of course do accumulate wealth. That's their main purpose.

  "Nevertheless, they see the social obligations and try to carry them out. On the other hand, there are those who do not appear to have moral values. I find that they tend to neglect their children,

"The faithful are fortunate...they are not only more likely to refrain from doing what they believe to be wrong, but also to have an advantage over others. Their faith helps them cope with stress and crisis, and to bring up their children properly."

"So long as you have firm convictions of what is right, what is wrong, what is good, what is bad, they will see you through."

"A person with moral principles is more likely to do well than a person without such principles."

and then the children sometimes end up in an awful mess."

- *"The faithful are fortunate … they are not only more likely to refrain from doing what they believe to be wrong, but also to have an advantage over others.*

  "Their faith helps them cope with stress and crisis, and to bring up their children properly. The agnostics, those with no religion, but who do not necessarily disbelieve in God, are not without character or resilience, provided they have strong moral principles."

- *"So long as you have firm convictions of what is right, what is wrong, what is good, what is bad, they will see you through.*

  "When you examine the great religions, the basic values are very much the same. If you believe in God and you believe in your religion, good luck to you. You are very fortunate.

  "I will never try to talk a Christian or a Hindu or a Muslim out of his religious belief. I think it would be absolutely wrong. You've got something when you have religious faith. A precious asset, isn't it?"

- *"Some people say that government is concerned only with secular matters—the economy, the banking system or whatever, employment; matters spiritual belong to the church and the bishops, and that is all right if you are a believer.*

  "I think a believing Christian is a very lucky man. He has achieved peace of mind because he believes in God and the Scriptures. I have noticed that Christians, generally speaking, conduct their lives in a very orderly way. They don't go for excitement and distractions, they don't waste money, and they raise their children very strictly according to moral principles. Their children will become moral persons, and a person with moral principles is more likely to do well than a person without such principles.

  "So those in Singapore who have true religious faith, whether it be Christianity, or Hinduism, or Islam, or Buddhism have a decided advantage over those who don't. But having said that, there are some agnostics who develop their own moral principles.

  "The Prime Minister [referring to then Prime Minister, Lee Kuan Yew], *for instance, is agnostic. But he was taught right and*

"We would be foolish not to learn from what the great religions and ethical disciplines can teach us, especially in our present scientific and materialistic age."

"We can readily observe what is happening to those societies that have abandoned or lost the time-tested moral and religious beliefs of their forebears."

"The teaching of religious knowledge and ethics can certainly reinforce the moral values of our children and provide them with a moral compass for life."

wrong by his grandmother. And he's a man of very strict moral principles. For that matter, so are other members of the old guard (referring to the first generation political leaders of Singapore).*"*

In February 1982, then Minister of State for Education, Dr Tay Eng Soon, also noted in a speech:

- *"The societies and civilisations from which we have descended have all been shaped and moulded by great religions and ethical teachings. Hinduism for example has permeated through Indian culture and thought for several thousand years. The Chinese civilisation has been profoundly influenced by Confucian ethics."*

- *"These civilisations have undergone great upheavals, wars, and change. It would be true to say that it was their moral and religious beliefs that have provided the continuity and given their people the strength to survive these changes."*

- *"We would be foolish not to learn from what the great religions and ethical disciplines can teach us, especially in our present scientific and materialistic age. We can readily observe what is happening to those societies that have abandoned or lost the time-tested moral and religious beliefs of their forebears. They have become amoral; they are permissive and self-indulgent, they are also turning to all kinds of fads and cults. And the thoughtful members of their societies are worried about these trends."*

- *"We do not want this to happen to us. The teaching of religious knowledge and ethics can certainly reinforce the moral values of our children and provide them with a moral compass for life even though we know there are many other factors such as the home, the example of elders and so on, which greatly influence the moral character of children."*

- *"The teaching of religious knowledge and moral education in our schools will not solve all our problems. But if well taught it could provide an anchor in the midst of the cross currents of change which are going on around us."*

Without Honour, one would not live out the values that one believes in, and changes to real life will not happen.

Having a common culture of Honour simplifies life for a diverse nation.

With a common code of ethics and understood rules of engagement, and with the common mission of improving the collective well-being of the nation in the long-term, we enjoy honourable relationships of trust and are free to live in harmony and to celebrate our diversity.

The true legacy of Lee Kuan Yew and the founding leaders is not buildings and wealth but their honourable and indomitable spirit, courage, and imagination to do all they could to secure the survival and well-being of the nation.

HONOUR AND RELIGION

While the merits of having a religion are well articulated by Dr Goh and Dr Tay, one should keep in mind the popular quote: *"Going to church does not make you a Christian, just like going to McDonald's doesn't make you a hamburger."*

Religion and religious rituals do not make a difference to one's life unless one lives out one's religious values and in a way that positively increases the well-being of others. Similarly, if one is agnostic but espouses strict moral principles, it will not make a difference to one's life or the lives of those in one's community unless these principles are lived out.

Since Honour is living by the virtues, Honour can be said to be the virtue of all virtues and the fundamental assumption of all religions and/ or moral principles, for without Honour, one would not live out the values that one believes in, and changes to real life will not happen.

The virtue of Honour is particularly important in Singapore due to its ideological commitment to be a multi-cultural and multi-religious nation. Having a common culture of Honour simplifies life for a diverse nation. With a common code of ethics and understood rules of engagement, and with the common mission of improving the collective well-being of the nation in the long-term, we enjoy honourable relationships of trust and are free to live in harmony and to celebrate our diversity.

WHERE IS SINGAPORE?

Thus far, we have made the following points:

- Being a "little red dot" in this huge wide world, Singapore's survival and success are two sides of the same coin.

- The true legacy of Lee Kuan Yew and the founding leaders is not buildings and wealth but their honourable and indomitable spirit, courage, and imagination to do all they could to secure the survival and well-being of the nation, and make a future for its people by imbuing a spirit of steadfastness, integrity, and trustworthiness in the nation.

HOME = HOpe + MEmory

Maslow's Hierarchy of Needs underscores the need for people to develop their spiritual impulses, moving from the "body" to address the needs of the "soul" and finally the needs of the "spirit".

Singaporeans need to take the time to think about what kind of Singapore they would like to have in the next 10, 20, 50, even 100 years.

- Honour is the virtue of all virtues. Honour is living out virtues, which are basically values in action. Without Honour, one would not live out the values that one believes in, and transformation in thought, action, and destiny will not happen. Honour is the foundation of trust for it has to be first offered before it can be reciprocated.

- The two dimensions of Honour that are particularly important for the continued survival and success of Singapore, so that Singapore will continue to be a **HOME**, which offers Uplifting **HO**pe and Heartfelt **ME**mory, to Singaporeans are:

  - **Honouring one's word**
  - **Honouring each other**

- **MASLOW'S HIERARCHY OF NEEDS,** which highlights a human being's natural need to progress from the physical realm to the mental realm then emotional realm, and finally the spiritual realm, with the highest need being Transcendence (i.e. helping others reach their potential), underscores the need for people to develop their spiritual impulses, moving from the "body" to address the needs of the "soul" and finally the needs of the "spirit". The lack of development of any of these three components of any human being will have a negative impact on one's well-being.

  This thesis has been underscored by the results of the 2015 National Values Assessment. Singaporeans need to compare their description of Singapore today with the descriptions of the US and the UK, and wonder why the lists are so different, as well as consider whether the differences have arisen from the differences in societal values.

  If the differences are the result of societal values, then would wishing for Singapore to embrace the values celebrated by popular culture, which is largely dominated by the West today, also result in Singapore becoming like Western societies today that experience social unrests, racial conflicts, religious tensions, unemployment, family breakdowns, etc.?

  Singaporeans need to take the time to think about what kind

The lifespan of great nations is about 250 years from their genesis to their decline.

Singapore at 50 years old is a teenager in "nation terms".

Singapore seems to be in the stage between the Age of Affluence and the Age of Decadence.

of Singapore they would like to have in the next 10, 20, 50, even 100 years.

- **THE FATE OF EMPIRES**: Sir John Bagot Glubb's profound essay, "The Fate of Empires and Search for Survival", notes that the lifespan of nations is about 250 years from their genesis to their decline. Glubb observes that over 3,000 years and different parts of the world, the "periods of duration of different empires at varied epochs show a remarkable similarity". If the average age of nations is 250 years, Singapore at 50 years old is a teenager in "nation terms".

In his essay, Glubb also describes many of the stages of empire, and many of the reasons why empires break down and eventually disappear. According to Glubb, the stages of the rise and fall of great nations seem to be as follows:

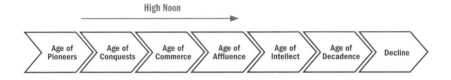

Singapore seems to be in the stage between the Age of Affluence and the Age of Decadence. The Age of Decadence arises due to

- Extended period of wealth and power
- Selfishness
- Love of money
- The loss of a sense of duty

Of the seven characteristics of the Age of Decadence, we note that there are already signs of five of them in Singapore, namely:

- Defensiveness
- Pessimism
- Materialism

For the continued success and survival of Singapore, it would be vital to conscientiously build a culture of Honour by:

- Honouring Our Word
- Honouring Each Other

To create a culture of Honour:

- Create conditions to bring out the best in others
- Think deeply about the Singapore we want in the future
- Know our history
- Arrest the pervasiveness and growth of selfishness, materialism, and the loss of a sense of duty
- Extend and expand our realm of responsibility by honouring ourselves and others
- Chase the opportunities, not the money
- Reintroduce norms with a moral vocabulary
- Take action

- Frivolity
- An influx of foreigners

Of the remaining two characteristics, "welfare state" and "weakening of religion", there have been signs of a negative shift in these two characteristics in our society.

WHAT CAN AND SHOULD SINGAPOREANS DO?

We think that for the continued success and survival of Singapore, it would be vital to conscientiously build a culture of Honour by:

- **Honouring Our Word**
- **Honouring Each Other**

In order to create such a culture of Honour, it would be imperative to:

- Create conditions to bring out the best in others
- Think deeply about the Singapore we want in the future
- Know our history
- Arrest the pervasiveness and growth of selfishness, materialism, and the loss of a sense of duty by strengthening familial relationships and honouring our elders
- Extend and expand our realm of responsibility by honouring ourselves and others
- Chase the opportunities, not the money
- Reintroduce norms with a moral vocabulary
- Take action

1. **CREATE CONDITIONS TO BRING OUT THE BEST IN OTHERS**: According to the 2015 National Values Assessment mentioned earlier in this part of the book, the self-perception of Singaporeans is highly positive—the top 10 values that they have chosen for themselves are all positive values with other-centred values, such as "family", "responsibility", and "friendship".

   This very much represents hope for Singapore since two of the reasons for the fall of a nation is due to "selfishness" and the "loss

Strong families, strong communities, and strong sense of responsibility make a strong nation.

Singaporeans should think deeply about the Singapore they want in the future and then honour the values needed to get there.

Singaporeans also need to study and know the history of Singapore, and be constantly aware of the vulnerabilities that Singapore faces as a small city-state with no natural resources.

of sense of duty".

Strong families and strong communities make a strong nation. If family ties are strong, the sense of responsibility is strong, and if the sense of responsibility is strong, the community and the nation will be strong.

What we need to do is to create good conditions for these positive self-perceptions to be manifested in positive public and group behaviour by:

- Acknowledging the good
- Praising the good
- Promoting the good in schools, workplaces, and communities
- Practising the good in leadership
- Setting them as priorities in life, choices, and relationships

2. **THINK DEEPLY ABOUT THE SINGAPORE WE WANT IN THE FUTURE:** Singaporeans should think deeply about the Singapore they want in the future and then honour the values needed to get there. Values are the compass when there is no map to get to the future. But first, it is important for us to ascertain where we want to go and reflect whether we are headed in the right direction.

3. **KNOW OUR HISTORY:** Singaporeans also need to study and know the history of Singapore, and be constantly aware of the vulnerabilities that Singapore faces as a small city-state with no natural resources, apart from its people.

When you ask most Singaporeans about what they know about Singapore's history, they will probably list "Sang Nila Utama", "Sir Stamford Raffles", "1965", or possibly "Lee Kuan Yew".

Yet, very few Singaporeans know about the momentous events leading up to Singapore's independence on 9 August 1965, after a failed two-year merger in Malaysia, or the strategic concerns that Singaporeans continually need to be sensitive about, due to the vulnerabilities of the country arising from its smallness and geography.

Why are Singaporeans mostly ignorant about our history?

Because it was never taught in its complexity to the majority

If the nation is not successful or does not survive, Singaporeans will have no chance to succeed themselves.

We should arrest the pervasiveness and growth of selfishness, materialism, and the loss of a sense of duty by strengthening familial relationships and honouring our elders.

We need to honour our own abilities and strengths by not expecting the Government to provide for all of our needs, and learning to create our own opportunities and exercising our own efforts and creativity to attain our dreams.

of Singaporeans unless they chose to study history in their upper secondary school days. In fact, many young Singaporeans have commented that they learnt more about Singapore's history from the documentaries that were telecast during the week of mourning following Mr Lee Kuan Yew's death in March 2015 than what they were taught in school.

While we can do nothing about the past, we need to know and honour our past to have a sense of identity. We need to know our past so that we can honour the spirit and live the values of our founding leaders, who personified Honour and moral courage, as well as strength in adversity.

Singaporeans need to be consciously and constantly aware that survival and success are two sides of the same coin for Singapore. If the nation is not successful or does not survive, Singaporeans will have no chance to succeed themselves.

4. **ARREST THE PERVASIVENESS AND GROWTH OF SELFISH-NESS, MATERIALISM, AND THE LOSS OF A SENSE OF DUTY BY STRENGTHENING FAMILIAL RELATIONSHIPS AND HONOURING OUR ELDERS:** As family is perceived to be the highest personal value in Singapore (both in 2012 and 2015), perhaps we can think more deeply about how we can strengthen familial relationships. We can start at home by honouring our parents and elders, and making Singapore a place where children are proud of their parents, not just a place where parents are proud of their children.

5. **EXTEND AND EXPAND OUR REALM OF RESPONSIBILITY BY HONOURING OURSELVES AND OTHERS:** Responsibility ranks as the second highest personal value for Singaporeans in 2015. It is manifested in our attitudes towards others and our attitudes towards work.

    Honouring ourselves by honouring our word, trying our best, and striving for excellence, are habits and behaviours that need to be emphasised again and again, not only in the workplace, but also in our families, communities, and organisations.

    We need to honour our own abilities and strengths by not

Our sense of responsibility also needs to be extended to the community.

"When those who reach the top fail to care for those below them, Singapore will disintegrate."

Honouring each other as fellow citizens and fellow human beings is the antidote for "Meritocracy Done Wrong".

We exist for others, not just for ourselves.

Chase the opportunities, not the money.

expecting the Government to provide for all of our needs, and learning to create our own opportunities and exercising our own efforts and creativity to attain our dreams.

As Jack Ma, the founder of e-Commerce giant Alibaba, shared: *"Whether you are doing business or working for other people, never complain about your competitors, your environment, and your life... instead of wasting time by complaining and attacking others, why not use the time to improve yourself?"*[30]

Our sense of responsibility also needs to be extended to the community. "Meritocracy Done Wrong, which has resulted in Meritocracy Gone Wrong" can be seen in some of the ills listed in Singapore Society as it is perceived today—particularly, *kiasu* (scared to lose), competitive, materialistic, self-centred, *kiasi* (scared to die), and blame.

As Lee Kuan Yew had once said: *"When those who reach the top fail to care for those below them, Singapore will disintegrate."*

Meritocracy is essential for Singapore—our smallness means we have to do whatever we can to benefit most from the abilities and talents of all our people. But meritocracy has to be tempered with the precept of "enlightened self-interest", where contributing towards the success of the group and of Singapore the nation is recognised as essential for the success and the future of the individual.

Thus the individual has to attend to the success of the group and not just look after himself or herself. Otherwise, meritocracy brings itself down to pride, disdain of others, condescension, and sense of entitlement. This is "Meritocracy Gone Wrong".

Honouring each other as fellow citizens and fellow human beings is the antidote for "Meritocracy Done Wrong".

It starts with us recognising that at the end of the day, life gets its full meaning when it is not about ourselves. We exist for others, not just for ourselves. It is what the extended Maslow's Hierarchy of Needs refers to as Transcendence, which is our highest as human beings.

6. **CHASE THE OPPORTUNITIES, NOT THE MONEY:** Money is what we get for the work we have done today using the knowledge and skills we have today, while opportunities determine what we get

Our qualifications and achievements today are not the end of our hard work, but the springboard to bigger ends and higher means.

With opportunities come obligations.

Work hard to ensure that your today is better than your yesterday.

We need to reintroduce norms and a moral vocabulary.

Reintroduction of norms will require:

- A moral vocabulary
- Holding people responsible for themselves
- Holding everybody responsible

for tomorrow as we gain new knowledge and develop new skills. A job done well today gives others the confidence that we can be trusted to do a job well tomorrow.

It is important for each of us to build a reputation for hard work, integrity, trustworthiness, reliability, quality, and excellence. Our qualifications and achievements today are not the end of our hard work, but the springboard to bigger ends and higher means.

Opportunities are for us to learn and to be the best we each can be. But with opportunities come obligations: the obligation to contribute to the well-being of those around us, and the obligation to offer others opportunities to discover themselves, just as we have benefitted from the opportunities given to us.

Anything less than doing the best that we can and being the best that we can be would be less than fair to ourselves and those around us. So enjoy today, but work hard to ensure that your today is better than your yesterday, so that you will have new opportunities tomorrow.

7. **REINTRODUCE NORMS AND A MORAL VOCABULARY**: In his article for the New York Times edition of 10 March 2015, "The Cost of Relativism", social columnist David Brooks notes that for circles in society that are in dysfunctional and destructive cycles of economic stress and family breakdown, *"sympathy is not enough…it's not only money and better policy that are missing in these circles; it's norms"*.

Brooks opines in the article that: *"The health of society is primarily determined by the habits and virtues of its citizens. In many parts of America there are no minimally agreed upon standards for what it means to be a father. There are no basic codes and rules woven into daily life, which people can absorb unconsciously and follow automatically."*

Brooks goes on to state that the reintroduction of norms will require:

- **First, a moral vocabulary**: *"These norms weren't destroyed because of people with bad values. They were destroyed by a plague of non-judgmentalism, which refused to assert that one way of behaving was better than another. People got out of the habit of setting standards or understanding how they were set."*

Are you living for short-term pleasure or long-term good?

A society will not have social repair "unless we are more morally articulate, unless we have clearer definitions of how we should be behaving at all levels".

"Constant dedication to discussion seems to destroy the power of action."

Choose to respond, not react.

Act upon reflection, not impulse.

Opportunities come to those who are prepared.

Create your own opportunities.

- **Second, holding people responsible for themselves:** *"People born into the most chaotic situations can still be asked the same questions:*
    - *Are you living for short-term pleasure or long-term good?*
    - *Are you living for yourself or for your children?*
    - *Do you have the freedom of self-control or are you in bondage to your desires?"*

- **Lastly, holding everybody responsible**: *"Social norms need repair up and down the scale, universally, together and all at once."*

Brooks states that a society will not have social repair *"unless we are more morally articulate, unless we have clearer definitions of how we should be behaving at all levels";* there needs to be an *"organic communal effort, with voices from everywhere saying gently: This we praise. This we don't."*

Brooks was commenting on American society. But the lessons are also for Singapore.

8. **TAKE ACTION:** In Glubb's essay, Glubb sagely notes that *"constant dedication to discussion seems to destroy the power of action"*.

   The 2015 National Values Assessment reflected the "perceptions" or "feelings" of the respondents. But the disconnect between the personal values that Singaporeans esteem and what these same respondents see as reflected in society underlines the point that we have to move deliberately from "thinking and feeling" to "acting and doing".

   For that we need to choose to respond and not react, and to act upon reflection and not impulse—reflection stirs purpose while impulse stirs emotion.

   Opportunities come to those who are prepared. Those who do not take the effort to prepare themselves will not be able to identify the opportunities to sow, and thus they will reap nothing.

   Finally, individuals must not only identify opportunities, but also create them. There is a limit to what the government can do for us. Our future depends on what we make of opportunities.

While Singaporeans should be proud about what we have achieved in the past, we cannot afford to be complacent about our future.

Honour our Past.

Honour the Present.

Honour our Future.

We need to create this spiritual mindset of honouring our past, present, and future, so that we can be energised collectively to move forward as one nation for the survival and well-being of our nation.

WINNING WITH HONOUR IN OUR NATION

In his essay, "The Fate of Empires and Search for Survival", Glubb writes: *"Nations of the past seem normally to have imagined that their pre-eminence would last forever."* While Singaporeans should be proud about what we have achieved in the past, we cannot afford to be complacent about our future.

It is important for us to honour our past—without honouring all that our founding leaders and pioneer generation have done, it would be very hard for us to be inspired to defend, cherish, and build upon the fruits of their labour that we enjoy today. By honouring our past, we have a sense of what it means to be Singaporean and where we should go moving forward.

By honouring the present, we are inspired to do our best to be of service to others, and to do more to honour our parents, our children, our leaders, our people, our country, and our environment.

By honouring our future, we reflect and think deeply about how our actions affect others and what kind of Singapore we want to build for our generation and future generations of Singaporeans.

We need to create this spiritual mindset of honouring our past, present, and future, so that we can be energised collectively to move forward as one nation for the survival and well-being of our nation.

CLOSING
THOUGHTS

HONOUR HONOUR

MAKING OUR FUTURE

Our hope is that we are able to find common ground as human beings, and that we agree that we need to honour humanity by seeking the collective long-term well-being of everyone.

Our right to be ourselves can only be to the extent that we do not undermine society today or for the coming generations.

Our interactions should increase our collective long-term well-being

Relationships are the building blocks of life.

Honour is the foundation for winning in relationships whether it be winning in families, communities, organisations, leadership, or life.

This has not been an easy book to write, because it concerns values and virtues, of which each of us can claim to be our own master.

There might have been generalisations and not everything might have resonated with you, but our hope is that we are able to find common ground as human beings, and that we agree that we need to honour humanity by seeking the collective long term well-being of everyone by being people who:

- **HONOUR OUR WORD:** We keep our promises. We are reliable and trustworthy.

- **HONOUR EACH OTIIER:** By honouring each other, we respect and esteem each other as fellow human beings.

But as members of a society, it also means that our right to be ourselves can only be to the extent that we do not undermine society today or for the coming generations. So we should not be trading insults, imposing our views on others, creating avoidable racial or religious disharmony, etc.

Our interactions should increase our collective long-term well-being by:

- Edifying Character
- Developing Trust
- Being Life-giving
- Building Relationships
- Strengthening Society
- Upholding Community
- Evoking Loyalty to the Country
- Honouring our Elders
- Building the Future
- Enhancing our Resilience and Capacity to Succeed

At the very least, we should not detract from one or more of these outcomes.

Relationships are the building blocks of life, and Honour is the foundation for winning in relationships whether it be winning in families, communities, organisations, leadership, or life.

Winning is the satisfaction that comes from doing good for someone and doing right according to our conscience.

If we want to win in life and to live a satisfied life, we have to remember that it is not about ourselves, but about others.

A strong society is one where the conscience in the individual is strong.

Honour plays the role of inspiring people to do what is right and good, even when there is no law to force them to do so, or no policeman around to apprehend them.

It is not about rights, but about the collective well-being of our society and future generations.

Winning is the satisfaction that comes from doing good for someone and doing right according to our conscience. Research has shown that the need for Transcendence—that is, helping others reach their personal growth and self-fulfilment, and doing good to others—is ranked as the highest of all needs in the human psyche. Hence, the highest need we all have is to move beyond just thinking of ourselves to contributing to the lives of others by doing good for their lives.

To put it simply, **if we want to win in life and to live a satisfied life, we have to remember that it is not about ourselves, but about others.**

But to win through Honour is not a matter of rules and formulas, for people are sensitive to and resentful of false pretences, insincerity, duplicity, and hypocrisy. If we simply become a society where what is legal is right and what is illegal is wrong, then we would have reduced morality to the law, and thereby the whole moral fibre of society would be damaged.

A strong society is one where the conscience in the individual is strong and where people are aware that they "reap what they sow"— people will then behave responsibly even when there is no one to catch or punish them. A weak society is one where people lose their sense of concern and responsibility for their fellowmen and need to be forced to do things.

Honour plays the role of inspiring people to do what is right and good, even when there is no law to force them to do so, or no policeman around to apprehend them. As Confucius had said of government:

"If the people are governed by laws and punishment is used to maintain order, they will try to avoid the punishment but have no sense of shame. If they are governed by virtue and rules of propriety are used to maintain order, they will have a sense of shame and will become good as well." (Analects 2.3)

In a small, multi-religious, multi-cultural, multi-ethnic and multi-lingual country such as Singapore, we need to establish and uphold a culture of Honour and honouring where everyone is considerate and conscious that our actions and our decisions have an effect on the well-being of others. It is not about rights, but about the collective well-being of our society and future generations—for if the nation does not survive, we are diminished, and if the nation does not succeed, we

Having a common culture of Honour simplifies life.

With a common code of ethics and understood rules of engagement, and with a common mission of improving the collective well-being of the nation in the long-term for ourselves and future generations, we enjoy honourable relationships of trust and are free to celebrate our diversity.

What makes it a matter of Honour is that we are driven to do these things out of a concern and regard for the well-being of others in the long run.

cannot succeed.

Having a common culture of Honour simplifies life. With a common code of ethics and understood rules of engagement, and with a common mission of improving the collective long-term well-being of the nation for ourselves and future generations, we enjoy honourable relationships of trust and are free to celebrate our diversity.

Honour, like love, is what comes from deep within us. We may be expressing courtesies and behaviours out of habit in observing the norms of society, but what makes it all a matter of Honour is that we are driven to do these things out of a concern and regard for the well-being of others in the long run.

Establishing a culture of Honour requires us to:

- Commit to a common mission to increase the collective well-being of the whole in the long-term
- Do unto others what we would have them do to us
- Not do anything to others that would be repugnant to ourselves
- Continually ask ourselves and others the question: "How can I help you be the best that you can be?"
- Actively ask ourselves what impact our actions and decisions will have on others
- Habitually ask ourselves how we can contribute good to the lives of others beyond ourselves

Maya Angelou was an American author, poet, dancer, actress, and singer. Of life, she said:

"I've learned that no matter what happens, or how bad it seems today, life does go on, and it will be better tomorrow.

"I've learned that you can tell a lot about a person by the way he/she handles these three things: a rainy day, lost luggage, and tangled Christmas tree lights.

"I've learned that regardless of your relationship with your parents, you'll miss them when they're gone from your life.

"I've learned that making a 'living' is not the same thing as making a 'life'.

"People will forget what you said, people will forget what you did, but people will never forget how you made them feel."

We need to honour all who cross our paths in life.

The well-known Russian folk tale about "The Enormous Turnip" illustrates the value of teamwork.

"I've learned that life sometimes gives you a second chance.

"I've learned that you shouldn't go through life with a catcher's mitt on both hands; you need to be able to throw something back.

"I've learned that whenever I decide something with an open heart, I usually make the right decision.

"I've learned that even when I have pains, I don't have to be one.

"I've learned that every day you should reach out and touch someone. People love a warm hug, or just a friendly pat on the back.

"I've learned that I still have a lot to learn.

"I've learned that **people will forget what you said, people will forget what you did, but people will never forget how you made them feel.**"

The last sentence bears particular significance: "*People will forget what you said, people will forget what you did, but people will never forget how you made them feel.*" It is a commentary on honouring all who cross our paths in life.

Perhaps a good way to appreciate the message can be found in the well-known Russian folk tale about "The Enormous Turnip".

The story is about a farmer who planted a turnip that kept growing… and growing…and growing until it became a real giant of a turnip. One day, he decided to pull the turnip out of the ground. He pulled and pulled, but it would not come out.

He asked his wife to help. The wife and the farmer pulled and pulled, but the turnip still would not come out. The wife asked a boy to help. So the boy and the wife and the farmer pulled and pulled, but the turnip was still stuck in the ground.

And so the story carries on. The boy called a girl, who then called a dog, who called a cat. And the cat and the dog and the girl and the boy and the wife and the farmer pulled and pulled, but the turnip would not come out.

The cat next called the mouse to help out. And the mouse and the cat and the dog and the girl and the boy and the wife and the farmer pulled and pulled…and finally the turnip came out of the ground! The wife then cooked the turnip and everyone had wonderful turnip soup for dinner.

Often the story is told to illustrate the value of teamwork. But in fact we can find not just one, but a total of five morals in the story.

If we all pull together (in the same direction), we can do things that we are not able to do individually.

Even natural enemies, like the cat and the dog, can find it worth their while to work together.

Everyone is important and valuable, even the smallest member of the team. We must appreciate everyone...no matter how small.

Ensure that there is fair and just reward after the job is done.

We must honour our word and honour each other.

Honour is the foundation of trust.

- **Moral #1:** If we all pull together (in the same direction), we can do things that we are not able to do individually. It is all about teamwork and synergy.

- **Moral #2:** Even natural enemies, like the cat and the dog, can find it worth their while to work together. It is a matter of "enlightened self-interest", a valuable idea for all of us.

- **Moral #3:** Until the smallest of them all, the mouse, joined in, the turnip would not come out. It shows that everyone is important and valuable, even the smallest member of the team. We must appreciate everyone…no matter how small.

- **Moral #4:** The farmer's wife gave turnip soup to everyone, and not just her favourites. "Reward for work and work for reward" is an important principle. Ensure that there is fair and just reward after the job is done.

- **Moral #5:** We must honour our word and honour each other (by respecting and valuing every effort and every person). It is a good way to conduct ourselves in life.

Trust is critical for long term, beneficial relationships, whether the relationships be personal or business. And **Honour is the foundation of trust.**

SINGAPORE, THE LITTLE RED DOT

Singapore is a little red dot among countries with large land areas and large populations. While Singaporeans may not like to be reminded of this, it nonetheless holds true that "no one owes us a living" and "no one else is responsible for our security".

The point about understanding history and geography of countries is not to hold the people back and hold them to the past—it is to give context for what needs to be done to make the country a great place for current and future generations. While countries cannot escape their geography, they should honour their history to inspire and galvanise their people to create a worthy future for themselves and the generations to come.

Honour is a matter of what legacy we want to leave for future generations.

Destiny is a matter of choice, not a matter of luck and hope.

Honour moves the perspective from "Me" to "Others".

So long as we will honour each other and honour the collective long-term well-being of our nation, we can end up with the "we" where we have the space to prosper as individuals, as families, as communities, as businesses and organisations, as country and nation.

Honour is a matter of what legacy we want to leave for future generations. **Destiny is a matter of choice**, not a matter of luck and hope. And we need to have the right perspective as to how we should think when we make choices.

An interesting mental exercise we each could undertake to think about the Singapore we want to have for the future, our children, and grandchildren is to list out in just four or five phrases that describes that future Singapore. It is important to limit ourselves to just four or five big ideas to keep focus and clarity.

Let us share with you our list:

- A Singapore that keeps succeeding despite its smallness
- Racial, religious, and community synergy
- A gracious society
- Children proud of their parents
- Citizens proud of their country

Dare we dream? Will we dream? Once we settle in our minds these big descriptors of the future Singapore we want, we can begin to work out the implications of how we need to think and what we need to do to get such a Singapore.

Carlos Slim, one of the world's richest men and a Mexican business magnate, investor, and philanthropist, is reputed to have heard someone say that *"what is needed is to have a good Mexico for the children of Mexico."* Slim countered that this is wrong and that *"what is needed is to have 'good children for Mexico'."*

This is a matter of morals, virtues, and values, and Honour is living by these morals, virtues, and values.

Honour moves the perspective from "Me" to "Others". **"Honour in Me"** is to honour my word and to honour myself by doing my best to be the best that I can be. **"Honour for You"** is to respect you as a human being and to do what is good for you, even if our stations in life might be worlds apart, and our views and ideals are different. And so long as we honour each other and honour the collective long-term well-being of our nation, we can end up with the "we" where we have the space to prosper as individuals, as families, as communities, as businesses and organisations, as country and nation.

Eulogy virtues are more important than the résumé virtues.

We should focus on developing a profound character.

For Singapore, survival and success are two sides of the same coin.

The drive to be exceptional in the way we think and act is not an option; it is destiny for Singapore.

It is destiny within our grasp for each of us to be individual "Little Red Dots" who:

- Honour our word
- Honour each other
- Honour ourselves

David Brooks, writer and commentator in the New York Times, began his book, "The Road to Character" (Random House 2015), with the words:

*"Recently I've been thinking about the difference between the résumé virtues and the eulogy virtues. The **résumé virtues** are the ones you list on your résumé, the skills that you bring to the job market and that contribute to external success. The **eulogy virtues** are deeper. They're the virtues that get talked about at your funeral, the ones that exist at the core of your being—whether you are kind, brave, honest or faithful; what kind of relationships you formed.*

"Most of us would say that the eulogy virtues are more important than the résumé virtues, but I confess that for long stretches of my life I've spent more time thinking about the latter than the former. Our education system [referring to the American education system] *is certainly oriented around the résumé virtues more than the eulogy ones. Public conversation is, too—the self-help tips in magazines, the nonfiction bestsellers. Most of us have clearer strategies for how to achieve career success than we do for how to develop a profound character."*

WE ARE LITTLE RED DOTS

Mr Lee Kuan Yew, Dr Goh Keng Swee, and the other founding fathers of Singapore impressed on the people of Singapore the need for Singaporeans to have a relentless drive for excellence, and to desire to be the best that we can be in everything we do. For Singapore, unlike for so many other countries, survival and success are two sides of the same coin.

There are countries that are independent but not sovereign, and countries that are sovereign but not independent. Singapore must seek to be friends with all who would be friends with Singapore, but never forget that no one owes us a living and that no one else is responsible for our security. The drive to be exceptional in the way we think and act is not an option; it is destiny for Singapore.

And it is destiny within our grasp for each of us to be individual "Little Red Dots" who:

- **Honour our word** to establish a reputation for being trustworthy and reliable

THE HONOUR CIRCLE

- **Honour each other** by always thinking about the collective long-term well-being and success of our society
- **Honour ourselves** by
  - ✓ Taking responsibility for our lives and our dreams
  - ✓ Having a relentless drive for excellence
  - ✓ Desiring to be the best that we can be in everything we do
  - ✓ Thinking through things for ourselves and not unthinkingly following the herd
  - ✓ Having the courage to try new things
  - ✓ Having the discernment to cut losses when things do not work out
  - ✓ Setting goals that are a stretch but achievable with effort and imagination.
  - ✓ Helping those in our spheres of influence be the best that they can be.
  - ✓ Leaving people and places better than how we found them.

WIN WITH HONOUR BY HONOURING YOUR HONOUR

A culture of Honour and honouring remains essential for the country's success and cohesion in the coming years, starting with the individual, then family, then others in society. This respect and concern for the well-being of others leads naturally to honouring our families, our communities, organisations, and nation to advance the peace, harmony, stability, and well-being of the collective whole in the long-term.

Honour enables respectful national discourse and constructive debate over issues of national life, and then further extends to caring for the global environment, peace, and security, for if planet earth does not survive, we do not survive.

There is much to look forward to in the future unfolding before us, but it is a future to be shaped and to be gained by honouring the goodness of the human spirit for the well-being of others. The survival, well-being, and success of our nation rests with being a people of Honour, and cultivating

A culture of Honour and honouring remains essential for a country's success and cohesion in the coming years.

Honour enables respectful national discourse and constructive debate.

The survival, well-being, and success of our nation rests with being a people of Honour, and cultivating children who learn, grow, and live with Honour.

Honouring our word and honouring each other is the Way to Win with Honour in our lives, as well as in relationships and leadership in our:

- Families
- Communities
- Organisations
- Nation

Will you honour your Honour?

children who learn, grow, and live with Honour.

Honouring our word and honouring each other is the Way to Win with Honour in our lives, as well as in relationships and leadership in our:

- Families
- Communities
- Organisations
- Nation

Will you choose to honour your Honour?

I HONOUR

I HONOUR MY NATION … by doing what I can to make my fellow countrymen proud of my country. I think not only for myself, but also for future generations. I actively consider how my actions affect those around me. If the nation is weak, I have no future and my home may be lost.

I HONOUR MY FAMILY … by helping to bring happiness to the home and to keep the family together. I will not speak words or do things that bring disgrace to my family. I cannot choose my family and I choose to make life better for them.

I HONOUR MY FATHER AND MY MOTHER … by helping to meet their holistic needs for they gave me life. I will care for them even if they do not appreciate it or have not earned it. They have given me life, and I honour them with my unconditional love and active regard.

I HONOUR MY ROLES AND RESPONSIBILITIES … by always doing my best. I do everything with pride and cannot be satisfied with myself if I do not do all I can according to my ability. I am blessed with unique talents that no one else has, and I will use them to do good to others in my life and the people I serve.

I HONOUR OTHERS … by respecting them as human beings and as fellow citizens. I recognise and respect the feelings and needs of others. I will treat them just as I would like them to treat me. I reap what I sow.

I HONOUR MYSELF … by looking after my body and taking responsibility for my life. I use my talents and abilities to do good and fulfil my unique calling. I will take steps each day to make my today better than my yesterday. My values, thoughts, and habits shape my destiny. I am the master of my fate. I am the captain of my soul.

Notes

1. http://www.virtuesproject.com/virtuesdef.html

2. https://medium.com/@frankdiana/digital-transformation-of-business-and-society-5d9286e39dbf

3. https://www.youtube.com/watch?v=Ck2Id3S9ct0

4. http://premierespeakers.com/mark_gungor/bio

5. https://appreciativeinquiry.case.edu/practice/organizationDetail.cfm?coid=852&sector=32

6. http://www.oprah.com/spirit/Oprah-on-Finding-Your-Calling-What-I-Know-For-Sure#ixzz3p5aQeyOZ

7. http://ritademaria.com/meet.php

8. http://www.marriagedoctor.com/article-7stages-of-marriage.htm

9. http://ideas.time.com/2013/10/04/why-second-marriages-are-more-perilous/

10. http://time.com/3966588/marriage-wedding-best-age/

11. http://www.xinli001.com/info/8028/

12. http://www.parents.com/parenting/dads/issues-trends/importance-of-fathers-involvement/

13. http://www.shinfanchang.com/resources/DiZiGui+part+1.pdf; http://tsoidug.org/dizigui/dizigui_web.pdf

14. https://www.autismspeaks.org/science/science-news/large-study-parent-age-autism-finds-increased-risk-teen-moms

15. http://www.eastasiaforum.org/2015/10/03/defusing-singapores-demographic-time-bomb/

16. http://www.rsis.edu.sg/wp-content/uploads/2015/08/CO15165.pdf?utm_source=getresponse&utm_medium=email&utm_campaign=rsis_publications&utm_content=RSIS+Commentary+165%2F2015+%E2%80%98Non-Zero+Sum%E2%80%99+Mindset+in+Inter-Faith+Relations+by+Mohammad+Alami+Musa

17. https://en.wikipedia.org/wiki/List_of_countries_by_GDP_(nominal)_per_capita

18. https://www.youtube.com/watch?t=26&v=w72uktH9P8Q

19. http://www.telegraph.co.uk/finance/newsbysector/retailandconsumer/11078890/Alibabas-Jack-Ma-Companies-must-help-solve-the-problems-of-society.html

20 Libor is the London Interbank Offered Rate, which is the average interest rate for lending and borrowing between banks, calculated through declarations by major banks in London of what are supposed to be the actual rates. The Libor scandal was a series of fraudulent actions uncovered in 2012, when it was found that banks had been falsely inflating or deflating their declarations to give the impression that they were more creditworthy than they were, or to profit from trades they were making.

21 http://labaton.com/en/about/press/upload/US-UK-Financial-Services-Industry-Survey.pdf

22 http://www.bmeacham.com/whatswhat/GoodAndRight.html

23 http://brandfinance.com/images/upload/brand_finance_nation_brands_2015.pdf

24 http://www.straitstimes.com/singapore/lee-kuan-yew-the-man-and-his-dream

25 http://www.singstat.gov.sg/statistics/browse-by-theme/national-accounts

26 http://www.bloomberg.com/visual-data/best-and-worst//most-efficient-health-care-2014-countries

27 http://www.eco-business.com/news/lee-kuan-yew-the-architect-of-singapores-water-story/

28 http://www.naturalnews.com/043518_happiness_nature_mental_health.html#ixzz3luG3q8kR

29 https://www.gfmag.com/global-data/economic-data/richest-countries-in-the-world

30 http://www.sgstemcell.com/blog/jack-ma-said-stop-complaining/